VICTORIAN SECRECY

Victorian Secrecy
Economies of Knowledge and Concealment

Edited by

ALBERT D. PIONKE
University of Alabama, USA

and

DENISE TISCHLER MILLSTEIN
Stephen F. Austin State University, USA

Routledge
Taylor & Francis Group
LONDON AND NEW YORK

First published 2010 by Ashgate Publishing

Published 2016 by Routledge
2 Park Square, Milton Park, Abingdon, Oxfordshire OX14 4RN
711 Third Avenue, New York, NY 10017, USA

First issued in paperback 2016

Routledge is an imprint of the Taylor & Francis Group, an informa business

British Library Cataloguing in Publication Data
Victorian secrecy: economies of knowledge and concealment.
1. Secrecy in literature. 2. English literature – 19th century – History and criticism. 3. Secrecy – Great Britain – History – 19th century. 4. Secrecy – Political aspects – Great Britain – History – 19th century.
I. Pionke, Albert D., 1974– II. Millstein, Denise Tischler.
820.9'3353'09034-dc22

Library of Congress Cataloging-in-Publication Data
Victorian secrecy: economies of knowledge and concealment / edited by Albert D. Pionke and Denise Tischler Millstein.
p. cm.
Includes bibliographical references and index.
ISBN 978-0-7546-6888-6
1. English fiction—19th century—History and criticism. 2. Secrecy in literature. 3. Secrecy—Great Britain—History—19th century. I. Pionke, Albert D., 1974– II. Millstein, Denise Tischler.
PR878.S423V53 2010
823'.809353—dc22

2009037545

ISBN 13: 978-1-138-25054-3 (pbk)
ISBN 13: 978-0-7546-6888-6 (hbk)

Contents

List of Illustrations

Notes on Contributors

Maria K. Bachman is Professor of English at Coastal Carolina University. She has edited scholarly editions of Wilkie Collins's *The Woman In White* (Broadview Press, 2006) and *Blind Love* (Broadview Press, 2004), as well as a collection of critical essays, *Reality's Dark Light: The Sensational Wilkie Collins* (University of Tennessee Press, 2003). She is currently working on a book project on embodied consciousness and the Victorian novel.

David J. Bradshaw teaches classical and British literatures at Warren Wilson College. With Suzanne Ozment, he has edited *The Voice of Toil: Nineteenth-Century British Writings about Work* (Ohio University Press, 2000). He is currently working on a study of autobiography in the nineteenth century.

Michael Claxton received his Ph.D. from The University of North Carolina at Chapel Hill in 2003 and teaches in the English department at Harding University in Searcy, Arkansas. He researches the history of performance magic and is currently writing a biography of an American female magician, Dell O'Dell (1902–62).

Robert P. Fletcher is Professor of English at West Chester University of Pennsylvania. He has published articles on W. M. Thackeray, Thomas Carlyle, Michael Field, Augusta Webster, and Mathilde Blind in such journals as *PMLA, Studies in the Novel, CLIO, ELH, Victorian Literature and Culture*, and *Victorian Poetry*. He also pursues research and teaches in the fields of cyberculture and electronic literature.

Sarah Hoglund is a Ph.D. candidate at the State University of New York at Stony Brook currently completing a dissertation on burial practices in eighteenth and nineteenth century Britain and India.

Deborah A. Logan is Professor of English at Western Kentucky University, where she teaches Victorian and world literatures. She is the author of *Fallenness in Victorian Women's Writing* and *The Hour and the Woman: Harriet Martineau's 'somewhat remarkable' Life*. Logan has edited eighteen volumes of Martineau's writings, including *The Collected Letters.* Current book projects include Florence Nightingale's political influence, Martineau's uncollected writing on Ireland, and an analysis of Martineau's writing on the British Empire. Logan is editor of *The Victorian Newsletter*.

John McBratney teaches English at John Carroll University in Cleveland, Ohio. He is the author of *Imperial Subjects, Imperial Space: Rudyard Kipling's Fiction of the Native- Born* (2002) and articles on nineteenth- and twentieth-century British literature and culture. He is currently working on a book about cosmopolitanism in the Victorian novel.

Denise Tischler Millstein is a long nineteenth-century scholar interested in tracing Lord Byron's influence on Victorian authors, especially female novelists. She is the Assistant Professor of nineteenth-century British Literature at Stephen F. Austin State University and lives in Lufkin, TX with her husband, Isaac.

Brooke McLaughlin Mitchell is an Associate Professor of English at Wingate University (NC). Her research interests focus on the Victorian novel and Scottish literature, particularly that relating to the Highland Clearances.

Albert Pionke is Associate Professor of English at the University of Alabama. The author of *Plots of Opportunity: Representing Conspiracy in Victorian England* (Ohio State UP, 2004), he is currently working on a book project about the prevalence and significance of ritual among the Victorian professional elite.

Eleanor Fraser Stansbie received her Ph.D. from Birkbeck College in 2006. Her dissertation is entitled *Richard Dadd; Art and the Nineteenth-Century Asylum*. She subsequently held a Paul Mellon Postdoctoral fellowship and is currently an Associate Lecturer in the School of History of Art at Birkbeck College, University of London.

Tamara S. Wagner obtained her Ph.D. from Cambridge University and is Assistant Professor at Nanyang Technological University. Her books include *Longing: Narratives of Nostalgia in the British Novel, 1740–1890* and *Occidentalism in Novels of Malaysia and Singapore, 1819–2004*. She is currently working on a study of financial speculation in Victorian literature.

Allison L. E. Wee received her Ph. D. in English from the University of Minnesota in 2003, specializing in British literature from the Victorian and Modernist periods. Her additional teaching subjects range widely, from Classical to contemporary Young Adult literature. She is an Assistant Professor at California Lutheran University in Thousand Oaks.

Acknowledgements

Individual publications rarely come to be without the personal and intellectual support provided by their authors' networks of mentors, colleagues, students, friends, and families. It is all but impossible to appraise completely or to acknowledge adequately the contributions of these persons to our work. This difficulty is magnified in a multi-authored collection like this one, and so, rather than futilely attempt to enumerate our many supporters, we offer a collective thanks to all of those who, consciously or not, helped us to discover our respective secrets.

These secrets might have remained hidden, however, without the financial and professional support of a variety of individuals and institutions, and it is with a keen sense of good fortune and gratitude that we acknowledge such debts. The volume itself grew out of the collective conversation at the 2007 meeting of the Victorians Institute, hosted by the University of Alabama. Albert Pionke offers his sincerest thanks for the financial support provided to the conference by Dr. Judy Bonner in the Office of Academic Affairs, Dr. Robert Olin in the College of Arts and Sciences, Dr. Patti White in the Department of English, Dr. Jim Hall in New College, Dr. Russell McCutcheon in the Department of Religious Studies, and Dr. Ida Johnson in the Department of Women's Studies. He also gratefully acknowledges the able and willing volunteers who donated their time to the event, including Elizabeth Buckalew, Ben Fishkin, Heather Humann, Kate Matheny, Denise Millstein, and Susan Reynolds.

A number of the individual contributors also received funding and other forms of direct professional support during their research and writing. David J. Bradshaw undertook his research concerning John Henry Newman during a sabbatical leave awarded by Warren Wilson College and supported by a grant from the Appalachian College Association. He acknowledges with gratitude these institutions and also with special thanks Professor David Goslee, who arranged for him to serve as the John B. Stephenson Visiting Scholar with the Department of English at the University of Tennessee at Knoxville while he was conducting research. Sarah Hoglund wishes to thank both the American Historical Association and the North American Conference on British Studies for grants that made this research possible. Brooke McLaughlin Mitchell would like to thank the Wingate University Summer Research Program, which funds the work of a professor and student during the summer term; "Secret, Silence, and the Fractured Self" is the result of her work in this program. Eleanor Fraser Stansbie is grateful to the Associated Humanities Research Council, UK, for their funding of her doctoral research, from which this material is drawn. She would also like to express her gratitude to the Paul Mellon Centre for Studies in British Art, UK, for their granting of a Postdoctoral Fellowship, which allowed her to transform her thesis into publishable form.

She is also indebted to Professor Lynda Nead and Dr Nicola Bown, both of whom so carefully guided her through the Ph.D. process.

Finally, our editor, Ann Donahue, and the staff at Ashgate Publishing have combined unstinting enthusiasm and thorough professionalism throughout the publication process. We gratefully acknowledge their efforts.

Introduction

Victorian Secrecy: An Introduction

Albert D. Pionke

> The benignant efficacies of Concealment,' cries our Professor, 'who will speak or sing? SILENCE and SECRECY! Altars might still be raised to them (were this an altar-building time) for universal worship. Silence is the element in which great things fashion themselves together; that at length they may emerge, full-formed and majestic, into the daylight of Life, which they are thenceforth to rule.
>
> —Thomas Carlyle, *Sartor Resartus*

It may be tempting, given the still-popular view of the Victorians as afflicted with "hyper -honesty"[1] and opposed to "subtlety and obliquity of any kind,"[2] to dismiss this rhetorical effusion from Diogenes Teufelsdröckh as just another example of Carlylean hyperbole. Indeed, Carlyle's great North American disciple and popularizer, Ralph Waldo Emerson, admiringly identifies "national sincerity" as a defining "English Trait,"[3] one that sets the English apart from both Americans and, crucially, the French: "An Englishman understates, avoids the superlative, checks himself in compliments, alleging that in the French language one cannot speak without lying."[4] In his 1970 Charles Eliot Norton Lectures at Harvard University, subsequently republished as *Sincerity and Authenticity*, Lionel Trilling draws upon these remarks by Emerson and other contemporary observers to conclude that, "in the nineteenth century there was widespread belief that England produced a moral type which made it unique among nations ... This moral type which England was thought uniquely to have produced had as its chief qualities probity and candour."[5]

---

1 John Kucich, *The Power of Lies: Transgression in Victorian Fiction* (Ithaca: Cornell UP, 1994), 6.

2 James Eli Adams, *Dandies and Desert Saints: Styles of Victorian Masculinity* (Ithaca: Cornell UP, 1995), 65.

3 Ralph Waldo Emerson, *English Traits*, in *The Complete Works of Ralph Waldo Emerson*, Centenary Edition, 12 vols. (Boston: Houghton Mifflin, 1903), 5:117.

4 Emerson, 5:118. On pp. 4–17 of *The Power of Lies*, John Kucich offers a fascinating "sketch of the cultural prominence of Victorian truth-telling" that places Emerson's remarks among a broad range of assertions of honesty made by Victorian moral philosophers, Utilitarian reformers, social and natural scientists, and many others.

5 Lionel Trilling, *Sincerity and Authenticity* (Cambridge: Harvard UP, 1971), 110.

This type famously assumed normative and ahistorical dimensions in 1983 during the run- up to the general election, when Britain's Conservative Prime Minister, Margaret Thatcher, called repeatedly for a return to "Victorian values."[6] Had Thatcher been more cognizant of the direction in which our modern hermeneutics of suspicion was leading Victorian studies, she might have reconsidered her prescriptive nostalgia.[7] Already four years prior to Trilling's lectures, and then again five years after—and thus thirteen and eight years before Thatcher's election-year rhetoric—Steven Marcus and U. C. Knoepflmacher, in *The Other Victorians* and "The Counterworld of Victorian Fiction," respectively, had unearthed a set of Victorian values distinctly at odds with probity and candor, not to mention the Conservatives' 1983 political agenda.[8] Much subsequent research has revealed the extent of the Victorians' rather poorly concealed fascination with sexual and criminal transgression broadly conceived.

A more particular selection of scholarship has investigated Victorian secrecy itself. Alexander Welsh's foundational *George Eliot and Blackmail* (1985), for example, charts the emergence of our modern information culture in the Victorian period and explains how the resulting pressures exerted upon individuals' privacy

---

6 Thatcher first used the phrase "Victorian values" during a January 16 interview with Brian Walden for London Weekend Television's *Weekend World*. She subsequently repeated it during a January 28 speech to the Glasgow Chamber of Commerce, a February 17 address to the House of Commons, and a May 31 press conference on the general election. These and all of Thatcher's subsequent uses of the phrase "Victorian values" are reprinted and fully searchable on the website for The Margaret Thatcher Foundation, http://www.margaretthatcher.org/ speeches/default.asp (accessed September 11, 2007). To be precise, the values to which she principally alludes are self-reliance and personal responsibility, both values popularized in Victorian England by Samuel Smiles's *Self-Help* (1859). However, as Kucich has shown, a demand for honesty forms the basis of Smiles's doctrine. See *The Power of Lies*, 9, esp. n.16.

7 My use of the phrase "hermeneutics of suspicion" is intended to invoke the sense in which Paul Ricoeur defines this term in *Freud and Philosophy: An Essay on Interpretation*, trans. Denis Savage (New Haven: Yale UP, 1970). In this work, Ricoeur locates two opposing poles in modern hermeneutics, poles which he labels the hermeneutics of faith, dedicated to restoration of meaning and descended from theological inquiry, and the hermeneutics of suspicion, "a tearing off of masks, an interpretation that reduces disguises" derived from the works of Marx, Nietzsche, and Freud (30). Although either hermeneutic has the potential to uncover secrets—witness second-wave feminists' recovery of forgotten Victorian women writers—since the 1970s it is predominantly scholarship grounded in a hermeneutics of suspicion that has revealed those aspects of the Victorian scene most at odds with Thatcher's Conservatism.

8 Steven Marcus, *The Other Victorians: A Study in Sexuality and Pornography in Mid-Nineteenth-Century England* (New York: Basic Books, 1966). U. C. Knoepflmacher, "The Counterworld of Victorian Fiction and The Woman in White" in *The Worlds of Victorian Fiction, Harvard English Studies* 6, ed. Jerome H. Buckley, 351–69 (Cambridge: Harvard UP, 1975).

led inexorably to widespread practices of secrecy.[9] Focusing his argument specifically through the life and works of George Eliot, Welsh contends that Victorian novels with blackmail plots often end by reconcealing the truth as the proper end of ethical behavior.[10] John Kucich, in *Repression in Victorian Fiction* (1987) and *The Power of Lies* (1994), draws upon psychoanalytic theory and historically-attentive close reading to argue for the productive power of repression, whether sexual or textual, in the development of Victorian emotional, intellectual, and professional life.[11] According to Kucich, managing secrets, through behaviors ranging from sublimation to outright deception, grounded middle- class claims to cultural authority. James Eli Adams shifts the emphasis of this prolonged inquiry in Victorian secrecy onto the question of manliness by showing how those accorded the public status of gentlemen had subtly to indicate that they were reserving an essential part of their characters from the public gaze. This performance of reserve leads Adams, in *Dandies and Desert Saints* (1995), to reinsert the subversive and unstable figure of the dandy back into such popular Victorian constructions of manliness as the priest, the prophet, the soldier and the gentleman. Finally, in *The Culture of Secrecy* (1998), David Vincent uses the Post Office scandal of 1844—when it was discovered that the Post Office regularly opened suspicious mail, including potentially that of Radical MPs—as an introduction to the ways in which certain forms of information were secreted from public view in the name of national security.[12]

*****

Perhaps prompted by such scholarship, careful readers of Victorian texts will perceive a tremendous variety of positions on the issue of secrecy adopted by Victorian authors. As he does on many subjects, Anthony Trollope comes close to articulating the normative Victorian middle-class standard on the practice and valence of secrecy. Reflecting on the difficulties experienced by the too-clever police in solving the multiple thefts of the titular Eustace diamonds, Trollope's narrator remarks, "Perhaps, on the whole, more power is lost than gained by habits of secrecy. To be discreet is a fine thing—especially for a policeman; but when discretion is carried to such a length in the direction of self-confidence as to produce a belief that no aid is wanted for the achievement of great results, it will

---

9 Alexander Welsh, *George Eliot and Blackmail* (Cambridge, MA: Harvard UP, 1985).

10 Welsh, 13–15.

11 John Kucich, *Repression in Victorian Fiction: Charlotte Brontë, George Eliot, and Charles Dickens* (Berkeley: U of California P, 1987).

12 David Vincent, *The Culture of Secrecy: Britain 1832–1998* (Oxford: Oxford UP, 1998). Welsh also briefly addresses the Post Office scandal on p. 54.

often militate against all achievement."[13] It is important not to take the narrator's declaration on secrecy at face value; however, since Trollope's narrative openness is not normative but strategic, a part of his larger effort to secure authoritative status for the realist novel at the expense of sensation fiction,[14] and professional status for the realist novelist on par with that enjoyed by doctors, lawyers, and, in this case, the detective police.[15]

From the eschewal of secrecy, for whatever reason, in Trollope's *Eustace Diamonds* we pass to its celebration in Christina Rossetti's "Winter: My Secret."[16] The poem's first nine lines show Rossetti's finely nuanced appreciation for the practice of secrecy irrespective of the content of a particular secret. The poem begins bracketed by a vaguely threatening pair of "I's"—"I tell my secret? No indeed, not I" (1)—read as eyes, which appear to promise a secret of the self for the "too curious" auditor (4). It moves quickly, however, to the almost coy opening of the second stanza—"Or, after all, perhaps there's none: / Suppose there is no secret after all, / But only just my fun" (7–9)—which seems both supremely aware of the emptiness of the claims to knowledge embedded within appeals to secrecy and encouraging of the implicitly male auditor's attention. The speaker uses her "secret" to attract the auditor's opening gaze, even as she tweaks his now—impotent power to penetrate her mystery. The poem, argues Isobel Armstrong, "is … a poem about secrecy and reserve, prohibition, taboo, revealing and concealing … It is about and is itself a barrier."[17] Armstrong connects "Winter: My Secret"

---

[13] Anthony Trollope, *The Eustace Diamonds*, ed. David Skilton, intro. by P. D. James (London: Trollope Society, 1990), 456.

[14] Readers of sensation novels like Wilkie Collins's *The Moonstone* (1868), who have to undergo rather extreme measures to discover the fate of the titular jewel, for example, are told immediately the precise location of the stolen Eustace diamonds; the narrator goes on to declare that he "scorns to keep from his reader any secret that is known to himself" (422).

[15] Trollope's consistent commitment to establishing writing as a legitimate profession can be seen in his *Autobiography*, ed. David Skilton, intro. by John Sutherland (London: Trollope Society, 1999), 134; in *The Letters of Anthony Trollope*, ed. John Hall (Stanford: Stanford UP, 1983), 110; and in Trollope's work on behalf of the Royal Literary fund, the last painstakingly documented in Bradford Booth, "Trollope and the Royal Literary Fund," *Nineteenth-Century Fiction* 7 (Dec. 1952): 208–16.

[16] Christina Rossetti, "Winter: My Secret," in *The Complete Poems of Christina Rossetti: A Variorum Edition*, 3 vols., ed. R. W. Crump, 1:47 (Baton Rouge, LA: Louisiana State UP, 1979). Hereafter parenthetically cited by line number in the text. Angela Leighton, in *Victorian Women Poets: Writing Against the Heart* (Charlottesville: U of Virginia P, 1992), uses "Winter: My Secret" as a point of entry into a more pervasive "secretiveness which at times seems to be the very subject, rather than just the technique, of Rossetti's poetry" (155). See her entire subsection on "Winter Secrets" on pp. 154–63.

[17] Isobel Armstrong, *Victorian Poetry: Poetry, Poetics and Politics* (London: Routledge, 1993), 357. Figures of concealment appear throughout the poem. In the second stanza alone, the speaker refers to "a shawl, / A veil, a cloak" (10–11), "my wraps" (16), and "my mask" (17). And, of course, the ubiquitous secret runs throughout, acting as the

and its many modes of concealment to the nineteenth-century expressive theory of poetry.[18] However, Rossetti's speaker is not merely an expressive poet; rather, as her dismissal of the secret's content in stanza two suggests, she is a self-reflexive and self-critical performer of expressive theory. In other words, her denial of her own secret makes her appeal to an expressive aesthetics of the pre-linguistic secret into a parody, one acutely conscious of and ready to exploit the status, meaning, and power dynamics of secrecy itself.

Rossetti's fellow Victorian woman poet, Elizabeth Barrett Browning, offers an entirely different perspective on secrecy in "The Mask."[19] For Barrett Browning's speaker, secrecy is not a game, but an unavoidable fact of living in polite society, which unwaveringly requires "a smiling face" (1), "a jest for all" (2), a "prison-grate" for its members' "souls behind a smile" (11, 14). Her indictment of this almost pathological demand for gaiety is summarized in the penultimate seventh stanza:

> But in your bitter world, she said,
>   Face- joy's a costly mask to wear;
> 'Tis bought with pangs long nourishèd,
>   And rounded to dispair:
> Grief's earnest makes life's play, she said. (31–35)

Barrett Browning's speaker's secret is her grief, which her everyday auditors expect her to keep hidden behind "a costly mask." Among those enforcing the speaker's emotional self- repression the poem includes the reader, addressed

---

most effective method of concealment even as it complicates the meanings of these other items. If there really is "no secret after all," then there may also be no body beneath the shawl, no face behind the veil, no self apart from the mask. The speaker makes clear that power lies not in the revelation of content, but in the practice of secrecy and surveillance itself. However, her awareness of this hidden dynamic of power allows her to use secrecy to her advantage, to capture her auditor's gaze and force it to engage in a winless guessing game—winless because "there is no secret after all."

[18] Armstrong's reading of the poem in this way is useful less for its individual explanatory power than for its ability to provide a theoretical context for an alternate idea of secrecy: "Expressive theory becomes morbid either when the overflow of feeling is in excess or when it is unable to flow at all, and repressed into a secret underground life. For expressive theory is above all an aesthetics of the *secret*, the hidden experience, because the feeling which is prior to language gives language a secondary status and is often written as if it cannot take linguistic form at all" (339). By casting the secret as beyond or prior to language, expressive poetics appears to support the panoptical search for repressed truth. In fact, Armstrong's reading of "Winter: My Secret" as an expressive poem which both flaunts and conceals the truth of the speaker's sexuality demonstrates just how seamless such a connection between panopticism and expressive poetics can be (357–9).

[19] Elizabeth Barrett Browning, "The Mask," in *The Poetical Works of Elizabeth Barrett Browning*, Oxford Complete Edition, 287–8 (London: Henry Frowde, 1904). Hereafter parenthetically cited by line number in the text.

directly in the second person in lines 5, 10, and 36, and indirectly through the second-person possessive in lines 27 and 31. Ironically, the poem's own reliance on a dramatic speaker, the anonymous "she" indicated in the first and last lines of each stanza, implicates Barrett Browning in the very system of emotional self-censorship that her poem laments. Not only does the poem decline to expand upon the "death-chime" apparently at the root of the speaker's unhappiness (9), through the use of that speaker it manages to silence any overt echoes of the poet's own beloved brother Bro's drowning at Torquay: the likely impetus for the poem itself. "The Mask," then, is itself a mask, one that reveals an especially painful aspect of modern life even as it conceals the private inspiration for its own critique.

In the appropriately titled "Night Shadows" chapter of *A Tale of Two Cities*, Charles Dickens shows himself every bit as aware as, if considerably more sanguine than, Barrett Browning about the ubiquity of secrecy in everyday life. The chapter opens with the narrator's reflections upon this "wonderful fact," that

> every human creature is constituted to be that profound secret and mystery to every other. A solemn consideration, when I enter a great city by night, that every one of those darkly clustered houses encloses its own secret; that every room in every one of them encloses its own secret; that every beating heart in the hundreds of thousands of breasts there, is, in some of its imaginings, a secret to the heart nearest it![20]

As it is in all of his novels, secrecy in *A Tale of Two Cities* is both alluring and dangerous for Dickens, who attempts to manage the subject by constructing a binary opposition between the licit private sphere of the Manette family in England and the illicit conspiracy of the Jacquerie in France. The famous conclusion of the novel, in which Sydney Carton imagines the future happiness of the family that he has preserved through his own heroic, and secretive, self- sacrifice, appears designed to reassure readers that the omnipresent secrecy alluded to earlier need not be a source of anxiety or unhappiness, so long as it is practiced in the safety of the domestic sphere. As Catherine Gallagher observes, however, Dickens's solution to the problem of secrecy in the novel remains somewhat duplicitous, since it obscures the degree to which he as author manipulates the concealment and revelation of secrets in order to ensure a pleasurable reading experience.[21]

---

[20] Charles Dickens, *A Tale of Two Cities*, ed. Norman Page (London: J. M. Dent, 1998), 13.

[21] Catherine Gallagher, "The Duplicity of Doubling in *A Tale of Two Cities*," *Dickens Studies Annual* 12 (1983): 125–45. Gallagher writes, "Both the Revolution and the Dickens narrator need to transgress against the private, and, to justify their transgression, they must create a belief that dark things (plots, conspiracies, vices) lurk everywhere, needing to be revealed. The belief in secrets creates the need to expose, but the need to expose is reciprocally dependent on the invention of secret plots" (134). In other words, the novel relies on the very conspiracy that it labels illicit, the Jacquerie, to support its binary opposition between privacy and conspiracy.

Eighteen years before *A Tale of Two Cities*, in his first historical novel, *Barnaby Rudge*, Dickens had dealt at great length with the problematic of collective practices of secrecy and their potential to ignite social unrest. Set during the extreme anti-Catholicism of the last quarter of the eighteenth century, and culminating in the Gordon Riots of 1780, the novel devotes considerable attention to chronicling the rise and fall of George Gordon's Protestant Association. In the twenty-seventh weekly number, the narrator attempts to account for this organization's mass appeal by referring to its proclivity for keeping secrets:

> To surround anything, however monstrous or ridiculous, with an air of mystery, is to invest it with a secret charm, and power of attraction, which to the crowd is irresistible … when vague rumours got abroad, that in this Protestant association a secret power was mustering against the government for undefined and mighty purposes … when all this was done, as it were, in the dark, and secret invitations [were given] to join the Great Protestant Association … then the mania spread indeed, and the body, still increasing every day, grew forty thousand strong.[22]

Collective action of any kind is always suspect for Dickens, who reserves special condemnation and fictional retribution for institutional acts of concealment—these lead in *Barnaby Rudge* to "mania," to mob violence, and ultimately to death for the rioters and imprisonment for Gordon. Dickens's desire to punish those who have engaged in collective secrecy leads him quietly to violate the very history that he purports to represent, however: unlike his fictional counterpart, the real Dennis the hangman escaped without serious repercussions for his participation in the riots.

A less violent, but considerably more disturbing version of London serves as both the backdrop and the subject of the very peculiar invocation of collective secrecy in James Thomson's *The City of Dreadful Night*.[23] Before ever setting out on his evening tour of the metropolis, the poem's world-weary speaker seeks to bind himself to his reader through a series of rhetorical questions and answers, concluding with the following bleak pair:

> O sad fraternity, do I unfold
> Your dolorous mysteries shrouded from of yore?
> Nay, be assured; no secret can be told
> To any who divined it not before:
> None uninitiated by many a presage
> Will comprehend the language of the message,
> Although proclaimed aloud for evermore. (38–44)

---

22 Charles Dickens, *Barnaby Rudge*, ed. Gordon Spence (Harmondsworth: Penguin, 1997), 347–8.

23 James Thomson, *The City of Dreadful Night*, intro. Edwin Morgan (Edinburgh: Canongate Classics, 1993). Hereafter parenthetically cited by line number in the text.

This final stanza of the Proem employs a curiously strained rhetoric of secrecy to divide potential readers into two camps. The first group is cast as members of a "sad fraternity" who have already "divined" the secret of *The City*, and who therefore presumably do not need to read the poem. By contrast, the second group of "uninitiated" cannot "comprehend the language of the message," even if they hear it "for evermore," and so it seems that they need not read the poem either. The speaker thus appears to have eliminated all of his potential readers at once. Victorians did (and Victorianists still do) read the poem, of course, not least because its very appeal to a rhetoric of secrecy that discriminates between initiates and outsiders cannily plays off of readers' fascination with secrets and secrecy, thereby prompting them to keep reading. At the same time, Thomson's speaker warns these readers that the secret he is about to share may not be one that they will be glad to know. Ultimately, all those who read the poem and learn the secret join the "sad fraternity," a collective identity constructed out of this shared unpleasant knowledge.

*****

The range of representational strategies and qualitative judgments offered by this limited sample of period literature hints at the complex of motives behind the Victorians' secrets. Trollope's invocation of the police points to the many ways in which secrecy was brought to bear in the maintenance of existing networks of social control, from government censorship, to the suppression of the under-enfranchised, to the imaginative construction of conspiracies.[24] Rossetti's playful fun, by contrast, recalls how practices of secrecy were deployed to resist social control, and sometimes social change.[25] The question of whether such strategies actually resisted or merely contributed to the regimes of power that provoked them defies easy answer, and often requires critics to tack dialectically between the theoretical perspectives offered by early twentieth-century sociologist Georg Simmel and late twentieth-century post-structuralist Michel Foucault.[26]

[24] In his account of the draconian policies of the English government during the years of conflict with post-Revolutionary France, for instance, E. P. Thompson, in *The Making of the English Working Class* (New York: Vintage, 1966), contends that, for the first twenty years of the nineteenth century, "the Government *needed* conspirators, to justify the continuation of repressive legislation which prevented nation-wide popular organization." (485).

[25] Welsh cites some of the social changes during the Victorian period that might have prompted resistance in the form of secrecy: "we can discern three conditions of society that affected individuals directly and indirectly intensified the need for privacy or secrecy, and these conditions are interrelated: a self-regulating economy; social mobility and choice of occupation; and representative government. Each depends on the rise of knowledge and communication and partakes of that liberated condition that in turn enforces a new sense of accountability; each contributed to a weakening of the sense of community" (72).

[26] In "The Sociology of Secrecy and of Secret Societies," *American Journal of Sociology* 11 (1906): 441–98, Simmel shows not only the capacity for meaningful resistance offered by membership in a secret society (470–98), but also the inevitability,

"The Mask" hints at the many associations between secrecy and shame in the Victorian period, including Barrett Browning's own personal shame over having contributed the environs, at least, of Bro's death; and the shameful sexuality and habitual mendacity often projected on even acceptably demur women. At its extreme, this persistent association between secrecy and shame might grow to a connection between secrecy and criminality: not only would criminals conceal evidence of their wrongdoing, as Gashford does in Dickens's *Barnaby Rudge*; but even the possession of an innocent secret could make one suspected of a crime.

Victorian practices of secrecy could also be motivated by a desire for aesthetic, individual or corporate authority. Both Rossetti and Dickens, in *A Tale of Two Cities*, remain acutely aware of the aesthetic pleasure connected with the judicious concealment of information, and the way that pleasure can be deployed to secure readerly attention. Carlyle's chapter on "Symbols" in *Sartor Resartus*, a portion of which serves as this introduction's epigraph,[27] offers the period's most theoretically sophisticated explanation for how secrecy can be used to create an interior standard of value for the secret's holder. Adding to the natural fascination alluded to in Rossetti and Dickens, Carlyle's panegyric on silence and secrecy associates both implicitly with rulership and virtue,[28] thereby suggesting that secrecy, insofar as it derives from a privileged access to Truth, is an estimable practice. As Dickens, in *Barnaby Rudge*, and Thomson demonstrate, this accrual of charismatic authority through secrecy could be harnessed by collectives as well, especially when yoked to popular prejudice or notions of belonging to a privileged "fraternity." Recently, Mary Poovey has shown convincingly the degree to which secrecy, and even active misinformation, was central to Victorian business practices, ranging from

---

even desirability of secrecy in interpersonal relations: "the fruitful depth of relationships which, behind every latest revelation, implies the still unrevealed, which also stimulates anew every day to gain what is already possessed, is merely the reward of that tenderness and self-control which, even in the closest relationship, comprehending the whole person, still respect the inner private property, which hold the right of questioning to be limited by a right of secrecy" (462). Foucault's work in general evinces profound skepticism of such resistance through secrecy, and his specific comments on the "secret" of sexuality, in *The History of Sexuality: Volume 1: An Introduction.*, trans. Robert Hurley (New York: Vintage, 1990), reveal the ways in which secrecy can function as a ruse of power: "What sustains our eagerness to speak of sex in terms of repression is doubtless this opportunity to speak out against the powers that be, to utter truths and promise bliss, to link together enlightenment, liberation, and manifold pleasures; to pronounce a discourse that combines the fervor of knowledge, the determination to change the laws, and the longing for the garden of earthly delights" (7).

[27] Thomas Carlyle, *Sartor Resartus: The Life and Opinions of Herr Teufelsdröckh in Three Books*, Introduction and notes by Roger L. Tarr, Text established by Mark Engel and Rodger L. Tarr (Berkeley: U of California P, 2000), 161.

[28] This tacit connection of secrecy and virtue is reinforced by Teufelsdröckh's allusion to the Gospel of Matthew 6:3 in the next paragraph: "Thought will not work except in Silence: neither will Virtue work except in Secrecy. Let not thy right hand know what thy left hand doeth!" (162).

the protection of trade secrets to the solicitation of investment capital.[29] Indeed, Victorian professionals in most fields relied upon collective practices of secrecy to create and maintain their intellectual, disciplinary, and social authority.[30]

This bewildering range of secrets and motives for keeping them exerts tremendous pressure on any hermeneutic deployed to make sense of Victorian secrecy as a general cultural practice. Faced with specific examples of secrecy, the Victorians themselves tended towards normative qualitative judgments based upon the actual or imagined contents, motives, and keeper(s) of a given secret. In general, secrecy that could be located within the private sphere and attributed to individuals met with greater approbation than secrecy deemed public and associated with non-familial collectives. This process of qualitative evaluation can be productively represented as a parallelogram divided into quadrants according to, from left to right, licit versus illicit and, from top to bottom, individual versus collective, forms of secrecy. Individual privacy would likely appear in the upper left quadrant; criminal behavior in the upper right; and trade unionism, Roman Catholic monasticism (aka, Jesuitism), and other supposedly dangerous group practices amenable to accusations of conspiracy would certainly be placed in the bottom right quadrant. In the bottom left quadrant, slightly offset to reflect Victorian middle-class suspicions of all collective behavior, one would find business secrecy and acts undertaken by the government in the name of national security. The more publicity such tacitly licit activities received however, the less acceptable they became, as is evident from widespread public hostility towards the kinds of clandestine accounting practices that precipitated the financial panics of 1847, 1866, and 1878, as well as the Home Office use of informers and the Post Office scandal mentioned earlier.[31] Moreover, since Victorian normative

---

29 "If the twin imperatives to disclose information and keep secrets are inherent in the modern market economy, then these agendas assumed a particularly intimate—and fraught—relationship in nineteenth-century Britain…the incentive to keep business secrets was heightened by increased competition in nearly every sector of the business community, and it was supported by the long-standing assumption that every man has a right to keep his financial dealings to himself" (Poovey, "Writing about Finance in Victorian England: Disclosure and Secrecy in the Culture of Investment," *Victorian Studies* 45, no. 1 [Autumn 2002]: 17–42, 30, 31). In her Introduction to *The Financial System in Nineteenth-Century Britain* (New York: Oxford UP, 2003), Poovey also notes, "This curious relationship between the financial community and the press, in which secrecy and misinformation were sometimes considered more valuable than accuracy, meant that the members of the public could not always find out what they wanted to know or know when they could trust what they read" (25).

30 As Adams succinctly notes, "Victorian obsessions with secrecy are manifold and powerfully overdetermined" (13).

31 According to Foucault, "power is tolerable only on condition that it mask a substantial part of itself. Its success is proportional to its ability to hide its own mechanisms … For it [power], secrecy is not in the nature of an abuse; it is indispensable to its operation" (86).

standards remain notoriously amenable to influence from class bias, religious preference, racial stratification, and other forms of individual and national caprice, there were numerous exceptions to the general rule, and often disagreements about the exceptions.[32] Finally, judgment, however capricious or debated, presumes discovery: should the keepers of a given secret be successful, judgment becomes impossible; unfortunately, secrets actively and successfully concealed risk becoming secrets passively forgotten in the absence of their original keepers. There is no way of knowing how many times this transition to cultural amnesia occurred, but the ever-increasing volume of Victorian scholarship dedicated to the recovery of historically under-enfranchised constituencies suggests that we still have a lot to remember.

*****

Given the fluidity and scope of the Victorians' practices of and attitudes towards secrecy, it is not the intention of this volume to privilege a single hermeneutic or disciplinary approach to the subject. Written by scholars working in the fields of art history, cultural studies, political and social history, and literary studies, the individual essays interrogate their shared subject using archival research, contemporary psychological theory, formalist textual analysis, historical reconstruction, and post-structuralist critique. Collectively, they offer multiple points of entry into the productive range of possible approaches to, and highlight the potential for interdisciplinary inquiry that emerges from, unearthing the Victorians' secrets.

The essays are arranged chronologically according to their primary objects of analysis; beginning with Sarah Hoglund's reconstruction of the multifaceted debate over intramural burial that occupied the late 1830s. Ultimately a question of where to hide the bodies of the dead, this debate united those concerned with public health, public morality, and class conformity in advocating against the practice of neighborhood burial and in favor of suburban "garden cemeteries" as historically and ideologically appropriate repositories for the departed. In a more figurative consideration of where bodies are buried, Deborah Logan investigates Harriet Martineau's largely forgotten intervention into the debate over the repeal of the Corn Laws in 1846, an intervention somewhat disingenuously labeled by Martineau as her "only political plot." Logan's essay, "Harriet Martineau's 'only political plot,'" reconstructs the instrumental role played by Martineau in repairing the personal breach between then-PM Robert Peel and radical MP Richard Cobden

---

[32] English Freemasonry is perhaps the most noticeable exemption from the general principles outlined above, whereas one of the more contentious disagreements that emerged from the Victorians' fungible approach to secrecy concerned the appropriate response to Italian unification in the 1860s. Both subjects are treated at some length in my own *Plots of Opportunity: Representing Conspiracy in Victorian England* (Columbus: Ohio State UP, 2004), the Freemasons on pp. 1–21 and Italian unification on pp. 101–32.

that had been impeding the process of repeal, and goes on to detail the ways in which Martineau's efforts remained "secret history" until posthumously publicized in the *Autobiography*.

Shifting focus from a political reconciliation to a crisis of faith, David Bradshaw's "Secrecy and Reticence in John Henry Newman's *Loss and Gain*," explores the links between secrecy, religious conversion, autobiography and the novel made perspicuous in the fictionalized Oxford experience of Charles Reding. Written in 1848, only three years after Newman's conversion to Roman Catholicism, this early semi-autobiographical *Apologia*, Bradshaw argues, represents the concealment of religious conviction and doubt as a practical defensive strategy against theological zealotry, a necessary element of personal religious growth, and a first step towards the perception of the divine. A much less sanguine representation of the connection between secrecy and faith emerges from John McBratney's "'What Connexion Can There Be?'" which reconsiders the criminal, social, and narratological modes of detection employed by Inspector Bucket in Charles Dickens's *Bleak House* (1852–3). A powerful figure for much of the novel, Bucket cannot discover all of its secrets in time to save Jo or Lady Deadlock, and his failure, McBratney argues, calls into question both the idea of Providential design and its novelistic corollary, the omniscient third-person narrator.

The example of panoptical detection and its failures provided by *Bleak House* paved the way for the troubling interpenetration of individual, institutional, and aesthetic forms of secrecy that characterizes the "sensational sixties." The next four essays in the collection concern themselves with a variety of secrets from this most secret-obsessed of decades. In "Concealing Minds and the Case of *The Woman in White*," Maria K. Bachman deploys a hybrid of narrative theory and cognitive psychology, most recently formulated by Lisa Zunshine in *Why We Read Fiction: Theory of Mind and the Novel*, to trace the links between secrecy, cognition, and narration in Collins's narrative. At the same time, by noting that *The Woman in White* (1860) steadfastly refuses to reveal all of its secrets, Bachman also uses the text to test the limits of Theory of Mind as a strategy for reading novels. At least in part, Collins may have intended his novel to undermine facile definitions of lunacy and the forcible confinement of troublesome relations to private asylums, but even he, one suspects, would have endorsed the medical incarceration of Richard Dadd, the Royal Academy trained painter confined to Bethlem Asylum for patricide in 1844, and the subject of Eleanor Fraser Stansbie's "A Victorian Picture Puzzle." Locating Dadd's *The Fairy Feller's Masterstroke* (1864), perhaps his most famous painting, in the context of mid-century shifts in the treatment of the insane—the painting was commissioned by Dadd's doctors as a form of expressive therapy—she argues that the crowded and enigmatic canvas can be read as a strategic response by Dadd to the panoptical clinical scrutiny directed at his art and interior life.

In "Detecting Business Fraud at Home," Tamara Wagner explores the destabilizing effects of white collar crime in Charlotte Yonge's *The Clever Woman of the Family* (1865), the plot of which turns on the detection and trial of a fraudulent clergyman. According to Wagner, the exposure of Mauleverer does more than simply permit Yonge a moment of sensational anti-Catholicism: it radically undermines the moral authority of the worlds of home, finance capitalism, and religion. A different threat to the moral authority of home occupies Denise Tischler Millstein in "George Eliot, *Felix Holt, The Radical* and Byronic Secrets." Using Felix Holt's accidental discovery, and subsequent self-righteous denunciation, of Esther Lyon's carefully secreted copy of Byron's works as a window into the revival of interest in the late 1860s in Byron's infamous sex life, she argues that the inclusion of Byron in *Felix Holt* (1866) indicates Eliot's recognition of Byron's enduring importance to Victorian political, literary and gendered self-conceptions, and her distrust of excessively radical political and sexual liberty.

Even as he shifts the volume from the sensational 1860s to the more eclectic 1870s, Robert Fletcher still evinces interest in sensationalism, sexuality and textual secrecy in "The Perverse Secrets of Masculinity in Augusta Webster's Dramatic Poetry." Focusing on Webster's attentive figurations of masculinity in "The Snow Waste" (1866), "With the Dead" (1866), and "The Manuscript of Saint Alexius" (1870), Fletcher reads all three poems as ambivalently poised between ethical identification with their monomaniacal male subjects and radical rejection and revision of the concealed ethos of masculinity revealed by their monomania. Working fully within the 1870s, although on an entirely different stage, Michael Claxton traces the tensions between professional secrecy and public respectability encountered by Victorian magicians. In "Victorian Conjuring Secrets," Claxton shows how those who thought of themselves as "true conjuring artists" were eager to distinguish themselves from, often by publishing the secrets of, spirit mediums, Eastern magicians, and street-side card sharps and other hustlers; to guard their own professional secrets from exposure in publications like *Modern Magic* (1876); and to profit from the increased popularity that such exposés produced.

Allison Wee's "A Secret Censorship" exposes a previously unknown secret of the Victorian Home Office, which in 1885 sought to prevent the publication of salacious accusations of homosexuality in the military, the police, and the aristocracy in the small weekly newspaper *Town Talk*. Using unpublished material from the Home Office archive, Wee traces the unwillingness of Home Office officials to censor directly the paper's editor, Adolphus Rosenberg, who preemptively sought their approval before publication; instead, the threat of a likely non-existent arrest warrant for obscene publication caused Rosenberg to close his own paper and disappear, effectively censoring himself. The volume concludes with a similarly unrevealed secret in *Tess of the d'Urbervilles* (1891) which provides Brooke McLaughlin Mitchell with a crucial link between contemporary trauma theory and the experience of reading Hardy's novel. In "Secrets, Silence, and the Fractured Self," she uses the narrator's reticence about what, precisely, happens to Tess at The Chase to argue that the text relies upon a prescient formulation of still-developing notions of psychological trauma to undermine the self-righteous prurience of some of Hardy's late-Victorian readers.

Together, the essays in this collection allow the Victorians to reveal their own uneasy, fractious, and unavoidable reliance on secrecy in their individual, aesthetic, professional, and national lives. Whether they adopt Victorian practices of and attitudes toward secrecy as objects of analysis or as points of interpretive departure, they show the relevance of the Victorians' practices of secrecy to issues central to current scholarship of the period, including individual self-formation, class and gender construction, political liberalism, and disciplinary and professional identity. Moreover, the essayists' productive diversity of approaches to their common subject reflects the increasing theoretical heterogeneity of Victorian studies, and the collective impulse of Victorianists to reappraise the interpretive legacy of Foucauldian accounts of the period and its secrets. Finally, by revising the popular misperception of Victorian England as largely free from concealment, the essays also provide an historical explanation for more modern investments in individual secrets, national security, and conspiracy theory. In other words, they suggest that certain Victorian values have been with us all along.

Chapter 1
Hidden Agendas: The Secret to Early Nineteenth-Century British Burial Reform

Sarah Hoglund

> And is it not most indecent, not to speak of frightful infection, that custom and cupidity should be permitted, without arousing public indignation, or being felt to violate the sanctity of some of the deepest and dearest principles of our nature, that the secrecy and silence of the grave should be disregarded.
>
> —"London Grave-Yards," *Monthly Review* (Feb. 1840)

By the time this censure was published burial grounds, in use for generations, had grown so saturated with the dead that they were unable, literally, to conceal what to many should have been the central secret of the graveyard—the dead body. Space for subsequent interments was secured by the removal of previous tenants whose dismembered bodies and bones were strewn wantonly about graveyards. With the physical and moral health of the nation at risk, physicians, theologians, landscape gardeners, urban planners, public health officials, and barristers of every political persuasion across Britain became increasingly convinced that the reformation of burial practices was a matter of grave significance. Many believed, as George Alfred Walker wrote, that "burial places in the neighborhood of the living" were a "national evil—the harbingers, if not the originators of pestilence; the cause, direct or indirect, of inhumanity, immorality, and irreligion."[1] Walker, and many like him, felt that the creation of new institutions of burial was an obligation "no less to the sacred ashes of the dead than to the health of the living" (4). They cited a litany of lurid details—the urban graveyards' stench, rumors of partially decomposed bodies exhumed and burned by church sextons, coffins burned as firewood, human bones unearthed and ground into fertilizer—in an attempt to rally support for the cause of burial reform.[2] While these authors worried over the effects of intramural

---

1 George Alfred Walker, *Gatherings from Graveyards: Particularly those of London; with a Concise History of the Modes of Interment Among Different Nations from the Earliest Periods; and a Detail of the Dangerous and Fatal Results Produced by the Unwise & Revolting Custom of Inhuming the Dead in the Midst of the Living* (London: Longman, 1839), iii. Hereafter cited parenthetically in the text.

2 See, for example, [Robert Southey], "Cemeteries and Catacombs of Paris," *Quarterly Review* 21, no. 42 (April 1819): 380; A Friend to Decency, "Bad Effects of Contracted Burying Grounds," *Imperial Magazine* 1, no. 5 (May 1819): 451–3; "New Place

burial on public health, others argued that the urban churchyards were simply unfit for the proper memorialization of their loved ones. In 1831, for example, John Strang wrote that the churchyard, "instead of proving ... either the solemn and affecting shrine of devotion, or the resort and consolation of the weeping individuals, is little better than a disgusting charnel house avoided by general consent, as if infected with a pestilence, and calculated even when entered to call forth rather the feelings of aversion and disgust, than of sympathy and sorrow."[3] For both of these groups, British burial grounds had become a site of national crisis, the cause of "inhumanity, immorality, and irreligion." They saw the various social ills that plagued the nation as the result of a failure to conceal the dead, to keep the corpse properly hidden. If only the dead body could be secreted away, concealed within the verdant acres of the new Victorian garden cemeteries or the proposed municipal cemeteries, these authors claimed, any number of problems could be rectified. While they spoke of the need to keep the process of physical decay secret, however, the desire that appears to have motivated these treatises lay elsewhere. In this essay, I look closely at the work of Walker to demonstrate that beneath his discussion of the implications of overcrowded inner city burial for matters of public health and social equilibrium lay another secret, namely a desire to reconfigure the relationship between nineteenth-century Britons and the history of Western culture.[4]

---

of Public Sepulture," *Newcastle Magazine* 8, no. 3 (May 1829): 109–11; H., "On Crowded Churchyards, and a Metropolitan Cemetery," *Mirror of Literature, Amusement, and Instruction* 16, no. 446 (August 1830): 141; J. A. Picton, "On Cemeteries," Architectural Magazine 4, no. 43 (September 1837): 429; Basil Holmes, *The London Burial Grounds: Notes on their History from the Earliest Times to the Present Day* (London: T. F. Unwin, 1896), 214.

3 John Strang, *Necropolis Glasguensis: with Observations on Ancient and Modern Tombs and Sepulture* (Glasgow: Atkinson, 1831), 24.

4 A number of recent authors have addressed the question of burial reform in nineteenth-century Britain. The majority have focused on the writings of bureaucrat Edwin Chadwick, particularly his parliamentary enquiry into urban poverty, and his spin-off investigations into the problems of urban interment. Though Chadwick remains a key figure in the historiography of public health, it is important that we not overlook the contributions his predecessor, George Alfred Walker (1807–84) to whom Chadwick's influential *Supplementary Report on Interment in Towns* (1843) owes a great deal. Indeed, Chadwick drew much of the evidence in his *Supplementary Report* straight from Walker, either in the form of direct testimony, or quotes lifted verbatim from Walker's published works. This is not, of course, to downplay the importance of Chadwick's *Supplementary Report*, which was in many ways more comprehensive than Walker's investigations. Chadwick widened the scope of inquiry to include the problem of urban sanitation more generally, and was interested in larger questions of morbidity and mortality. See for example Chris Brooks, *Mortal Remains: the History and Present State of the Victorian and Edwardian Cemetery* (Exeter: Wheaton, 1989); Julie Rugg, "A New Burial Form and Its Meanings: Cemetery Establishment in the First Half of the Nineteenth Century" in *Grave Concerns: Death and Burial in England 1700 to 1850*, ed. Margaret Cox (York: Council for British Archaeology,

Walker's *Gatherings from Grave Yards* attracted a great deal of attention soon after it was published in November 1839 and was favorably reviewed in publications ranging from medical and scientific journals, to cheap weeklies, popular monthlies and established quarterlies. But arguments against unsavory urban burial grounds had been raised long before his salacious exposé became something of a best seller. In a 1552 sermon, Bishop Hugh Latimer wondered why "London, being so rich a city, hath not a burying ground without"? After all, "many a man taketh his death in Paul's church-yard," and Latimer himself had "felt such an ill-favored unwholesome savour" when giving sermons. For Latimer, Londoners should follow the "good and laudable custom" of the citizens of Nain, whom Christ witnessed carrying a dead body on a funeral procession toward their extramural burial ground.[5] John Evelyn took a similar stance in "Silva," his 1664 essay on tree cultivation, when he suggested that burial should be moved north of the walls of the City of London. There, "a grated inclosure [sic], of competent breadth for a mile in length, might have served as a universal cemetery to all parishes … distinguished by like separations, and with ample walks of trees, the walks adorned with monuments, inscriptions, and titles, apt for the contemplation and memory of the defunct."[6] Not much had changed by 1672, when Evelyn described churchyards in Norwich with layers of bodies stacked so high around the perimeter that "the churches seemed to be built in pitts."[7] Just a few short

1998); Karen Sanchez–Eppler, "Decomposing: Wordsworth's Poetry of Epitaph and English Burial Reform," *Nineteenth-Century Literature* 42, no. 4 (March 1998): 415–31; Mary Elizabeth Hotz, *Literary Remains: Representations of Death and Burial in Victorian England* (Albany, NY: SUNY P, 2009), and "Down Among the Dead: Edwin Chadwick's Burial Reform Discourse in Mid-Nineteenth-Century England," *Victorian Literature and Culture* 29, no. 1 (March 2001): 21–38; Tara White Kee, "No Place for the Dead: The Struggle for Burial Reform in Mid-Nineteenth-Century London," (Ph.D. diss. University of Delaware, 2006). Nevertheless, a gap remains in the history of death and disposal during the first half of the nineteenth century, one which I hope to go some way toward filling. While not the "full narration" of Walker's burial reform campaign, called for by Peter Jupp in 1997, this essay seeks to reorient discussions of Walker by portraying him not solely in relation to the later burial reform movement, but as an important intellectual voice in his own right. See Peter Jupp, "Enon Chapel: No Way for the Dead," in *The Changing Face of Death: Historical Accounts of Death and Disposal*, ed. Peter C. Jupp and Glennys Howarth (New York: Palgrave Macmillan, 1997), 96.

5 Hugh Latimer, *Select Sermons* (Boston: Hilliard and Gray, 1832), 276.

6 See John Evelyn, *Silva; or a Discourse on Forest Trees*, 5th ed. (London: J. Walthoe, J. Knapton, D. Midwinter, A. Bettesworth, J. Tonson, 1729), 147. In the first half of the nineteenth century, this passage from Evelyn was quoted repeatedly in support of arguments for new burial space. This diverse array of publications included: *the Quarterly Review* (1819), *London Medical Gazette* (1830), *The Court Journal* (1833), *the Penny Magazine* (1834) and *Household Words* (1850).

7 William Bray, ed., *Memoirs of John Evelyn: Comprising His Diary, from 1641–1705–6, and a Selection of His Familiar Letters* (London: Frederick Warne and Co., 1871), 360.

years later, John Vanbrugh and Christopher Wren recommended the construction of extramural cemeteries following the Great Fire of 1666. When Vanbrugh, with Wren, submitted his plan for fifty new churches in London in 1712, he pressed that the new churches

> ... may be free'd from that Inhumane custome of being made Burial Places for the dead. a Custome in which there is something so very barbarous in itself besides the many ill consequences that attend it; that one cannot enough wonder how it ever has prevail'd amongst the civiliz'd part of mankind.[8]

Like Evelyn, of course, Vanbrugh believed Londoners could rectify the situation by establishing a series of cemeteries on the "outskirts of Town."[9]

In 1721, London curate Thomas Lewis wrote of the need to end urban interment in *Seasonable Considerations on the Indecent and Dangerous Custom of Burying in Churches and Churchyards*. The custom of burying in churches and churchyards was both indecent to God, as "the Church is his House, and it is not to be prophaned, nor polluted," as well as dangerous to man.[10] Contemporary practice allowed "great Numbers [to be] buried promiscuously of all Sorts of Distempers; and many in Coffins as hardly hold together."[11] Compounding this threat to Londoners health and wellbeing, vaults and graves in congested crypts and churchyards were commonly left unsealed for days. As a result, visitors to the churchyards had on more than one occasion been exposed to the sight of decaying corpses. The conditions that Lewis decried as "an Act of Profanity, Indecency, and of most Pernicious Consequences to the Living," had hardly improved by 1838 when a letter sent to the *Morning Chronicle* and *Weekly Dispatch* shamefully noted that "in this place of 'Christian burial,' you may see human heads, covered

---

[8] John Vanbrugh, "Mr Van–Brugg's Proposals about Building ye New Churches (1712)," *British Architectural Theory 1540–1750: An Anthology of Texts*, ed. Caroline van Eck, with contributions by Christy Anderson (Burlington, VT: Ashgate, 2003), 138.

[9] Vanbrugh referred to the spacious cemetery established by the East India Company outside of Surat, which he had seen while a junior merchant in the company. In 1711, he produced a plan for a six-acre cemetery on the periphery of London, which he based largely on his experiences at Surat. See Kerry Downes, "Vanbrugh's India and his Mausolea for England," in *Sir John Vanbrugh and Landscape Architecture in Baroque England 1690–1730*, ed. Christopher Ridgway and Robert Williams (Stroud, UK: Sutton, 2000), 122; and Joseph Roach, *Cities of the Dead: Circum-Atlantic Performance* (New York: Columbia UP, 1996).

[10] Thomas Lewis, *Seasonable Considerations on the Indecent and Dangerous Custom of Burying in Churches and Churchyards: with Remarkable Observations, Historical and Philosophical, Proving that the Custom is not only Contrary to the Practice of the Antients, but Fatal, in case of Infection* (London: A. Bettesworth, 1721), 54. See also Mark Jenner, "Death, Decomposition and Dechristianisation? Public Health and Church Burial in Eighteenth-Century England," *English Historical Review* 120, no. 487 (2005): 615–32.

[11] Lewis, 57–8.

with hair, and here, in this 'consecrated ground,' are human bones with flesh still adhering to them."[12]

Walker's condemnation of urban burial was not, therefore, particularly novel by the time he published his text in 1839. Indeed, he appears to have been familiar with many of these earlier arguments, citing both Latimer and Thomas Pennant's eighteenth-century observations of St. Giles's churchyard, in which, for example, coffins were said to have been "piled one upon the other, all exposed to sight and smell."[13] Yet, given the number of authors who had addressed this issue in the seventeenth and eighteenth centuries, why, one must ask, did these practices become such an important matter in the first half of the nineteenth century? Why did this debate gain such urgency more than 150 years after it had first been raised? In addition, by the time Walker's *Gatherings from Graveyards* appeared in 1839, extramural burial was not uncommon. With the opening of Kensal Green cemetery in 1832, Norwood cemetery in 1837 and Highgate cemetery in 1839, great numbers of Londoners had begun to be interred in what was then the countryside. Walker's treatise thus articulated an underlying sense of shame that Britain, one of the most successful and prosperous nations of the world, had failed the least of its citizens by neglecting to enact a thoroughgoing official reform of burial practices. Opening his text with a nationalistic cry for reform, he asked why London

> the seat of science, the arena of inventions, the vast amphitheatre where all that is great, good and noble; all that is conducive to the comforts and pleasures of life—all that the mind can conceive for good or evil—that London, with its thousands of busy minds and observant eyes, anxiously exploring the dimly shadowed outline of the future, yet neglecting the awful monitors of the past;—should bear upon its breast those awful plague spots, the BURIAL GROUNDS, must appear to every reflecting mind, an anomaly not easily explained (1).

Surveying forty-two public and private burial grounds in London, all situated in close proximity to private residences, Walker found them "overcrowded," "disorderly" and "disgusting" places of interment. Even more alarming, there was no corner of the capital immune to the problem: Westminster, Southwark, Spitalfields, all, according to Walker, were home to burial spaces that were simply unsuitable to basic human decency. The intermingling of the living and the dead was, as noted, a "national evil" responsible for any number of physical and social

---

[12] T. James, "Disgusting State of Churchyards," *Morning Chronicle*, September 27, 1838. Ensuring a wider audience, James also sent his observations to the *Weekly Dispatch*, where it was published on September 30, 1838. Ruth Richardson has noted that St. Giles's churchyard was a popular source of the cadavers "bodysnatchers" or "ressurectionsts" unearthed to satiate the demands of London's numerous anatomical schools. See Richardson, *Death, Dissection and the Destitute* (Chicago: U of Chicago Press, 2000), 60. However, by the time this scandalous re-appearance of St. Giles's corpses was published in the metropolitan papers, the practice had been rendered virtually obsolete by the Anatomy Act of 1832, which awarded researchers the unclaimed bodies of paupers.

[13] See Pennant, *Of London* (London: Robert Faulder, 1790), 162.

ills. And these problems would only intensify as the population of Britain continued to grow and gather in metropolitan areas. The population of London alone had more than doubled between 1801 and 1841, from 958,000 to 1,948,000, but adequate accommodations had not been made for the burial of the city's dead.[14]

For *Blackwood's*, these "dead-pits," were "admirable specimen[s] of the art of packing—of compressing the greatest possible quantity into the smallest possible space."[15] But for Walker, such carefully contrived configurations were the exception rather than the rule. The bulk of his 258-page opus cataloged in gory detail the many and varied abuses associated with burial in London. At a graveyard in Southwark, he tells his audience, "a body partly decomposed was dug up and placed on the surface, at the side slightly covered with earth." Worse still, "a mourner stepped upon it, and the loosened skin peeled off, he slipped forward and had nearly fallen into the grave" (20–2). At Enon Chapel Walker was struck by "the total disregard of decency exhibited—numbers of coffins were piled in confusion—large quantities of bones were mixed with the earth, and lying upon the floor of this cellar (for vault it ought not to be called), lids of *coffins* might be trodden upon at almost every step" (157). As sensationalistic as these stories may sound, according to Walker experiences of this sort were all too common. Living and working in the Strand, he explained, had brought him into daily contact with the disrespectful practices of any number of unsanitary churchyards.

Walker's understanding of the dangers posed by these unsanitary churchyards was undoubtedly influenced by continental European discussions of contagion. Of particular influence was the work of French physician and anatomist Félix Vicq d'Azyr. d'Azyr's pioneering research in public health and epidemiology led him in the late-eighteenth century to challenge existing funerary practices and to advocate the construction of new burial grounds outside of French cities.[16] He published influential tracts based on his investigations that detailed the dangers of burial in church vaults.[17] Perhaps the most detailed of these examples, one which would be repeated by later burial reformers, concerned University of Montpellier professor, Dr. Henri Haguenot's account of the churchyard and crypt at the parish church of Notre Dame in Montpellier. On the evening of 17 August 1744, the

---

[14] S. E. Finer, *The Life and Times of Sir Edwin Chadwick* (London: Methuen, 1952), 213. In 1841, a reader estimated in the *Times*, based on a recent Parliamentary return, that in 1832 alone, London's 134 parish churches and burial-grounds had been forced to accommodate an average of 217 bodies per acre. See, Anti-Pestilence, "The Dead versus The Living," *Times* (London) October 9, 1841.

[15] [Henry King], "Post-Mortem Musings," *Blackwood's Edinburgh Magazine* 48 (December 1840): 829.

[16] See André Parent, "Félix Vicq d'Azyr: Anatomy, Medicine and Revolution," *The Canadian Journal of Neurological Sciences* 34, no. 1 (February 2007): 32–3.

[17] Of d'Azyr's many publications, most influential to the cause of burial reform was his *Essai sur les lieux et les dangers des sepultures* (Paris: Didot, 1778), in which he translated and expanded an earlier work on sepulchral emanations in Modena by the Italian cleric Scipione Piattoli.

portefaix, in the process of partially exhuming a common grave, was overcome by mephitic exhalations and fell into a state of apoplexy. A horrified onlooker was lowered by rope to extract the motionless grave-digger, but scarcely reached the bottom of the pit before his body went limp and was quickly retrieved in a state close to death. Miraculously, the samaritan soon regained consciousness but languished in a debilitated state for some time thereafter. Less fortunate were the three subsequent men who attempted to withdraw the body—even the most robust constitution could not withstand the dangers of the grave, and all were said to have perished from the noxious effluvia.[18]

Also important in the development of Walker's thinking was the work of Felix Pascalis. In 1823, Pascalis, a respected Italian-American physician, translated into English d'Azyr's and Scipione Piattoli's writings on the dangers of urban interment. In his *Exposition of the Dangers of Interment in Cities*, described by one reviewer as "partly translation, partly a compilation, and partly original," Pascalis linked the outbreak of the 1822 yellow fever epidemic in New York to the surfeit of decaying corpses in the burial ground of Trinity Church.[19] As Pascalis's text had played an important role in the 1823 prohibition of burials in lower Manhattan, Walker lamented that it "had not fallen into [his] hands at an earlier period." Time and again Walker deferred to Pascalis, d'Azyr and Piattoli and cited the French and American debates on urban burial as examples of sepulchral progress.

The ideas of these public health specialists were crucial for Walker. Written before the germ theory of disease causation was understood, his text brims with the language of poisoned air, miasmas and humors. He discussed the "nature and effects of the various deleterious products of human putrefaction," claiming that

---

18 d'Azyr, xii–xiv. d'Azyr was not alone. Many physicians and surgeons presented strong opposition to popular burial practices in late-eighteenth-century France. As a result, in 1765, the Parlement of Paris restricted burials in urban churchyards and churches, and eleven years later burials in church vaults were restricted. Further state intervention in burial matters occurred in the 1780s, when the famed Cemetery of the Holy Innocents in Paris was closed and the human remains cleared. Then, in 1804, a Napoleonic decree that places of interment be moved to the outskirts of urban areas led to the creation of the celebrated Père la Chaise cemetery in northwest Paris. These acts all drew on Enlightenment discussions that portrayed the dead body as both a source of contagion and an object subject to oppressive ecclesiastical control. See Richard A. Etlin, *The Architecture of Death: The Transformation of the Cemetery in Eighteenth-Century Paris* (Cambridge, Mass.: MIT Press, 1984), 3–39; Thomas A. Kselman, *Death and the Afterlife in Modern France* (Princeton, N.J.: Princeton UP, 1993), 169–74.

19 See Felix Pascalis, *An Exposition of the Dangers of Interment in Cities: Illustrated by an Account of the Funeral Rites and Customs of the Hebrews, Greeks, Romans, and Primitive Christians; by Ancient and Modern Ecclesiastical Canons, Civil Statutes, and Municipal Regulations; and by Chemical and Physical Principles. Chiefly from the Works of Vicq d'Azyr and Prof. Scipione Piattoli with additions by Felix Pascalis* (New York: W. B. Gilley, 1823); "Pascalis on the Danger of Interment in Cities," *The New York Medical and Physical Journal* 4, no. 13 (January–March 1825): 113–121.

"miasmata from animal putrescencey not only may cause the loss of life, but it exacerbates the intensity of pestilential diseases" (vi, iv). To readers, his accounts of the smell of rotting bodies would have sounded quite familiar, but Walker's goal was to emphasize a very direct connection between the corpse's stench and the spread of disease (101). Deferring to the writings of experts like d'Azyr, Pascalis and others, Walker repeated his basic assertion that the exhalations from dead bodies were "very afflicting and dangerous" to the living (105). Burying the dead body was an inherently risky proposition, he wrote, but never more so than when undertaken in close, public quarters, as the "atmosphere of churches is ordinarily moist and heavy," and the "putridity of the air" within churches was directly connected to the practice of frequently opening tombs to inter new bodies (109). In nearly every burial ground he surveyed, Walker commented upon the "noxious odors" that permeated the air, frequently mentioning the various fevers with which those odors were associated.[20] Those who lived near graveyards, he suggested, suffered an almost incalculable acceleration of disease and degradation. Upon entering these quarters, the "disgusting," "offensive," "loathsome" air "produce[d] a feeling of nausea." How, he asked, could the proprietors of these grounds maintain a clear conscience while crowding bodies into such small spaces? The living and the dead, he averred, would have to be separated.[21]

However, it is important to note that for Walker, the encroachment of the dead endangered more than the health of local residents; it threatened to corrupt their sense of decency. In Clerkenwell, for example, all four of the parish churchyards were not only overcrowded and fetid, with the sheer number of bodies causing the ground "saturated with human putrescence" to rise to the level of the first floor windows, they were also a moral danger: as he put it, in "this filthy neighborhood fever prevails, and poverty and wretchedness go hand in hand" (176). How could the poor be expected to better themselves, he asked, when they were surrounded by such "degradation" and "noxious disorder"?[22] Intramural burials of this sort "disgrace and degrade … civilized beings. They teach us the sad, the humiliating truth, that the holiest of feelings are openly trampled on in this land which boasts so loudly of its Christianity, and that abuses of the most revolting kind are winked at and tolerated for the sake of gain."[23] Worse still, it was the crowded neighbourhoods

---

[20] For a discussion of how late-eighteenth-century medical and scientific theory came to be led by the nose, see Alain Corbain's seminal *The Foul and the Fragrant: Odor and the French Social Imagination* (Cambridge, Mass.: Harvard UP, 1988).

[21] Much of the medical community stood behind Walker's assertions, with the *Lancet*, *British and Foreign Medical Review*, *Edinburgh Medical and Surgical Journal*, *Medical Times* and the *Medico-Chirurgical Review* reproducing large tracts of his writings.

[22] Quite famously, Edwin Chadwick took up this point in some detail in his 1843 *Supplementary Report on the Results of a Special Inquiry into the Practice of Interment in Towns* (London: W. Clowes, 1843).

[23] George Alfred Walker, *On the Past and Present State of Intramural Burying Places: with Practical Suggestions for the Establishment of National Cemeteries* (London: Longman, 1851), 8.

of the poor, where bodies were scarcely laid in the grave before they were unearthed to create room for more, that were most harmed by the physical and moral "evils" of intramural burial. The middle classes had already fled both the city centers and the urban churchyards, making their homes in the garden suburbs, and burying their dead in the newly constructed garden cemeteries. It was here that Walker called quite explicitly for the state to become involved in the reformation of burial practices: "the attention of the Government cannot too anxiously be directed" to these matters … who will not venture to affirm that the health of a community is not of first importance to the stability and prosperity of society?" (6)

For Walker, as well as many of his contemporaries, it was shameful that in a country as "advanced" and commercially successful as Britain such "sad mementoes of ignorance, cupidity, and degraded morality still exist" (157). Because he believed in the "inseparable connection existing between physical agencies producing disease, and their demoralizing results," the exhalations of the dead that "increased, if not generated" disease had to be addressed. Though Walker was unwilling to accept that individuals "never can be quite bereft of the means of making ourselves better or worse," it could not be denied

> that upon circumstances depends the moral and social elevation or depression of all sorts and conditions of mankind in the mass. Let circumstances be favourable, virtue and happiness will prevail,—let them be adverse,—vice and misery will abound (253–4).

While "the power of mere circumstances," Walker felt, could "never be absolute over a *rational* and *responsible* being," the poor were far less able to overcome environmental challenges to their character.[24] Thus, the commercial garden cemeteries were not a solution to the problem as Walker saw it, for not only were those concerned only with profit more likely to abuse the dead body than to respect its sanctity, but they also failed to extend the benefits gained by hiding the dead body to those at the greatest risk.

In spite of Walker's apparent disdain for these new for-profit garden cemeteries, it is important to note the power they exerted on his argument. In these new burial grounds, which, for Walker, spoke of opportunity rather than responsibility, the middle classes could purchase a secluded plot that would ensure them a peaceful eternal slumber.[25] Because of their cost, plots at places like Kensal Green cemetery in London could never have offered a viable alternative for most of those who buried their dead in city churchyards. Instead, they offered the middle classes a

---

[24] Emphasis mine. As Hotz notes, this notion that "environmental conditions determine the subjectivity of those who inhabit them," was a common conviction amongst burial reformers. See Hotz, 2001, 25.

[25] For the most detailed discussion of the establishment of one of the London cemeteries, see James Stevens Curl, ed. *Kensal Green Cemetery: the Origins and Development of the General Cemetery of All Souls Kensal Green, London, 1824–2001* (Chichester, UK: Phillimore, 2001).

grave secure not only from the activities of potential "bodysnatchers," but also from the corruption and disarray of the city and its inhabitants. Cemetery companies erected high perimeter walls and gated entryways, and repeatedly emphasized the new burial grounds' separateness from the city through the calculated use of landscape architecture. In cemeteries like Highgate, Kensal Green, and Abney Park, mourners were to be greeted with scenes that suggested the restorative power of "nature." The cemetery landscape was designed to convey a sense of controlled organicism. The arboretum at Abney Park in northeastern London contained 2,500 varieties of trees and shrubs while its "rosarium" boasted 1,029 varieties of rose—all of which were individually labeled for the "enlightenment of all who walked there."[26] As commentator William Justyne wrote in 1865, "No Cemetery near London [could] boast so many natural beauties" as Highgate. Describing the scenic landscape, he wrote that the

> … irregularity of the ground, rising in terraces, the winding paths leading through long avenues of cool shrubbery and marble monuments, and the groups of majestic trees casting broad shadows below, contribute many natural charms to this solemn region.[27]

While it seems obvious that these cemeteries' appearance of order and salubriousness would have appealed to Walker, I believe that the burial grounds themselves held another, more subtle appeal.

It was, of course, not the model of ownership that appealed to authors like Walker, but the particular model of Britishness and the narrative of cultural progress presented in these spaces. Walking through a suburban cemetery one would see Egyptian pyramids, hieroglyphics, and obelisks, Roman cinerary urns and sarcophagi, the pointed arches, rose windows, and flying buttresses of the Gothic cathedral, coats of arms. The middle class had appropriated these historical forms and others to make a series of claims about the relationship between the present and the past, the living and the dead. More than just memorializing the dead, these structures and figures situated them within an idealized historical narrative, one that lent a new significance to the individual, while recasting the whole of British culture. These monuments are essential to any attempt to understand the Burial Reform movement. For as much as the practice of intramural burial was said to threaten public health and safety, Walker's ultimate justification for the reformation of burial practices was to be found in his discussion of "traditional" Western burial practices. Burial reform was not just a matter of medical urgency; it was a historical necessity.

Although burial of the dead in the heart of the living may have been "so familiar from its frequent or daily occurrence … that the most perfect indifference appears to prevail upon the subject," Walker reminded his readers that it was in fact a fairly

---

[26] James Stevens Curl, *The Victorian Celebration of Death* (Stroud, UK: Sutton, 2000), 106.

[27] William Justyne, *Guide to Highgate Cemetery* (London: Moore, 1865).

recent introduction, while the secrecy that accompanied the separation of the dead and the living had long been sanctioned by history. Indeed, he told his readers, secreting the dead from the living was "the universal custom of all times, and of the most polished nations" (115). Thus he felt it important to open his volume with a "comprehensive sketch of the modes of interment among different nations, and in different periods"(14). Choosing very specific examples, Walker attempted to convince Britons that intramural burial was, simply put, historically inappropriate. Focusing only on the most "reverent" practices—or, as he put it, those in which "we shall find … the elements of our own customs" (15, 23)—he pointed out that in ancient Egypt, for example, there was a "flattering idea of honor" attached to the tomb, and to "break open the tombs—to scatter here and there" was a "horrible sacrilege" (17–8). Moreover, the Egyptians, "from whom other nations have learned whatever polishes and softens the manners," also invented the art of embalming, making the dead body "innoxious to the living" (19). In the case of the ancient Jews, Walker informs his readers, burial spaces were generally amongst the caves and fields far removed from the cities. In both their inhumation and cremation, the ancient Greeks too adhered to the "very salutary custom of conveying the dead to a distance from the cities" (224). However the best model, at least in Walker's opinion, was to be found in the practices of the ancient Romans, insofar as they "preserved the custom indicated by nature, that of *inhuming* the dead" (30). The Romans had even decreed, in the Law of the Twelve Tables, that no body should be burnt or buried within the walls of the city (30). By the time of the early Christians, he noted, burial outside city walls was an "obligation upon all" (34). It was only after the death of Constantine, with, as he called it, a "perversion of Christian doctrine," that the dead were allowed to return to the realm of the living. And once an exception was made, individuals increasingly sought burial near the altar, "till at length … from veneration, ambition, or superstition, the abuse was carried so far, that interment, in the vicinity of churches, was granted to Pagans and Christians,—to the impious and the holy" (225).

Walker's narrative of historical death-ways elides and modifies both existing and nascent nineteenth-century historiographic traditions, articulating an uncomfortable ambivalence toward the function of history. Where authors like Pascalis made reference to historical practices in an effort to establish their medical credibility and authority, there is in Walker's text, I believe, something else at stake.[28] As a number of scholars have suggested, the wider British relationship with the past underwent a series of shifts as British hegemony became more entrenched in the years after Waterloo.[29] As Britons increasingly began to see themselves as

---

[28] See Ludmilla Jordanova, *The Sense of the Past in Eighteenth-Century Medicine* (Reading: U of Reading P, 1997).

[29] History, as Catherine Hall points out, "was immensely popular in the mid-nineteenth century, a time of self-conscious nation formation and of nationalist enthusiasm, and historians played a vital part in defining this nation." See Hall, "At Home with History: Macaulay and the *History of England*," in *At Home with the Empire: Metropolitan Culture*

an unchallenged world power they began to construct new histories accordingly. *National* histories began to rival the more classically-oriented texts that conceived of "history" as the record of Antiquity. Where it had long been common to conceive of Britain's or England's history through a series of analogies with the ancient Greeks and Romans, drawing parallels between, say, the democracy of Athens and the constitutionalism/democracy of England, or between the Roman and the British Empires, during the early-nineteenth century, a specifically British narrative replaced classical antiquity as the dominant historical frame.[30] Stressing the continuity between the past and the present, these histories displayed a growing tendency to see historical events in England, Scotland and/or Britain as foretelling the present greatness of the nation. History, as renowned Whig historian Thomas Babington Macaulay put it, was important "not because it furnished a contrast to the present, but because it had lead to the present."[31] But as much as Walker moved through a succession of historic death rituals and customs, rather than offering his readers the increasingly common Whiggish "march of progress," i.e., marshaling the past to praise the greatness of contemporary Britain, he presents contemporary Britain as a disastrous *break* with historical precedent. Churchyard burial did not respect tradition; it did not even respect humanity. British sepulchral practices had failed to maintain the secrecy of the dead, and as a result they served only to cast doubt upon British cultural, economic and political superiority.

Walker was not alone. John Strang, George Collison, Edwin Chadwick, William Justyne, any number of authors looked to cast the issue of burial reform in terms of a necessary respect for Western cultural heritage. The texts that engaged burial and the new cemeteries were almost formulaic, beginning nearly every time with an extended historical narrative before moving into a more detailed discussion of the churchyards' filth and pestilence.[32] Collison's 1840 text *Cemetery Interment*, for

---

and the Imperial World, ed. Catherine Hall and Sonya O. Rose (Cambridge: Cambridge UP, 2006), 32.

[30] A. Dwight Culler remarks upon this move toward national histories, noting that for Sir Walter Scott and Macaulay, "the analogy of history was not with some other civilization at a comparable stage of its development but with their own civilization in an earlier stage. The circumstances were different but the issues and processes were the same." See *The Victorian Mirror of History* (New Haven: Yale UP, 1985), 20. Nevertheless, the shift was not definitive, and the universalizing histories of the seventeenth and eighteenth centuries, more focused on ancient Greece and Rome, would overlap with the nineteenth century interest in a national past. See Rosemary Mitchell, *Picturing the Past: English History in Text and Image, 1830–1870* (Oxford: Clarendon, 2000), 5.

[31] Thomas Babington Macaulay, "History," in *The Works of Lord Macaulay*, ed. Lady Trevelyan (London: Longmans, Green and Co., 1871), 5:141.

[32] See for example James Peggs' 1840 text, *A Cry from the Tombs; or, Facts and Observation on the Impropriety of Burying the Dead among the Living, in Various Ages and Nations* (London: John Snow, 1840). Also following the same formula was John Richards, *Essay on Cemetery Interments* (London: Pelham Richardson, Cornhill, Richard Welch, Reading, 1843); George Milner, *Cemetery Burial; or, Sepulture, Ancient and Modern*

example, opened with an extensive history of burial in the West. After outlining the "various modes practised by the ancients in the disposition of their dead" he states, "in almost all cases, it was customary and frequently obligatory, to erect their cemeteries, or burying-places, at a proper distance from cities and towns, or other populous districts."[33] Collison's treatise echoed Walker's populism, emphasizing a particular concern that those living in the City of London and the East End had little or no access to extramural burial grounds, and that roughly a quarter of the population was still forced to bury loved ones in the grossly overcrowded city churchyards.

While less concerned with the lives of the poor than either Collison or Walker, John Strang made a similar argument regarding the current burial provision in his native Glasgow. In 1831, Strang argued that "every square yard" of Scottish sepulchres held "piles of mouldering bodies," and, situated in the center of densely populated cities, were "little better than a generator of plague and pestilence."[34] It was because they failed to conceal the dead body that these "sepulchral nuisances" prevented "heavenly communing" at the tombs of beloved friends and relatives.[35] According to Strang, the "Ancients" were "never polluted with the idea of a charnel house, nor their feelings roused by the revolting emblems of mortality," for they knew how important it was to maintain the secrecy of the corpse.[36] The Ancients "contemplated death without terror, and visited its gloomy shrine without fear."[37] Death was calmness and serenity for them; it signified "tranquility, and the only images that were associated with it, were those of peaceful repose and tender sorrow."[38] For this reason, Strang called upon the people of Scotland to abandon their churchyards, and to erect a necropolis that would rival the most magnificent of the new garden cemeteries. After all, "A garden cemetery and monumental decoration afford the most convincing tokens of a nation's progress in civilisation and in the arts, which are its results."[39] Lest Scotland lose the prominence it had

---

(London: Longman and Co., 1846); Elizabeth Stone, *God's Acre; or, Historical Notices Relating to Churchyards* (London: John W. Parker and Son, 1858).

33 George Collison, *Cemetery Interment: Containing a Concise History of the Modes of Interment Practised by the Ancients; Descriptions of Père la Chaise, the Eastern Cemeteries, and those of America; the English Metropolitan and Provincial Cemeteries, and more Particularly of the Abney Park Cemetery, at Stoke Newington, with a Descriptive Catalogue of its Plants and Arboretum* (London: Longman, Orme, Brown, Green, and Longmans, 1840), 67.

34 Strang, 34.

35 Strang, 34–5.

36 In Strang's account, the "garden" cemetery, of which the Parisian Père la Chaise was for him the finest example, owed its lineage, to the "Ancients," who were "never polluted with the idea of a charnel house, nor their feelings roused by the revolting emblems of mortality."

37 Strang, 59.

38 Strang, 59

39 Strang, 62.

gained as an arbiter of knowledge during the Enlightenment, Strang reminded his readers that "the most celebrated nations of which history speaks, have adorned their places of sepulture, and it is from their funereal monuments that we gather much of what is known of their civil progress and advancement in taste."[40] Was not, he wrote, "the story of Egypt written on its pyramids, and is not the chronology of Arabia pictured on its tombs? Is it not on the funeral relics of Greece and Rome, that we behold those elegant images of repose and tender sorrow with which they so happily invested the idea of death?"[41]

In contemporary writings on cemeteries and burial practices, historical narratives of this sort were exceedingly common. Throughout the literature on burial reform the history of burial, and, by extension, the history of Britain, was as much of a concern as was public health, overcrowding, or any of the other explanations offered. What makes these narratives so interesting, and particularly in Walker's case, is that the historical and cultural precedents cited for the necessity of burial reform were the very same as those that had inspired the more ostentatious sepulchral monuments. In much the same way that Egyptian pyramids and Roman cinerary urns in the early garden cemeteries made a set of claims about the relationship between the British middle classe and the history of Western culture, Walker's narrative effectively applied that legacy and heritage to the whole of Britain. This was more than a matter of simply secreting dead bodies tastefully out of sight. In the discussion of burial reform, nothing less than the cultural identity of Britain was at stake. Of course, the evolving public concern with hiding the dead in nineteenth-century Britain was tied to a concern with public health and morality. Moreover, the issues of death and burial cannot be separated from the contemporary obsession with the writing of British history.

---

40 Strang, 62.

41 Strang 63.

Chapter 2
Harriet Martineau's "only political plot": Assassins, Duels, and Corn-Law Repeal

Deborah A. Logan

> I want to be doing something with the pen, since no other means of action in politics are in a woman's power.
>
> —Harriet Martineau

Writer Harriet Martineau occupied an anomalous position in Victorian political and social history. [1] Triply disadvantaged according to the ideological values of the era—a woman, a dissenter (later, agnostic), and informally educated—her keen intellect and compulsive "need of utterance" early positioned her as a socio-political commentator whose insights were sought by prominent men. Prompted by a concern for political sensitivity during the mid-century revolutionary period, Martineau declared herself satisfied with the invisibility of her role in the passage of significant legislation; this apparent humility continues through her account of Corn-Law Repeal in *History of the Peace* (1849–51). But when diagnosed with terminal illness in 1855, her clarity about the "jealousy of men" prompted her to break her own best-kept secret. This discussion of a singular episode in Martineau's career dramatizes how thoroughly women have been written out of Victorian political history, and how one woman made sure that the success of her "only political plot" would not be lost to posterity.

Throughout her career, Martineau was approached by an array of special interest groups, who recognized in her literary prominence and political influence a means to promote social reforms. One such episode was particularly distinguished by its sensitivity, its urgency, and its political implications: the repeal of the Corn Laws during the great Irish famine. Notable too is the cast of characters involved: Prime Minister Sir Robert Peel,[2] reformist MP Richard Cobden,[3] and the controversial

---

[1] Harriet Martineau (1802–76), was an author and journalist who wrote on issues of political economy, sociology, history, national and imperial politics.

[2] Sir Robert Peel, 2nd Baronet (1788–1850), statesman, MP, Tory Prime Minister. Initially, Peel favored gradual Corn Law reform, seeking "to preserve old institutions, while diligently reforming their abuses"; later, he advocated complete, immediate repeal. William Harvey, *The Life of the Right Honourable Sir Robert Peel, Bart* (London: Routledge, 1853), 117.

[3] Richard Cobden (1804–65), radical politician who advocated free trade. Arguing that the Anti-Corn-Law League's propagandizing was insufficient to resolve the issues,

Harriet Martineau—an unlikely trio of political bedfellows, to be sure. This tale of moral assassination and political suicide, covert intrigues and overt agendas, punctuated by rhetorical duels and even the threat of a pistol-duel, comprises a Victorian secret that was revealed—not through subterfuge, but by design—in *Harriet Martineau's Autobiography*. An overview of certain antecedents in Martineau's career establishes her as a socio-political authority whose opinions were valued and respected, and whose influence extended to the political movers and shakers of the period generally, without acknowledgement.

While Martineau was an outspoken advocate of economic reform even before her *Illustrations of Political Economy* (1832–4), her most pronounced assertion of political influence dates from that period. Quaintly characterized by Lord Chancellor Brougham as "the little, deaf woman from Norwich," this provincial unknown—with impressive self-confidence—sent each MP a copy of her prospectus, thereby inserting her voice in the intense political debates of the Reform Bill era. Her modest aim was simply to inform "our legislators that a book was coming out on their particular class of subjects."[4] Inexperienced though she was, Martineau did not operate from delusions of grandeur: following her arrival in London and the immediate success of the *Illustrations*, she was aggressively courted by politicians and reformers who sought to engage her to write on behalf of their causes. Within two years, Martineau produced three series of "little books" on political economy, poor laws, and taxation, thereby playing a central role in the "diffusion of useful knowledge" aimed at empowering the rising industrial classes.[5] "I became the fashion," she notes, with influential writers and politicians calling at her walk-up flat, and blue-books and social invitations pouring in; nevertheless, she asserts, she was not "spoiled" by such "lionization" but preserved her professional integrity—a primary consideration to this eclectic, idiosyncratic author (*AB* 1:185).

Martineau's initial London period (1832–4) established an enduring pattern for her literary and political influence. As a result, her American tour (1834–6) was an extended exercise in negotiating the attempts of special interest groups to secure her influence—already established as international in scope—to promote their agendas.[6] In her aim to maintain sociological neutrality, Martineau strove valiantly

Cobden urged more aggressive political tactics, for example, electing free-trade candidates like himself.

4 Harriet Martineau, *Harriet Martineau's Autobiography,* 2 vols., ed. Gaby Weiner (London: Virago, 1983), 1:175 (hereafter *AB*). The "book," *Illustrations of Political Economy* (London: Charles Fox, 1832–34), consists of a series of twenty-five novelettes (averaging 130 pp.), issued monthly between 1832–34.

5 While completing the *Illustrations of Political Economy*, Martineau wrote two series for the Society for the Diffusion of Useful Knowledge—*Poor Laws and Paupers Illustrated* (1833) and *Illustrations of Taxation* (1834), both published by Charles Fox. The three series are "didactic fiction," tales designed to entertain while teaching economic principles.

6 R. K. Webb, in *Harriet Martineau. A Radical Victorian* (New York: Columbia UP, 1960), estimates readership of *Illustrations of Political Economy* at approximately 144,000,

with the pro-slavers, the gradual emancipationists, and the colonizationists, keenly engaged in the debates shaping what she came to regard as *the* defining issue of the century; but it was the compelling ardor of the abolitionists that resonated with her humanitarian views, prompting her to abandon neutrality for a commitment to abolition that informed the remainder of her career.

While some critiqued her antislavery polemic in *Society in America* (1837), *Retrospect of Western Travel* (1838), and *The Martyr Age of the United States* (1839), others viewed that body of work as a model for what might be accomplished in alternative frameworks. For example, in 1839, Daniel O'Connell[7] sought Martineau's acquaintance, "looking round anxiously for every means of making the Irish question popular in England,—even requesting an English author whom he thought likely to be listened to, to travel in Ireland ... in order to report upon the condition of the country."[8] In his view, Martineau's work on American culture demonstrated her "capacity to understand and represent the political and social condition of another country" and thus, by extension, her suitability to write about Ireland "in a way which the English were willing to listen to" (*AB* 2:312).[9]

She was similarly approached by a representative from Sweden, who invited her for an extended stay as a houseguest of the Prime Minister, because "he conceived that my books on America showed me to be ... capable ... of understanding the working of the constitutions of foreign nations" (*AB* 2:311). Sir James Brooke, the "White Rajah" of Sarawak, sought her services as a "legislator for the Eastern Archipelago";[10] more ignominiously, she was offered "an estate of several thousand acres ... if I would bind myself to live for five years in Texas, helping to frame their Constitution, and using my influence to bring over English settlers" (*AB* 2:51–2). This plan, she suspected, was a ruse to get her to sanction the territory's bid for

based on sales figures averaging 10,000 for each of the twenty-five numbers and on estimates relating to lending-libraries (113). The series was purchased by the Austrian and Russian courts, adapted into the French public school system, and translated into German, Spanish, French, Russian and Dutch.

7 Daniel O'Connell (1775–1847), Catholic politician and MP, Union repealer and radical reformist, Irish nationalist.

8 *Harriet Martineau's History of England,* 6 vols. ed. Deborah Logan (London: Pickering & Chatto, 2004), 5:107 (hereafter *History*). The "English author" was Martineau, whose writing about Ireland includes *Letters from Ireland, Endowed Schools of Ireland,* "Ireland" (reprinted in *Harriet Martineau's Writing on the British Empire* [London: Pickering & Chatto, 2004], vol. 4), and an additional forty-eight periodical articles.

9 The proposed meeting between Martineau and O'Connell was delayed by her European tour (1839), her illness (1839–45), and her tour of the Middle East (1847–48); O'Connell died before her return.

10 Maria Weston Chapman, *Memorials* (Boston: J. R. Osgood, 1877), 346. Sir James Brooke (1803–68), the "white Rajah of Sarawak" in Malaysia, established a hereditary protectorate on his own initiative; his request that the British government annex Sarawak as a colony generated controversy.

statehood—as a slave state. Martineau was even aggressively courted to promote British railway interests in Egypt in *Eastern Life, Present and Past*:

> [W]hat was wanted was that I should write a book on Egypt, like Mrs. Romer, ... and that, like Mrs. Romer, I should be flattered into advocating the Egyptian Railway scheme by which the English in Egypt hoped to gain an advantage over the French.[11] (*AB* 2:276).

More flamboyantly, she was pursued across the North African desert by an Italian patriot, Count Porro, on horseback. Porro's proposal to establish her in Milan as part of Italy's independence and unification movement "was as nearly as could be a repetition of O'Connell's plea and request" (*AB* 2:315). As "a traveller of reputation," Martineau had proven her ability "to understand and report of a foreign state of society"; the "strong resemblance" these examples share "seems to show that there must be something in them which makes them worth the telling" (*AB* 2:316). They are indeed "worth the telling" in their capacity to reconcile the unlikely role she was to play in Corn-Law Repeal.

While flattered by such acknowledgments of her socio-political acuity, Martineau refused all requests to intervene in foreign politics, preferring to exercise her influence over domestic politics and collaborating with virtually every significant reform movement active between the 1820s and 1870s. When she terms her role as peacemaker between Richard Cobden and Robert Peel "my only political plot," she is far too modest, given that most of her writing aimed to influence political opinion, pending legislation, and public policy-makers (*AB* 2:257–64 *passim*). As pressure to repeal the Corn Laws intensified in the 1840s, fueled by a decade of drought, famine, and cholera, Martineau became affiliated with the Anti-Corn-Law League, for which she wrote the tale *Dawn Island* and contributed needlework for its fund-raising bazaars.[12] It was from this association that her "only political plot" evolved beyond such muted modes of social activism into a genuine political intrigue.

The remainder of this discussion centers on Martineau's self-styled singular intervention, through private correspondence, as a liaison between Cobden and Peel, whose mutual antagonism she viewed as responsible for delaying passage of the repeal bill in which the starving masses had an urgent interest. Martineau succeeded in her endeavor: peace was made, apologies accepted, and the Corn Laws were repealed shortly after. While the episode demonstrates her influence,

---

[11] Isabella Romer, *A Pilgrimage to the Temples and Tombs of Egypt, Nubia, and Palestine, in 1845–46* (London: R. Bentley, 1846); see also, Martineau's *Eastern Life, Present and Past* (*Harriet Martineau's Writing on the British Empire,* vols. 2–3).

[12] Corn Laws (1816–46), enacted after Peninsular Wars, taxed imported grains in order to bolster the domestic agricultural economy. But domestic grain was also prohibitively priced; Corn Law repeal aimed to restore competitive pricing through free-trade. The Anti-Corn-Law League was established in October 1838 in Manchester and dissolved in July 1846.

including this intrigue in Martineau's *Autobiography* raises several questions: what was her purpose in making public the details of this event? For all her insistence on epistolary privacy, why did she consider *this* exchange particularly essential to the image bequeathed to posterity in her *Autobiography*? Since she assumed (wrongly, as it turns out) that her letters had been destroyed, as she required of her correspondents, did she envision that her role in this adventure would otherwise be lost to history? Insofar as the answer to the last question is a resounding "yes," the following narrative proves that Martineau was certainly correct in assuming that, unless she claimed credit for herself, no one would do it for her.[13]

The "Hungry Forties" were marked by uprisings and such "muscular" demonstrations as Chartist rallies, Irish "Monster Meetings," European socio-political revolutions, and the mobilization of the Anti-Corn-Law League, a group with a somewhat mixed reputation. On the one hand, notes Martineau, the League was "led by men of station, character, and substance,—men of enlarged education, and of that virtuous and decorous conduct which distinguishes the middle class" (*History* 5:69), society's "Golden Mean." But on the other hand, because of their aim to disrupt the economic status quo, Leaguers were considered radicals and were rumored to "sanction" and "patronize" assassination in order to achieve their political goals—a bizarre claim reflecting "the tribulation of the time."[14] As a political newcomer, Cobden was an unknown and as yet unproven factor, whereas Peel was in the midst of an illustrious career. The Anti-Corn-Law League were socio-economic reformers, not assassins; but anyone, clearly—particularly repeal opponents—could easily evoke fear and paranoia during a period when even Queen Victoria was targeted by radical extremists.[15]

Martineau regards Cobden's election to the House of Commons "as [the] representative of the bread-winners of the kingdom" a significant turning point in parliamentary politics (*History* 5:157). A Manchester textile manufacturer and son of a farmer, Cobden palpably demonstrated the rise of middle-class industrialists to economic, social, and particularly, political, power. On the occasion of Cobden's first parliamentary speech (August 25, 1841), "the people's tale was for the first time fully and properly told in Parliament ... in a way which fixed the attention of every thoughtful observer of the times ... a new era in the history of England

---

[13] Neither G. H. Francis (*The Late Sir Robert Peel, Bart. A Critical Biography.* London: Parker & Son, 1852) nor William Harvey (*The Life of the Right Honourable Sir Robert Peel, Bart.* London: Routledge, 1853) mentions Martineau in their biographies of Peel; it is likely that she read both, as she was an avid reader of contemporary literature. Martineau's *Autobiography* was completed (1855) and printed (1856) a decade before Cobden died, although not distributed until 1877. John Morley's discussion of this episode in his biography of Cobden (*The Life of Richard Cobden,* 2 vols. London: Chapman and Hall, 1881) utilizes both her *History of England* (which does not reveal her role) and *Autobiography*, but does not give Martineau the credit she so clearly deserves.

[14] Martineau quoted in John McGilchrist, *Richard Cobden, the Apostle of Free Trade* (New York: Harper, 1865), 113.

[15] Queen Victoria's life was threatened on three occasions in 1842.

had opened" (*History* 5:157). Martineau depicts Cobden as a man who sacrificed a potential fortune in the industrial sector in order to represent those whose material well-being was held in thrall to protectionism. The sufferings of the operative classes, whose accessibility to affordable food was severely compromised by the prohibitive tariffs protecting landed interests, were dignified by Cobden's compelling speech, delivered despite the hoots and cat-calls of jaded MPs bent on intimidating the junior MP from the manufacturing class.[16]

In 1842, shortly after Cobden's "maiden" speech, Peel introduced legislation designed to remedy the ailing economy by eliminating certain tariffs altogether and revising the Corn Laws: "one of the most extended and best considered efforts ever made to reduce the necessaries of life to the people at large."[17] By thus "seal[ing] the fate of the old commercial system," the fears of those opposed to the 1832 Reform Bill were made manifest in this confrontation between upper- and middle-class economic interests.[18] The protectionist question was revealed to be more a matter of class than of party politics: "Despite his masterly defence of a sliding scale of corn duties, Peel was gradually falling into odium with the chiefs of the Protectionist party ... 'if the minister did not please the agricultural members, they, by whose aid he would be placed in office, would turn him out again' ... [this threat] contributed not a little to his subsequent tendency to the utter abolition of the taxes on food."[19] Christine Kinealy adds "[w]ithout majority support Peel was aware that repeal of the Corn Laws would be political suicide for him and would probably lead to the downfall of the government," which indeed occurred twice before the matter was resolved.[20] The path from corn-law legislation, to compromise through gradualism, to unequivocal repeal challenged all those attempting to negotiate this pivotal test of the democratizing principle on which the Reform Bill was based.[21]

An indirect source for the political quarrel between Peel and Cobden dates from 1843, during an incident illustrating "the extraordinary ferment and excitement

---

16 Cobden "reminded the House that it was the condition of the nation, and not the interests of a class, or the abstract doctrines of the economist, that cried for a relief which it was in the power of the legislature to bestow ... [He] represented a new force with which the old parties would one day have to deal." John Morley, *The Life of Richard Cobden*, 2 vols. (London: Chapman and Hall, 1881), 1:178; 1:180.

17 Harvey, 141.

18 George Francis, *The Late Sir Robert Peel, Bart. A Critical Biography* (London: Parker & Son, 1852), 89.

19 Harvey, 141.

20 Christine Kinealy, *This Great Calamity. The Irish Famine 1845–52* (Boulder: Roberts Rinehart, 1995), 36.

21 "While all shouted out, *'No sliding scale*,' some called for a fixed duty, and others clamoured for '*Total and immediate repeal*'" (Morley 1:218). Harvey adds, "The measure for the repeal of the Corn Laws was the culminating point of this series of ameliorative measures" (143).

of feeling which the Corn Law agitation produced in England."[22] In January of that year, Peel's close friend and private secretary, Edward Drummond,[23] was shot in the back in Whitehall, London, by Scottish-laborer-turned-assassin Daniel Macnaghten. While there was some concern that Macnaghten had mistaken Drummond for Peel and had intended a very different outcome than the murder of a secretary, he was acquitted on the ground of insanity and confined to an asylum for life. Not surprisingly, Peel was quite shaken over the event, and over the indeterminacy of Macnaghten's intended target. During a parliamentary debate on Corn Law repeal on February 17, 1843, just weeks after Drummond's assassination, Cobden—who was himself suffering from ill health and mourning the death of his infant daughter[24]—accused Peel of being "personally responsible" for "the misery of the people." Peel, frustrated, anxious for his own life, grieving for his friend, charged Cobden "with exposing him to fatal consequences" and "with being answerable for assassination," language evoking the League's rumored association with hired assassins and suggesting, to the more excitable, that this sort of talk inevitably leads to a duel (*History* 5:70; *AB* 2:260). After a brief verbal altercation, Peel extended what he thought a sufficient retraction and forgot about the incident, at least in terms of its capacity to continue rankling wounded egos.

Cobden biographer Wendy Hinde offers fuller insight on what appears to be more a question of semantics than politics. During his speech, Cobden denounced Peel's "responsibility" for the country's economic and agricultural distress: "you are responsible for the consequences of your act ... I throw on you all the responsibility of your own measure."[25] Peel responded that it was indeed his *responsibility* to take action on the matter, to which Cobden retorted "it is the duty" of every MP to hold Peel "responsible for the present position of the country." At this point, any further attempts to repair the damages of linguistic hair-splitting were lost in the general "uproar" and "hubbub" of shouting MPs; if there was an *amende* and it was accepted, apparently no one heard either through the ensuing row.

John Morley's version of this "most painful incident in Cobden's parliamentary life" evokes the image of a hazing initiation, illustrating "the ungenerous, the unsparing, the fierce treatment for which a man must be prepared who enters public life in the House of Commons. The sentiment of the House itself was against Cobden ... [who was] known to have a serious influence outside, and to be raising the public opinion of constituencies to an inconveniently strong pitch."[26] The harsh "boot camp" mentality by which new MPs were initiated into parliament

---

22 McGilchrist, 111.

23 Edward Drummond (1792–1843), civil servant who served as private secretary to the Earl of Ripon, Canning, Wellington and Peel.

24 Wendy Hinde, *Richard Cobden. A Victorian Outsider* (New Haven: Yale UP, 1987), 118–19.

25 Hinde, 119.

26 Morley, 1:256 and 1:262–3.

was not just an attempt to intimidate Cobden: it was an acknowledgment of his "inconvenient" power.

Stung by the implications of Peel's assassination comment, Cobden and the Leaguers nursed wounded pride and animosity for three years. Although dueling was essentially anachronistic by this time, some claimed that only this confrontation could resolve an insult of such intensity and duration.[27] Between the 1843 and the 1846 debates, Cobden visited Martineau at her sickroom in Tynemouth, telling her that her opinions "might be of use to the leaders of the agitation" and asking her to write to him "if at any time I had any thing to criticise or suggest in regard to League affairs. I had not much idea that I could be of any service; but I made the desired promise" (*AB* 2:259). The occasion arose soon after for her to act on that promise.

As the 1845 parliamentary session began, notes Martineau, "the one troublesome controversy was ... about the corn-laws" (*History* 5:223). While wavering between gradual reform and outright repeal, Peel had been "rising yearly in the favor of the manufacturing and commercial classes, by whom he was regarded ... a free-trader" (*History* 5:223). The year 1845 marked the beginning of the potato famine; and, as many "discerning" commercial men argued,

> the first pressure upon the food-market must occasion a repeal of the corn-laws ... Sir R. Peel was more likely to effect the change than any other man, because he knew and had done most about free-trade ... he was the only man we had who could govern under difficulties. (*History* 5:223)

The issue of Corn Law repeal came to a point in December 1845 when the *Times* announced that the Conservatives, led by Peel, were determined to abolish the corn-tax; pressured by the opposition, Peel's Cabinet was dissolved. Also in December, Cobden's unappeased antagonism surfaced during two political speeches in which he insulted Peel in "outrageous terms," first at Stockport and then at Covent Garden, both events well-publicized in the press.[28] Indeed, insofar as Peel's spontaneous remarks in the heat of that boisterous exchange in 1843 *might* be construed as requiring a duel to resolve, Cobden's slanderous accusations in these prepared public speeches offer sufficient retaliation. An admirer of both the illustrious statesman and the reformist politician, Martineau perceived that their shared political aim—repeal—was threatened by something other than political partisanship: "the great middle-class body, including the Anti-corn-law League, showed ... little earnestness in supporting Peel; so that when the matter was placed

---

[27] Associated with the privileged classes, dueling was not only outmoded and officially discountenanced: it was hardly appropriate to the modernizing perspectives of the upwardly-mobile middle classes.

[28] At Stockport, which Cobden represented, "the distress was fearful; one out of every five houses ... was untenanted, half of those occupied were not paying rent; nearly half of the manufacturers' mills were closed" and thousands were unemployed (McGilchrist 74–5). See also *Autobiography* 2:260.

in Peel's hands by his restoration to power, it did not seem to *get on*" (*AB* 2:259).[29] Because of her association with Cobden, she asserts, "I had occasion to know where the hitch was; and, as it appeared to me, to act upon that knowledge, in a way quite new to me"—adding pointedly, "indisposed as I have always been to meddle in matters which did not concern me." Martineau decided that it was time to act on Cobden's invitation, and she wrote to him "as a member of the League, and not as a censor ... I asked him whether he thought the object of the League would be furthered" by publicly insulting Peel, particularly at this crucial juncture in pending corn-law legislation. In her December 27, 1845 letter to Cobden, she firmly assumed the role of peacemaker:

> No one ever dreamed of excusing Peel's conduct that night. But there is something more to be said in accounting for it than is commonly known.... He had been out of health ... he was shocked and grieved by the loss of his friend Drummond ... ill, sleepless, harassed, ... surrounded by boding men, crying women, & a starving people, ... his mind morbidly full of the idea of his being a mark for assassination ... He was exactly in a condition to misapprehend the words "personal responsibility," & his attack on you was a burst of constitutional rage ... something very different from a cool & premeditated attempt to destroy your character ... While my strongest interest is in your great objects, you will let me put what I think a fair construction on a man who cannot yet be viewed from afar by any of us.[30]

John Morley observes, "At this time circumstances naturally began to work a complete change in Cobden's attitude towards Sir Robert Peel," but he neither articulates the origins of the change nor acknowledges Martineau's role in it.[31] As is now clear, reconciliation was fostered by those positioned to support and encourage the junior MP through his political growing pains: "It was wrong to exult in Peel's fall," Cobden admitted to George Combe; "I was quite taken aback, and out came that virulent attack upon Peel, for which I have been gently rapped on the knuckles by Miss Martineau, yourself, and many other esteemed correspondents."[32] Since Morley employed Martineau's account in her *Autobiography* to construct his own version, it is curious how thoroughly her participation in these events was written *out* of his biography of Cobden.

Consistent with her utilitarian mindset, Martineau wrote: "I did not see why the [repeal] cause should suffer for such individual griefs. I had plenty of evidence ...

---

29 Attempts by Russell to establish a new cabinet failed, forcing Peel back into the position temporarily.

30 Harriet Martineau, *The Collected Letters of Harriet Martineau*, 5 vols. ed. Deborah Logan (London: Pickering & Chatto, 2007), 3:33–4 (hereafter *CL*).

31 Morley, 1:351.

32 Morley 1:352 (Cobden to Combe, December 29, 1845). Compare with Morley's account of the same incident: "[when] Cobden was betrayed ... into some strong language about Sir Robert Peel, Miss Martineau, George Combe, and others, rebuked him rather sharply" (1:207).

that the great manufacturing classes were holding back [their support] on account of this unsettled reckoning" (*AB* 2:261). Some Leaguers revived the duel question, urging Cobden "to seek personal satisfaction from his enemy"; but he refused, agreeing with Martineau that private feuds should not compromise public matters. Ironically, of course, this was exactly the case, with or without actual swords or pistols; but once both Cobden and Peel admitted culpability, as happened soon after, the potential for healing personal and political rifts was assured.

At this point, Martineau asked her friend, Richard Monckton Milnes, to intervene. Milnes was "a neutral friend ... a Conservative MP, wholly opposed to the repeal of the Corn Laws ... I had little doubt that he would be glad of the opportunity of bringing two earnest men to a better understanding with each other" (*AB* 2:261).[33] Considering the crucial significance of rhetorical precision in this matter, it is most odd that Martineau perceived no conflict-of- interest between neutrality, conservatism, and an anti- repeal platform: indeed, she implies that such a combination ensures a balanced viewpoint. On December 31, 1845, she wrote to Milnes:

> I have large ground for believing that the greatest obstacle to peace in the House & the country between the Govt & the really ruling party out of doors is Peel not having retracted or apologized for his attack on Mr. Cobden ... [T]he hatred & contempt of [the] public grow deeper with every year that Peel allows that slander to remain unretracted ... Cobden owns his fault, & does not attempt to excuse it ... Now, can you do any thing in this? If you can, rely upon it, you will be doing the greatest service to the public morals that any man can at this moment do. (*CL* 3:35–7)[34]

On the same day, Martineau also wrote to Cobden: "By your kind & frank tone I see that you acquit me wholly of any notion of interfering with you as you ... It is as a piece of League business, & because once asked for an opinion on League business that I have done it" (*CL* 3:37). But Cobden's February 2, 1846 letter to George Combe reveals that, although he accepts emotional distress about *physical* assassination as a viable explanation, he still holds Peel accountable for *moral* assassination:

> I am eager to avow my regret at having been betrayed into a vindictive attack upon Peel ... [But] I must say that Peel's atrocious conduct towards me ought not to be lost sight of.—I do not complain of his insinuating that I wished to incite to his assassination ... [this] might have been excused on account of his state of mind ... [but] it did not atone for his having failed to retract

---

33 Richard Monckton Milnes, 1st Baron Houghton (1809–85), MP and writer. See also Martineau's *Autobiography*, 1:342–4.

34 The "really ruling party out of doors" is the Anti-Corn-Law League and the manufacturing and industrial classes associated with it.

> or explain his foul charge subsequently which in fact, made & now makes it a deliberate attempt at moral assassination.[35]

"It was not many weeks from this time," notes John Morley, "before a curious incident had the effect of finally effacing the last trace of enmity between these two honoured men."[36] Once again, Morley does not articulate the circumstances, the significance, or the source of this "curious incident." Although he clearly alludes to the fact that, what Martineau calls "the greatest service to the public morals that any man can at this moment do", was left to the woman in the equation to accomplish without credit.

Martineau had both overestimated Peel's culpability and underestimated the neutrality of her friend Milnes; the latter waited three weeks before responding with a "fierce vituperation of his abjured leader [Peel]" that eliminated any hope that it would be he, rather than Martineau, who would facilitate peace (*AB* 2:261). Disappointed but undeterred, she decided to contact Peel directly: "He would probably think me meddlesome, and be vexed at the womanish folly of supposing that, while the laws of honour which are so sacred in men's eyes remain"—dueling—"he could make any move towards a man who had insulted him as Mr. Cobden had recently done. But ... his opinion could not weigh for an instant against the remotest chance of abridging the suspense about the Corn Laws" (*AB* 2:262).[37] In her letter, she notes, "I laid the case before him; and, when I came to the dueling considerations, I told him what a woman's belief is in such a case,—that a devoted man can rise above arbitrary social rules; and that I believed him to be the man who could do it":

> I write to you on a matter which concerns yourself ... [and] whatever concerns you concerns the country ... Mr Cobden ... has suffered most bitterly ... from your not having made any sort of amende ... I almost tremble to write this. But a woman may put in a peacemaking word where a man might not venture ... a woman may have faith in the impossible which men do not entertain ... you are a great doer of the impossible,—in the government of yourself, as well as in the government of the country. (*CL* 3:43–5)[38]

---

[35] Richard Cobden, *Letters of Richard Cobden.* Ed. Anthony Howe (New York and Oxford: Oxford UP, 2007).

[36] Morley, 1:353.

[37] The suggestion that a textile manufacturer would face off with a Prime Minister in this way and during this period is unlikely, particularly given the personalities involved. However, both Peel and Cobden probably adhered to the ideology underpinning dueling: the vindication of personal honor.

[38] In the *Autobiography*, Martineau notes that she wrote to Peel on New Year's Day, 1846, but the extant copy of this letter is dated February 22. Her letter to Milnes was December 31, 1845; she was prompted to write to Peel after receiving Milnes's ambivalent reply three weeks later.

Of his reply by return of post, she wrote, "nothing could be more frank, more cordial, or more satisfactory" (*AB* 2:262–3). Peel expressed surprise at her disclosure, believing the matter had been resolved in 1843. Martineau also replied by return of post, "acknowledging the honour you have done me by your courteous reply to my letter":

> It appears to me that the thing now to be done is to impress him & others with your view ... One cannot but deeply lament that there is so little of the peacemaking spirit abroad as that no one should ... have brought Mr Cobden & yourself to a clear understanding ... the mistake is at present seriously injurious to the great cause which you both have at heart. (*CL* 3:45–6)

Lest Cobden be caught off guard by Peel's unanticipated conciliatory overture, Martineau wrote him "the most artful letter I ever penned. It really was difficult to manage this, my first intrigue, all alone"—an amazing admission, given that she does not seem to have had any difficulty intriguing thus far:

> Sir R. Peel considers that the *amende* was made & accepted three years ago ... My hope now is that Sir R. Peel & you being led to one another's point of view, you may soon attain to doing each other justice ... I inclose a copy of a statement of Sir R. Peel's view ... of the matter ... I don't expect that you & he will fully appreciate each other: but I don't despair of seeing you civil enough for your peace of mind & the public good. (*CL* 3:46–7)

According to Peel, Cobden charged him with responsibility for "the misery of the people"; when Peel accused Cobden of "exposing him to fatal consequences," Cobden responded:

> "I intended (& I believe every body but the Rt Hon: Gentn understood what I meant) to throw the responsibility of his measures upon him as the Head of the Government: & in using the word *individually* I used it as he uses the first person when he says 'I passed the Tariff & you supported me'." (*CL* 3:46–7)

Peel replied:

> "I am bound to accept the construction which the Hon: Member puts upon the language he employed. He used the word *individually* in so marked a way that I & others put upon it a different interpretation. He supposes the word *individually* to mean *public responsibility* in the situation I hold, & I admit it at once" (*CL* 3:46–7).

This response he believed was conciliatory; if it was insufficient, he asks, why did no one so indicate? The answer to his query is simple: amidst the riotous hubbub of ill-behaved MPs, both Cobden and Peel gave up their attempts to be heard; and what one considered to be more or less resolved, the other regarded an unsettled affront.

Pressing her advantage at this moment of mutual accountability, Martineau suggests that verbal dueling is a sufficient defense of one's honor, and that establishing peace and getting on with the business of governing the country is the most honorable course. She conveyed to both Cobden and Peel that each was positioned to welcome "an occasion of reconciliation" and was prepared "to merge his private grief in the great public cause of the day" (*AB* 2:263–4). Within two days, Martineau received the *Times* account of renewed efforts to secure repeal, personally signed by Peel, which

> "told me how immediately...[he] had acted on his new information and that that union of effort was now obtained under which the immediate repeal of the Corn Laws was certain" (AB 2:264). She also received a note from Cobden asserting that "he could not lay his head on his pillow till he had sent me the blessing on the peace-maker...his mind was eased of a load which had burdened it for long and miserable years; and now he should be a new man."

While these events illustrate post-Reform Bill power shifts from the declining privileged class to the ascending middle-class, they also affirm the unexpected political influence of women—at least, this particular woman—for whom official representation, through the franchise, was still many decades in the future. Although unacknowledged, Martineau's influence was evident during the final Corn Law debates in Spring, 1846, when Benjamin Disraeli contentiously recalled that the Prime Minister had "accused a member of the League of abetting assassination." If it was Disraeli's aim to spark a row, it was deflated by Peel's admission that he had previously "put an erroneous construction on some expressions used by the honorable member for Stockport."[39] On this occasion, Peel's *amende* was unmistakable—and audible, not now being shouted down by rowdy hoots—as he sought "to relieve Mr. Cobden ... from the imputation ... he had put upon him."[40] Cobden responded in kind, expressing "regret at the terms in which he had more than once referred to Sir Robert Peel. And so," concludes Morley, "with the expression of a hope that the subject might never be revived, the incident came to an end."

Christine Kinealy notes, "As expected, [repeal] resulted in the fall of Peel's government";[41] and, on June 29, 1846, three days after repeal of the Corn Laws, Peel resigned as Prime Minister. During his final speech, he announced: "The name which ... will be associated with the success of these measures, is the name of one who, acting, I believe, from pure and disinterested motives, has, with untiring energy, made appeals to our reason, and has enforced those appeals with an eloquence the more to be admired because it was unaffected and unadorned ... the name [is that] of Richard Cobden."[42] The name of Harriet Martineau would have

---

[39] Morley, 1:354. See also McGilchrist, 113–14.

[40] Morley, 1:354.

[41] Kinealy, 36.

[42] McGilchrist, 137.

suited Peel's tribute just as well; apparently, "a woman may put in a peacemaking word where a man might not venture," but the masculine code of honor required that it remain unacknowledged.[43]

When, in 1842, Peel boldly introduced his gradualism policy, he hoped it would ameliorate conflicting economic concerns through compromise. Perhaps because of his misunderstanding with Cobden—whom he respected and whose cause he supported—and the desperate circumstances of the time, which made rhetorical dueling the pastime of the privileged while millions starved, Peel took the even bolder step of complete, unequivocal repeal. He had "shown that what he did he would do with all his strength; and it was in this spirit that he resolved on utterly abandoning the tax on corn, rather than effect any compromise."[44] Peel's actions transcended party concerns, placing him beyond political partisanship and earning him the cautious admiration of opponents, the grudging respect of colleagues, and the gratitude of the hungry masses. According to some theorists, the "continental convulsions" of 1848 were avoided in England largely because of the preemptive strike of Corn Law repeal. The Condition of England during the Hungry Forties prompted Peel "to anticipate, by a bold initiative, an inevitable concession" to the lower classes by the upper classes; thus, "England passed tranquilly through the year 1848 solely because it had complied with the popular wants of commercial reform."[45] Of his various positions on the Corn Laws, Peel asserted:

> I will not withhold the homage due to the progress of reason, and to truth, by denying that my opinions on the subject of Protection have undergone a change. It may be supposed that there is something humiliating in making such an admission ... but I should feel the deepest humiliation if, having changed or modified my opinions, I declined to acknowledge the change, for the base fear of encountering the charge of inconsistency.[46]

Similarly, Cobden also resisted party affiliation in favor of Free Trade, viewing repeal as a necessarily collaborative endeavor: "I don't think Manchester [alone] will carry the repeal of the Corn Laws, but that we shall carry it by making it a national question."[47] In this instance, at least, utilitarianism fostered a nationalism that rejected internal class divisions as detrimental to political cohesion; perhaps it is no coincidence that the post- repeal period ushered in the Empire's greatest era of global economic expansion.

---

[43] Since, at this time, Martineau's name was associated with an embarrassing notoriety resulting from her enthusiasm for mesmerism, acknowledging her service in Parliament would probably have generated another row, heaping ridicule rather than honor on the three primary players.

[44] Francis, 89.

[45] Francis, 90–91.

[46] Harvey, 144.

[47] McGilchrist, 97.

Notwithstanding the positive outcome between Cobden and Peel and the issues each represented, unfinished business yet remained, Martineau being especially fond of getting the last word. She wrote two letters on 2 March 1846, the first to Cobden: "I must just wish you joy of your release from that galling weight upon your mind which has vexed you so long. And here let the subject be buried for ever" (*CL* 3:49). The second letter was to R. M. Milnes, seeking accountability for his failure to intervene as she had asked: "Am I wrong in thinking you not quite right about the affair I commended to you? Thank God it has ended well" (*CL* 3:48). She outlines how she positioned Peel and Cobden "at each other's point of view ... most cordial are the acknowledgments of both to me" and demands, "Don't you think you ... should have let me know the moment you resolved not to stir? ... it is inconceivable ... that you would leave me to grope, & perhaps blunder, in the dark ... I trust you will live to rejoice, without any mixture of regret, in the present measures. The day of free trade in food will be a blessed one for land-owners, depend upon it."

Written during what proved to be just the beginning of Ireland's apocalyptic famine years, Martineau's enthusiasm for Corn Law repeal is poignant, if not naive, in its optimism about the benefits of free-trade.[48] Too little, too late, argued the starving, whose hunger, exacerbated by the potato famine, continued unrelieved; too much, too soon, claimed the land-owners, who feared economic loss. Since 1816, the Corn Laws had represented landed interests; that Martineau facilitated peace between government and opposition, between Lords and Commons, between landed gentry and starving masses, thus enabling crucial legislation to move forward, attests both to her political influence and to the spirit of the age of reform, during which the needs of the many finally began to outweigh the profit margins of the few.

Without doubt, Martineau's efforts at peacemaking were enabled by the historical inevitability sparked by the Reform Bill. Of the significance of Corn Law Repeal, she wrote, "the power under the Reform Bill, discovered by Mr. Cobden, of renovating county constituencies, must, sooner or later, bring forth vast political results" (*History* 5:243). Its work accomplished, the Anti-Corn-Law League was dissolved in Manchester in July, 1846; on this occasion, Cobden pronounced that, though Peel "had lost office, he had gained [the loyalty and gratitude of] a country ... For my part, I would rather descend into private life with that last measure of his ... than mount to the highest pinnacle of human power."[49]

Soon after, Martineau wrote to Cobden that she had burnt his letters, as he requested: "More than one interesting piece of secret history will die with me ... So your confidence is safe" (*AB* 2:264). Wendy Hinde notes, "Apparently he was not told of her correspondence with Peel, and so never learned the full extent of her

---

48 While the topic is beyond the scope of this paper, some argued (Irish nationalists like John Mitchel, for example) that Corn Law repeal and free-trade not only did not alleviate Ireland's famine but exacerbated its effects.

49 McGilchrist, 137.

peacemaking diplomacy."[50] But, also in the *Autobiography,* Martineau asserted that, while most know the outcome of this exchange—Corn Law repeal, and the public pronouncement of mutual regard between Cobden and Peel—"scarcely any body knows ... how they came to an understanding ... I should not have related the story here if I had not considered it honourable to every body concerned" (*AB* 2:264). As these two statements indicate, Harriet Martineau can hardly be accused of consistency: in 1846, she melodramatically pronounced that this history would die with her, yet less than ten years later, she incorporated the adventure into her autobiography. Another twenty-two years later, the *Autobiography* was published posthumously, after all three players in this drama had died: Peel in 1850, Cobden in 1865, and Martineau in 1876.[51] Since this episode was "honourable" to all concerned, its publication represents not a betrayal of confidence, political or epistolary, but the preservation of the history of a political crisis—and her role in it—not elsewhere recorded.

This Victorian-secret-revealed anticipates socio-cultural changes in other ways as well. The calico-print fabrics of manufacturer-turned-MP Richard Cobden became all the rage: "the wives and dependents of the great landowners, whose monopoly he assailed, were seen in public clad in his garments"; even Queen Victoria wore "Cobden's prints," as observed from one of the first passenger trains rolling past Windsor Castle.[52] In contrast, Peel's bizarre death after falling from a skittish horse—"a dire and irreparable loss to the country"—symbolized the old order giving way to the new.[53] Cobden's political career lasted through 1865, involving him in the Crimean War, the Indian Uprising, and conflicts with China. Martineau, though pleased by the outcome of her "only political plot," was content to retreat behind the relative anonymity of journalism; to my knowledge, she never wrote to another Prime Minister.

Martineau's terming this political intrigue an isolated incident is rather disingenuous. Perhaps she was "indisposed ... to meddle in matters which did not concern [her]," but there were surprisingly few matters that came under that category. Yet this episode was indeed unique among her political adventures: Cobden's appeal to her expertise opened the door, while his intemperate public speeches provided the opportunity. Further, her failed attempt to enlist the not-so- neutral R. M. Milnes as peacemaker, and her awareness that the well-being of millions hung in the balance, forced her to take the unprecedented step of writing to Peel directly. Martineau's Victorian secret was preserved for over thirty years, and her role in it is, accordingly, absent from the standard—or, at least, earliest—biographies of both men. To the questions I raised earlier concerning

---

[50] Hinde, 161.

[51] Of Peel's death, Martineau wrote: "I never felt or witnessed such grief at any public loss ... [I]t is a comfort to me to see that the judgment of Peel which I gave out [in the *History*] ... is now that which we read & hear on every hand" (*CL* 3:162–4).

[52] McGilchrist, 20–21.

[53] Morley, 2:76.

this episode, then, I will add a few more: why were these politicians so responsive to her suggestions and yet hesitant to acknowledge her role in resolving the conflict? What role did their respective biographers play in erasing Martineau's participation in this episode and why? To what extent, finally, is the reputation of Victorian statesmen dependent upon projecting an image of inherent autonomy and wherewithal, and how and why is that compromised or threatened by the contributions of an intellectual woman?

In the absence of answers to those questions, I find it highly plausible that Martineau's reputation as a shrewd political analyst is evidenced as much by her participation in these events as it is by her writing about and publishing them; there can be no question of self-aggrandizement here, since publication occurred more than thirty years after the event, and that posthumously. At the beginning of her career, she wrote: "I want to be doing something with the pen, since no other means of action in politics are in a woman's power" (*CL* 1:139). Those circumstances did not change during her lifetime, which necessitated her recording this episode in the *Autobiography*. Martineau's socio-political and intellectual authority is evidenced by requests for her expertise from around the world, and by her successful orchestration of peacemaking between feuding politicians. On the occasion of her "only political plot," the pen wielded by Harriet Martineau proved to be mightier than either the swords or the rhetoric of duelling MPs; but it is an unfortunate sign of the times that "petticoat-government" carried an even greater stigma than the peculiar "laws of honour which are so sacred in men's eyes."

Chapter 3
Secrecy and Reticence in John Henry Newman's *Loss and Gain*

David J. Bradshaw

> Religion is what the individual does with his own solitariness.
> —Alfred North Whitehead, *Religion in the Making*

In "The Buried Life," Matthew Arnold elucidates the perplexity experienced by many nineteenth-century writers as they turned, in different forms of autobiographical discourse, to understand and then present the authentic selves they wished their readers to acknowledge and affirm. Arnold posits that some providential agency, concerned that the fickle willfulness of man would lead him to tamper with a natural integrity and "well nigh change his own identity," has imposed a radical limit upon self-knowledge in order "That it might keep from his capricious play / His genuine self." Such providence or fate

> Bade through the deep recesses of our breast
> The unregarded river of our life
> Pursue with indiscernible flow its way;
> And that we should not see
> The buried stream, and seem to be
> Eddying at large in blind uncertainty,
> Though driving on with it eternally. (ll. 34–6; 38–44)[1]

Arnold discerns a safeguard in a sort of Carlylean anti-self-consciousness that preserves one's psychic well-being against a restlessness of the meddling intellect.[2]

---

[1] *Arnold: Poetical Works*, ed. C. B. Tinker and H. F. Lowry (New York: Oxford UP, 1945), 246.

[2] John Stuart Mill was, if not the first, certainly the most prominent thinker to credit Thomas Carlyle for developing an effective method of dealing with depression; in countering his own despondency, Mill found essential Carlyle's therapeutic strategy of cultivating a resistance to inhibiting introspection. Writing, in his *Autobiography*, about his gradual escape from the aridity of the analytic intellect and about his subsequent recovery from disabling depression, Mill refers to "anti-self-consciousness" as a preservative of psychic wholeness, attributing to Carlyle the significant articulation of this philosophical stance: "The experiences of this period … led me to adopt a theory of life, very unlike that on which I had before acted, and having much in common with what at that time I certainly had never heard of, the anti-self-consciousness theory of Carlyle … This theory

His central image of the buried stream of life suggests how central to nineteenth-century autobiographical writing was the predicament of repression. For Arnold, the true nature of a person is a secret quite providentially kept not simply from others but also from one's own probing intellect intent upon self-knowledge.

Arnold's assessment of the difficulties involved in self-knowledge may helpfully inform the study of autobiography. Analysis of Victorian self-writings, especially, involves consideration of different types of repression on the part of autobiographers, the critical disposition being to discern and make public what writers have kept private from others and perhaps have kept, consciously or not, secret from themselves.[3] Any writer claiming to be straightforward and ingenuous in constructing the autobiographical subject is likely to be construed as devious or disingenuous, while an assertion of secure belief or personal serenity is apt to be read as a pretense designed to mask anxiety and doubt. Writers themselves may seem hyperconscious of the suspect nature of statements that, in certain ways, they only are in an authoritative position to affirm. Consider one of the most well-known claims to resolved equanimity, which occurs in John Henry Newman's *Apologia pro Vita Sua*. Newman, who was writing in 1864, offers in a chapter titled "Position of My Mind since 1845" the following declaration that would seem to call for challenge:

> From the time I became a Catholic, of course, I have no further history of my religious opinions to narrate. In saying this, I do not mean to say that my mind has been idle, or that I have given up thinking on theological subjects; but that I have had no variations to record, and have had no anxiety of heart whatever. I have been in perfect peace and contentment; I never have had one doubt. (*ApVS*, 320).

That Newman intended to arrest readers by his assertion of assured, almost *ex morte* stability of perspective seems clear—note the dismissively parenthetical "of course" in the initial sentence, calculated, along with the excessive nature of his declarations, to provoke thought, possibly even to call forth a skeptical disbelief that is induced only to be forcibly quelled.

Some such postulation of steadied perspective, however, would seem a necessary assumption for most writers of autobiography, who need to assure themselves more so even than their readers that they enjoy an authoritatively distanced standpoint on their remembrances of things past, a security of retrospective serenity that

---

now became the basis of my philosophy of life." *Autobiography*, ed. John Robson (New York: Penguin Books, 1989), 117–18.

[3] R. A. York may expose some of the motivation for this critical disposition in remarking that secrecy "suggests a feeling that the *real* self of the other person lies precisely in his or her unwillingness to tell us everything." *Strangers and Secrets: Communication in the Nineteenth-Century Novel* (Madison, New Jersey: Fairleigh Dickinson UP, 1994), 18. What is secret is more valued, therefore understood as more authentic than what is publicly exposed.

Wordsworth calls "The calm existence that is mine when I / Am worthy of myself" (*The Prelude*, I.349–50).[4] This steadiness of viewpoint accords with a stance of the writer as truth teller, as someone who neither prevaricates nor conceals anything from readers. Yet writers' openly acknowledged concealments from others comprise significant features of many autobiographies. For some nineteenth-century thinkers, what proves efficacious in cultivating and preserving selfhood is not so much a complex or an unacknowledged repression as a simple secrecy evidenced in mindful reticence and silence. William Wordsworth, John Henry Newman, and Edmund Gosse all record, in distinctively different autobiographical narratives,[5] a deliberative turning toward prudent reserve that fosters individuation and spiritual growth. Such concern with secrecy and discretion would seem not some subliminal urge to repress or mystify what is disturbing but rather a conscious decision to acknowledge silence and secrecy as means through which a spiritual force can actualize the self.

Of the three writers, Newman is most commonly associated with secrecy, having been vilified by Kingsley as a crypto-Catholic prior to conversion, an equivocator whose transgressive concealments about ecclesiastical allegiances may have seduced blandly unsuspecting followers. Yet it is not the Newman of the

---

4 *Wordsworth: Poetical Works*, ed. Thomas Hutchinson, rev. Edward De Selincourt (New York: Oxford UP, 1936), 499.

5 Newman's *Apologia pro Vita Sua* is the most traditional of these autobiographies, fulfilling certain conventions of the religious conversion story. Wordsworth's *The Prelude* is a fourteen-book blank verse poem that aspires to epic status but is distinguished by lyric reflection. Edmund Gosse's *Father and Son* is generally regarded as a hybrid, a "biography/ autobiography," although Gosse wanted it to be received as somewhat a scientific report, subtitling it *A Study of Two Temperaments* and insisting that he offered it as a "*document*, a record of [certain] educational and religious conditions…the diagnosis of a dying Puritanism" (*FaS*, 3). The diversity of autobiographical writing in the nineteenth century is a register of the widespread interest in self-assessment and self-explication. Summaries of the development of various models for self-writing may be found in these now traditional studies: Wayne Shumaker, *English Autobiography: Its Emergence, Materials, and Form* (Berkeley: U of California P, 1954); Roy Pascal, *Design and Truth in Autobiography* (New York: Garland, 1960); Paul Delany, *British Autobiography in the Seventeenth Century* (London: Routledge and Kegan Paul, 1969); Elizabeth Bruss, *Autobiographical Acts: The Changing Situation of a Literary Genre* (Baltimore: Johns Hopkins UP, 1976); William C. Spengemann, *The Forms of Autobiography: Episodes in the History of a Literary Genre* (New Haven: Yale UP, 1980); Linda Peterson, *Victorian Autobiography: The Tradition of Self-Interpretation* (New Haven: Yale UP, 1986); Clinton Machann, *The Genre of Autobiography in Victorian Literature* (Ann Arbor: U of Michigan P, 1994). Two recent books are also instructive: Bruce Hindmarsh, *The Evangelical Conversion Narrative: Spiritual Autobiography in Early Modern England* (New York: Oxford UP, 2005) and James Treadwell, *Autobiographical Writing and British Literature, 1783–1834* (Oxford: Oxford UP, 2005). For consideration both of the urge to delimit what is, properly, autobiographical and also of the tendency to extend the boundaries defining autobiography, see Eugene Stelzig, "Is There a Canon of Autobiography?", *a/b Auto/Biography Studies* 7, no. 1 (Spring 1992): 1–12.

Kingsley calumnies and the familiar *Apologia* who provides the readiest example of deliberative secrecy but, instead, Charles Reding, the hero of Newman's 1848 autobiographical fiction *Loss and Gain*, a young and impressionable Oxford student whose honest doubts and spiritual anguish become resolved through conversion from Anglicanism to true Catholicism. Writing three years after his reception into the Roman communion, Newman creates Reding to be sufficiently distinct from himself that no one could assert an absolute identity between the two: Reding only reluctantly engages in theological speculation, is an unwilling controversialist, champions no movement, never actually takes an Oxford degree or assumes a university appointment, causes no national scandal by discovering the Church of England to be Duessa. However, the pointed similarities between Reding's doubts and those entertained by Newman, the consternation felt at the prospect of leaving behind, in the progress toward Rome, beloved family and friends, the ascetic bent and quixotically idealistic disposition all clearly link Reding to Newman.

Also connecting author and character is a resolute concern with secrecy, concealment, and privacy that sets Reding apart as he comes to engage in destabilizing controversy that consistently exposes him to attempts by others to define for him not simply the nature of orthodox beliefs but the distinctive character of his own inmost soul. Against impositions by anxious and sometimes outright neurotic colleagues eager to confirm their own beliefs by converting him, Reding cultivates a defensive strategy of concealing both convictions and doubts; he deploys even more assertively a similar tactic against quasi-inquisitorial university churchmen keen to pluck out the heart of his mystery. And, if Newman was determined to preserve through his own selective secrecies what biographer Ian Ker calls "the inner life of the individual, where conscience not logic reigns supreme,"[6] Reding, too, insists upon an internal seclusiveness that safeguards his genuine self from the capricious play of a sometimes meddling, sometimes irascible intellect. Notably, too, as Heather Henderson observes, following fast upon his admission into the Catholic Church, Reding registers the ultimate experience of ecstatic vision in "a near speechless moment,"[7] concealed in silence and seclusion from everyone but his fellow convert Willis; Willis, however, quoting Psalm 50, assures Reding of a time when reticence will not be needed, for '"Deus manifeste veniet, noster Deus, et non silebit"': "God shall be manifest, our God, and He will not be silent" (*LaG*, 297).[8]

Newman begins this novel with reflections by Reding's father, a thoughtfully benevolent Anglican cleric, concerning a natural inviolability of the human psyche. Quoting from *The Christian Year*, the father recalls John Keble's observation that

---

[6] Ian T. Ker, *John Henry Newman: A Biography* (New York: Oxford UP, 1990), 290.

[7] Heather Henderson, *The Victorian Self: Autobiography and Biblical Narrative* (Ithaca: Cornell UP, 1989), 63.

[8] John Henry Newman, *Loss and Gain: The Story of a Convert*, ed. Alan G. Hill (New York: Oxford UP, 1986), 297.

"'Each in his hidden sphere of bliss or woe, / Our hermit spirits dwell'" (*LaG*, 5). Anxious that he may not fully know his son's mind, he contemplates the (perhaps) reassuring idea that the "'heart is a secret with its Maker; no one can hope to get at it or to touch it'" (*LaG*, 5). That Newman sets the novel into motion with meditations upon young Reding's "secret thoughts" and characteristic "reserve" (*LaG*, 5) would seem not inadvertent, for the documentation of the progress of this soul is a record of ongoing quietist development engaged in as a defensive strategy against the fretful stir unprofitable of feverish theological controversy.

Newman presents Reding as, at first, unqualifiedly opposed to argument about matters of faith. At Oxford as a first-year student, Reding initially wants a smooth simplicity, not a problematical complexity, and the abundance of good will that distinguishes his personality disposes him to broadminded acceptance of diverse opinion (*LaG*, 18, 25). Teased by his friend William Sheffield to acknowledge the radical insufficiency of a particular Oxford don, Reding replies in a fashion that reveals a naïvely genial temperament ill-disposed to any irritable reaching after fact or reason:

> 'I am for taking every one for what he is, and not for what he is not; one has this excellence, another that; no one is everything. Why should we not drop what we don't like, and admire what we like? This is the only way of getting through life, the only true wisdom, and surely our duty into the bargain.' (*LaG*, 9)

A constitutional hankering after truth, however, steadily amends this disposition, as Reding comes to recognize that: "All doctrines could not be equally sound: there was a right and a wrong. The theory of dogmatic truth, as opposed to latitudinarianism ... had ... gradually begun to energise in his mind" (*LaG*, 27). The gradualism noted here is important, as is the secretive, personal deliberation that stands apart from the "talk, talk, in every quarter" of Oxford about which Reding complains (*LaG*, 25). Conversion for Charles Reding will come, as it had come for John Henry Newman, largely as the result of regularly evolving ideas that, over time, have been given sustained private consideration in a tranquil and independent mind.

> Some persons fidget at intellectual difficulties, and, successfully or not, are ever trying to solve them. Charles [Reding] was of a different cast of temper; a new idea was not lost on him, but it did not distress him, if it was obscure or conflicted with his habitual view of things. He let it work its way and find its place, and shape itself within him, by the slow spontaneous action of his mind. (*LaG*, 48)

If, for Newman, divine revelation itself unfolds progressively through time, for Reding, personal conviction about spiritual truths and, indeed, character itself, as George Eliot would insist, also comprise "a process and an unfolding."[9]

---

[9] George Eliot, *Middlemarch*, ed. Gordon S. Haight (Boston: Houghton Mifflin, 1956), 111.

For, in *An Essay on the Development of Christian Doctrine*, written just before *he* left Oxford for Rome, Newman had insisted that, "From the nature of the human mind time is necessary for the full comprehension and perfection of ... ideas."[10] (67). In his exhaustive and scrupulously documented study of Newman's Anglican career, Frank Turner finds this treatise vital to understanding Newman's complexly conflicted mindset during the later 1830s and earlier 1840s;[11] however, neither Turner nor others trace in *Loss and Gain* the significant ideas informing the *Essay on Development*, especially the insistence that time is essential for ongoing reflection to take place, for continuing revelation to occur. For Charles Reding, such time cannot be a hurried episode: "[T]he principle of dogmatism gradually became an essential element in Charles's religious views. Gradually, and imperceptibly to himself– ..." (*LaG*, 49). Again, the gradualism is crucial, as is the privacy of religious reflection, for mind and soul must grow organically, the season of silent thought being extended to whatever length is needed for maturation.

Maturation itself, meanwhile, Newman honestly presents as an unsettling process involving a sense of radical disaffection from self, others, and world, a perplexity experienced as what Wordsworth had termed the "Blank misgivings of a Creature / Moving about in worlds not realized."[12] As the result of his initially reluctant yet increasingly resolute theological deliberations, Reding becomes ill at ease with his fellows, uncomfortable with family, and conflicted within himself. In this condition, he mirrors the thirty-year-old Augustine prior to his conversion. For, whether by design or as the result of the diffuse influence of the *Confessions* upon the ways in which thinkers construed the conversion experience, Newman recreates in Reding the pre-conversion pattern that Augustine establishes in his seminal narrative: the perplexed wandering *in regione dissimilitudinis*, the realm of disaffected isolation or estranged dissimilarity from God (VII.x.16), and the ultimate release from such alienation through redemptive grace.[13] If he is like Augustine in describing both a subjection to fragmented, inauthentic life and a concluding providential liberation from such dissociated existence, Newman is also like Augustine in maintaining that ongoing self-development is the law of human nature. The pilgrim soul or human becoming must enter communion with others, but it does so only through perpetual struggle in a world that does, indeed,

10 John Henry Newman, *An Essay on the Development of Christian Doctrine*, ed. C. F. Harrold (New York: Longmans, Green, 1949), 67.

11 Frank Turner, *John Henry Newman: The Challenge to Evangelical Religion* (New Haven: Yale UP, 2002), 558–77, 629–40. Turner also gives recurring attention to the *Essay on Development* in the extended critical analysis forming the Introduction to his edition of *Apologia pro Vita Sua* (New Haven, Connecticut: Yale UP, 2008), but, even in treating this most famous of autobiographical works, he does not turn toward the autobiographical fiction that comprised Newman's first publication as a Roman Catholic.

12 "Ode. Intimations of Immortality from Recollections of Early Childhood" ll. 148–9; see also 461.

13 *The Confessions of Saint Augustine*, trans. E. B. Pusey. 1838 (London: Watkins, 2006), 153.

assume the aspect of a vale of soul-making. Newman puts the matter simply when, in speaking of the ineluctable growth of Reding's character, he insists upon the dynamic aspect of the young man's spiritual progression: "It is impossible to stop the growth of the mind" (*LaG*, 142). At the fractious Oxford of his time, however, Reding needs to cultivate a defensive reticence in order to nurture the natural growth of his thoughts.

Most pointedly, Newman has Reding learn the hard way not to speak too freely of his doubts and concerns. Faced with variances in beliefs among his fellows, Reding "did not wish to speak, but he was not sorry to listen" to their discussions (*LaG*, 36). When, however, he articulates his uncertainties and misgivings, he first finds himself zealously detained by Mr. Vincent, the tutor absolutely committed to the *via media* yet incapable of defining his own beliefs, for he "thought it enough to flee from extremes, without having any definite mean to flee to" (*LaG*, 54). Reding fairly quickly sounds the shallows of Vincent's Anglican soul, yet his interactions with Vincent lead him to increased reticence and hesitation to make known his own views.

Next, acknowledging to his High Church friend Bateman his uncertainties concerning the Thirty-nine Articles of the Anglican Church, Reding faces a barrage of accusations and recriminations that intensify rather than relieve his own anxieties. His response is to withdraw from conversation and engagement, to conceal the force of his doubt. Hiding from his fellows and in some measure from himself, like the modern men whom Arnold disparaged and pitied, he "live[s] and move[s] / Trick'd in disguises, alien to the rest / Of men, and alien to" himself.[14] This pattern of disengagement and concealment is repeated and extended when, subsequently, Reding and his friend Sheffield take a cottage during the summer months as they begin to read for honors and prepare for examinations. Exposed through interactions with their tutor to genuine theological controversy, Reding "began to feel uncomfortable misgivings and doubts" and "[a]ccordingly he kept silence, and ... attempted to change the subject" (*LaG*, 151).

Such efforts at concealment have success but success that is limited, for, in spite of his discretion, Reding faces official surveillance, having been "outed" as a man uneasy with the Thirty-nine Articles, a man "'papistically inclined'" (*LaG*, 162). "[T]here was at that time," Newman writes of Oxford, "a system of espionage prosecuted by various well- meaning men" to identify, mark, question, and censure any who were leaning toward Rome (*LaG*, 162). No one expects an Anglican Inquisition, certainly not the still trusting Charles Reding, and Reding is astonished and distressed to find himself interrogated by the University Vice-Principal and the Principal. His response to these men is lawyerly in the evasive concealment of his growing misgivings about the Church of England; once again, conscious reticence and prudent reserve enable Reding to maintain in privacy the integrity of his own thoughts, beliefs, and doubts. University administrators, meanwhile, dissatisfied with their inability to convict him of actual infidelity to

14 Matthew Arnold, "The Buried Life," ll. 20–22; see also 245.

the English Church, dismiss him for a time from the university, and, having been rusticated, Reding must continue his reflections upon dogma, church history, and ecclesiastical traditions largely at a second remove from fellows and friends.

In isolation, Reding continues to be perplexed, yet he conceals from his family the extent of his distress, the intensity of his doubt.[15] In contact, again, with Bateman, the High Churchman, he finds himself accused of being deceptively secretive about his supposed movement toward Rome and about his own most personal beliefs: "'why are you silent?'" asks Bateman. But Reding will not give a direct rejoinder. "Bateman could not make him out, and had not a dream how he was teasing him ... They paced down the walk in silence" (*LaG*, 189). Yet silence enjoyed in privacy also distinguishes the moments of epiphanic revelation that Reding is granted. At a dinner in the country attended by old friends from Oxford, Reding once again finds Willis, the man who already has converted to the Roman communion. As Willis and he walk for a short space together toward their separate lodgings, Willis calls for Reding to pray for faith so that he might embrace the true faith, and he tells him that he is the subject of Catholic prayers; then, "he drew Charles to him and kissed his cheek, and was gone before Charles had time to say a word. Yet Charles could not have spoken had he ever so much opportunity" (*LaG*, 229). Discreet secrecy and silence can act as a defense against that which threatens the self, yet they also serve as an appropriate acknowledgment of that which sustains or nourishes the psyche. In his private wonderment at Willis's invitation to join him in the crucial movement toward Rome, Reding "felt himself possessed ... by a high superhuman power ... With winter around him, he felt within like the springtide, when all is new and bright ... He felt he was no longer alone in the world" (*LaG*, 229).

Shortly thereafter, Reding does make conscious to himself and public to others the decision that, in fact, he had already long since made in his heart: he dissociates himself from the Church of England and declares his allegiance to Rome. In coming to awareness of the steady though slow workings of providential grace in him, however, Reding experiences none of the psychological trauma of a Hopkins wrestling with his God or the rhapsodic exhilaration of a Thompson fleeing a divinity who pursues him down the labyrinthine ways of his own mind. Epiphany for Reding is a gradually growing realization that he must patiently open himself to grace and submit himself to direction, not anxiously seeking after many

---

15 There is genuine pathos in Newman's own isolation from family during and following his conversion; Reding's estrangement from his sister Mary and especially his heartrending parting from his mother would seem to rehearse the ruptures that Newman experienced as he distanced himself from his sisters Jemima and Harriett and as he dealt with the distress expressed by his ailing mother during the Tractarian controversies. (Newman's mother died prior to his conversion.) Newman's situation—and Reding's—may best have been summed up by another celebrated writer who moved from Oxford to Rome, Gerard Manley Hopkins: "To seem the stranger lies my lot, my life / Among strangers. Father and mother dear, / Brothers and sisters are in Christ not near." *The Poems of Gerard Manley Hopkins*, 4th ed., ed. W. H. Gardner and N. H. MacKenzie (New York: Oxford UP, 1967), 101.

things but, rather, awaiting in quiet seclusion from partisan theological debate the emergence, in the fullness of time, of the one thing needful. "'Conviction,'" he has reflected,

> 'is the eyesight of the mind, not a conclusion from premises; God works it, and His works are slow. At least so it is with me ... I must move in what seems God's way; I can but put myself on the road; a higher power must overtake me, and carry me forward.' (*LaG*, 204)

Privacy, reticence, discreet reserve in conversation with others does not, for Reding, generate faith, but they foster its development. After two years of retirement (roughly the length of time that Newman spent in seclusion at Littlemore before being received into the Roman communion), Reding leaves home to begin his life as a Roman Catholic.

Before he makes his actual confession of faith, however, Reding is assailed in his temporary lodgings in London by various religious zanies who impose themselves upon him in attempts to "save" him from his rash decision to become a Roman Catholic. Newman presents, in this set of antic scenes, a comic parallel to the previous impositions of Reding's Oxford friends upon his privacy and deliberative silence.[16] The "talk, talk, in every quarter" about which he had complained at Oxford (*LaG*, 25) is parodied by the babble of the mottled zealots that confronts Reding when he has concealed himself so that he might reflect earnestly upon his momentous decision. "Reding naturally wished to take the important step he was meditating as quietly as he could" (*LaG*, 266), but successive intrusions by importunate and noisy enthusiasts make impossible his successful seclusion and his simple desire "to be to [him]self" (*LaG*, 274). Oppressed by the clamor of those who thrust themselves upon him, he abandons his plan to engage in prayerful meditation, almost relapses into the disquieted incertitude that distinguished his pre-conversion unrest, and even ceases his attempts to avoid further visitations from emotionally unstable extremists. Purposive action now seems impossible, and Reding is overwhelmed by a sense of futility, yet, even in his bewildered exhaustion, he yearns for silence: "It mattered little now whether he was left to himself or not, but conversation harassed and fretted him" (*LaG*, 280). The repeated episodes in which Reding is beset by multiple erratic proselytizers

---

[16] This section of the conclusion of *Loss and Gain* is not without serious satiric purpose. While Newman indulged in bursts of happy laughter as he composed certain segments of the narrative, this episode seems invested with bitter anger rather than with gaiety. Robert Lee Wolff tellingly notes that, "This procession of members of the lunatic fringe of mid-nineteenth-century English religion is funny, of course, even hilarious,...But it is also a serious expression of Newman's intolerant disgust with the proliferating sects that were, in his view, sure to spring up like evil fungi so long as every man, no matter how illiterate or how crazy, indiscriminately exercised his reason and his private judgment, acknowledging no higher authority than his own." *Gains and Losses: Novels of Faith and Doubt in Victorian England* (New York: Garland, 1977), 59.

reinforce through comic exaggeration a theme that Newman has more decorously developed in presenting Reding's Oxford experiences: Public display of matters of personal spiritual consequence results in erosion of meaningful development; by contrast, keeping secret from others one's spiritual reflections can promote devotion and personal religious growth.

As Newman moves Reding from the farcical to the sacred, from interaction with fanatics to entrance into the Roman Church, he only intensifies his insistence upon the importance of seclusion, silence, and secrecy. For, at the Passionist House in London, where Reding turns with now urgent concern to escape the cacophony of religious squabbling and quibbling, he makes his profession of true faith and finds himself in a silence that is a blessing from divine love rather than a defense against earthly bickering: "It was Sunday morning about seven o'clock, and Charles had been admitted into the communion of the Catholic Church about an hour since. He was still kneeling in the church of the Passionists before the Tabernacle, in the possession of a deep peace and serenity of mind, which he had not thought possible on earth" (*LaG*, 298). To him comes Willis, with the decisive assurance of a blessed time when, in place of creaturely concealment, there will be divine manifestation, a time when the silence maintained by individual persons will be superseded by the joyful noise made by the triumphantly covenanting God: "'Deus manifeste veniet, noster Deus, et non silebit'": "God shall be manifest, our God, and He will not be silent" (*LaG*, 297). No longer, then, will there be need of secrecy or concealment, for manifest divinity, the Word of God, makes unnecessary any silence other than that of reverent contemplation.

As was to be the case with his composition of the *Apologia pro Vita Sua*, Newman wrote *Loss and Gain* in response to an apparent attack on Roman Catholicism and, in part, on himself. Elizabeth Harris was a woman who had, perhaps sincerely, asked for acceptance into the Roman communion but then had returned to her Anglican origins. In 1847, she published, anonymously, a novel titled *From Oxford to Rome: And how it fared with some who lately made the journey. By a Companion Traveller*.[17] Harris hinted that those who had converted to the Roman Church might take part in the retrogression that defined her life, and Newman, who, living in Rome, had heretofore kept a disciplined silence about his all-important spiritual decision, felt compelled to speak out and give a true account of a story of conversion. It may have been the effect of the self-imposed seclusion and silence that led him to make secrecy, reticence, and prudent speech so distinctive a feature of this novel. Whatever the reason, Newman makes both concealment of doubt and confession of belief problematic concerns for Charles Reding. Those who find *Apologia pro Vita Sua* an account of spiritual development

---

[17] Alan G. Hill, in his introduction to the Oxford World's Classics edition of the novel, provides the essential information concerning the Harris novel. Newman's "Advertisement to the Sixth Edition" (1874) explains the prompting that led him to compose the work. Joseph Ellis Baker, in *The Novel and the Oxford Movement* (New York: Russell & Russell, 1965), 54–68, provides helpful historical context for reading *Loss and Gain*.

that is altogether too cerebral and devoid of personal emotion can discern in *Loss and Gain: The Story of a Convert* what Newman was too circumspect to advance before readers as a private testimony: the highly personal account of a soul in angst-ridden religious crisis. The *Apologia* is Newman's record of intellectual progress, a careful and polemical discrimination of theological distinctions offered to define and defend a resolution to acknowledge the singular and absolute legitimacy of the Roman Catholic Church. *Loss and Gain* is Newman's depiction of passionate spiritual struggle, a typically Victorian portrayal of a soul subject to anxiety, depression, and emotional discord because of honest doubt about religious certitude.[18] That such doubt needed to be concealed, that the struggle needed to be undertaken in isolation and defensive secrecy, makes the pathos of the spiritual disquiet all the more powerful. The novel makes available the "way of the soul," the journey to faith that Newman's contemporaries understood as the core of spiritual autobiography, and, though fiction, it renders real the suffering and distress that Newman underwent as, in the early 1840s, he heroically repudiated one life in order to enter upon another.

---

[18] Ed Block, Jr., notes that, "Choosing the mode of fiction rather than autobiography, Newman was able to universalize as he explored the dynamics of personal transformation and development with greater liberty and consequently greater psychological complexity than had he begun a work like the *Apologia*." "Venture and Response: The Dialogical Strategy of John Henry Newman's *Loss and Gain*," in *Critical Essays on John Henry Newman*, ed. Ed Block, Jr. (British Columbia: U of Victoria P, 1992), 24.

Chapter 4
"What Connexion Can There Be?": Secrecy and Detection in Dickens's *Bleak House*

John McBratney

Nineteenth-century writers sought to expose the dark, disturbing secrets of their psycho-social worlds for readers who, it was felt, were too apt to avert their eyes. This desire was particularly strong among writers about England, the first nation to experience the Industrial Revolution on a major scale. There, the often wretched results of that social and economic transformation were at once plainly on view and just as plainly ignored. From Friedrich Engels to John Ruskin to Charles Kingsley to Annie Besant, writers of the period urged their audiences to enlarge their field of vision—to take off their blinders or peer beneath the veneer of middle-class prosperity—in order to apprehend more clearly the distorted and iniquitous psychic and social arrangements of England as a preliminary to individual and collective reform.

Charles Dickens, who shared his peers' impulse to reveal injustice and inspire repair, often saw the project of exposure as detection; the lifting off, etymologically speaking, of roofs or covers to reveal hidden corruption and suffering. In *Dombey and Son*, he made the act of detecting secrets—secrets at once private and public—seem literal: "Oh for a good spirit who would take the house—tops off, with a more potent and benignant hand than the lame demon in the tale, and show a Christian people what dark shapes issue from amidst their homes, to swell the retinue of the Destroying Angel as he moves forth among them!"[1] But it was in *Bleak House* (1852–3), among all his novels, that Dickens pushed the concept of detecting hidden knowledge to its furthest point. Indeed, in the figure of the detective, Inspector Bucket, he expanded the idea far beyond the simple uncovering of the "dark shapes" of sin and crime to include two others kinds of detection: the revelation of those hidden human connections that bind a society together and the identification of those obscure means by which he himself as a novelist constructed his own social narratives. Yet, ironically, it is also through the figure of Bucket that Dickens explored most fully and incisively the difficulty of detection on the three levels—the criminal, the social, and the narrational—I

[1] Charles Dickens, *Dombey and Son* (London: Penguin, 1970), 738. The "tale" concerning "the lame demon" refers to Alain René Lesage's *Le Diable Boiteux*, in which the spirit Asmodée removes the roofs of houses so as to spy on the inhabitants.

identify above. The police inspector suggests that the English project of detection can go only so far when confronted with the riddles of crime and sin, the mysteries of the English social system, and the ambiguities of narration.

In a central passage of the novel, the third-person narrator asks,

> What connexion can there be, between the place in Lincolnshire, the house in town, the Mercury in powder, and the whereabout of Jo the outlaw with the broom, who had that distant ray of light upon him when he swept the churchyard-step? What connexion can there have been between many people in the innumerable histories of this world, who, from opposite sides of great gulfs, have, nevertheless, been very curiously brought together?
>
> Jo sweeps his crossing all day long, unconscious of the link, if any link there be.[2]

The third-person narrator—and implicitly Dickens himself—poses these questions in all seriousness. Indeed, they provide the impetus behind the novel's inquiry into the detection of secrets on the levels of the criminal, the social, and the narrational. The first sentence asks what links the aristocratic Dedlocks to the crossing-sweeper Jo—a question that bears ultimately on the solution of the mysteries of Tulkinghorn's murder and Lady Dedlock's disappearance. The second sentence goes beyond mere crime or imputed sin to ponder both social relations in general ("many people…from opposite sides of great gulfs") and the narratives about those relations ("the innumerable histories of this world"). On all three levels, the efforts of detection are rendered complicated. In the people "very curiously brought together," we see at once an investigative conundrum, a social oddity, and an aesthetic strangeness—inexplicabilities that will perplex Bucket and his creator. Moreover, in the "distant ray of light" that strikes Jo when he sweeps the churchyard-step, we encounter an issue that will intimately concern detection of all kinds: the question of the existence of Providence. That the ray of spiritual illumination that touches Jo's soul is "distant"—and that its distance seems all the greater for the boy's ironic proximity to a church—raises doubts about the assistance of the divine in answering any of the questions this passage poses. The qualifier "if any link there be" underscores those doubts, extending Jo's unconsciousness of connection to include potentially the narrator's. Are there any life-affirming links at all among persons? Are the links forged by Providence? Or are they, instead, wrought by some other agency: a totalizing social discipline, for example; or a mysterious fate; or mere chance? I will examine these questions, at once metaphysical and ideological, in tracing the detection of criminal, social, and narrational secrets in *Bleak House*. However, before I do, let me address briefly a possible objection to my method.

---

[2] Charles Dickens, *Bleak House* (London: Penguin, 1971), 272. Subsequent references to this work, with chapter numbers followed by page numbers, will be included in the text.

In seeing Bucket as crucial to a wide range of detective enterprises, I might be accused of placing too much emphasis on a minor character in the novel. Although I will implicitly address this objection throughout my argument, I want to give a general response here. Many critics have discussed *Bleak House* as a detective novel—an approach that has been particularly popular since the publication in 1983 of D. A. Miller's elegant, ground-breaking essay "Discipline in Different Voices: Bureaucracy, Police, Family, and *Bleak House*," later included in his 1988 *The Novel and the Police*.[3] In almost all of these readings, Bucket has figured heavily, whether as a figure of social regulation, social and political legitimation, psychological splitting and reintegration, failed Panopticonism, passively dominant masculinity, modern professionalism, or predatory atavism.[4] I argue his prominence based not only on his close involvement with the key mysteries of the plot, but also on his role as a potential nexus of social connection and as an analogue of the novelist himself. Although Bucket is a secondary character, his function in *Bleak House* is wide-ranging and central.[5]

I

Although *Bleak House* is about the detection of crime, it is not a detective novel in the pure sense of the term: a long narrative fiction whose central action is the solution of a crime. According to Ian Ousby, *Bleak House* is more properly a sensation novel: "Sensation novels are rarely concerned solely with crime and are hardly 'crime stories' in the literal sense of the term. Characteristically, they create a pervasive air of mystery to which mysterious crime is merely one contributing

---

3 D. A. Miller, *The Novel and the Police* (Berkeley: U of California P, 1988).

4 For these representations of Bucket, see respectively D. A. Miller, *Novel*, 58–106; Jan B. Gordon, "Dickens and the Transformation of Nineteenth-Century Narratives of 'Legitimacy,'" *Dickens Studies Annual* 31 (2002): 203–65; Albert D. Hutter, "The High Tower of His Mind: Psychoanalysis and the Reader of *Bleak House*," *Criticism: A Quarterly for Literature and the Arts* 19, no. 4 (1977): 296–316; Simon Joyce, "Inspector Bucket versus Tom-all-Alone's: *Bleak House*, Literary Theory, and the Condition-of-England in the 1850s," *Dickens Studies Annual* 32 (2002): 129–49; Michael Steig and F. A. C. Wilson, "Hortense Versus Bucket: The Ambiguity of Order in *Bleak House*," *Modern Language Quarterly* 33, no. 1 (1972): 289–98; Ronald R. Thomas, *Detective Fiction and the Rise of Forensic Science* (Cambridge: Cambridge UP, 1999), 131–49; and Peter Thoms, "'The Narrow Trace of Blood': Detection and Storytelling in *Bleak House*," *Nineteenth-Century Literature* 50, no. 2 (1995): 147–67.

5 Bucket's role beyond the confines of this novel has also been significant. As Ronald R. Thomas in "Detection in the Victorian Novel," in *The Cambridge Companion to the Victorian Novel*, ed. Deirdre David (Cambridge: Cambridge UP, 2001), points out, his influence on the development of the detective novel as a genre was decisive: "Mr. Bucket is not the first detective to appear in the English novel, but he is the most important early representative of this emerging literary and cultural hero" (178).

factor."[6] Yet, I want to consider the novel for a moment simply as a "crime story," since Bucket's performance as a detective in the strict sense will hold significance for his performance as a potential agent of social "connexion" and as a surrogate for the author.

Bucket is, no doubt, a detective of great, almost superhuman talent. "[A]ttentive" (22: 361) and, to Mr. Snagsby, with "an unlimited number of eyes" (22: 368), he has an almost panoramic vision of the world. Moreover, as he "dips down to the bottom of his [Snagsby's] mind," he has an equal power to fathom moral and psychic worlds within (22: 362). He is at once everywhere—he "strolls about an infinity of streets" (53: 768)—and nowhere, having materialized, it seems, out of thin air when he first appears before the law-stationer. Calm, pleasant, tolerant, and affable, he has a "fondness for society" and an "adaptability to all grades" (53: 777). Yet he is capable, in a professionally detached way, of great firmness, pointing his iconic forefinger, at once phallic and regulatory, at the target of his peremptory will. He knows "so much about so many characters, high and low" that there is no "move on the board that would surprise [him]" (54: 782). Finally, he is an expert at disguise, which he uses effectively, impersonating a physician to insinuate himself into Trooper George's shooting gallery. All these qualities make him not only an "omnicompetent" detective, but also the fitting embodiment of a new disciplinarity, at once legal, social, and political, that seeks to permeate all social space in order to produce the modern, urban, bourgeois subject as we know him or her.[7] (I say "seeks" because I will qualify this characterization of Bucket's agency below.) He is, in short, a walking Panopticon, seeing all, it seems, without being seen, as Mercury, the footman, discovers (53: 779).[8] At times, he appears supernatural, even god-like. He has a "ghostly manner" (22: 361); he seems "to vanish by magic" (24: 404); and when he arrests Hortense, he sweeps her away like "a homely Jupiter" (54: 799). Given his semi-divine omniscience, he seems one for whom there are no secrets, whether in the domain of the psychological or the social.

Yet, despite his apparently superhuman qualities, Bucket has a mixed record as a detective. He is involved in two cases in the novel: the apprehension of the murderer of Tulkinghorn and the recovery of the missing Lady Dedlock. The two cases are different in kind; in the first, Bucket acts as a public official and, in the second, as a private hire. However, this cross-over from public to private

[6] Ian Ousby, *Bloodhounds of Heaven: The Detective in English Fiction from Godwin to Doyle* (Cambridge, Mass.: Harvard UP, 1976), 81.

[7] The adjective "omnicompetent" is that of Philip Collins, *Dickens and Crime*, 3rd ed. (New York: St. Martin's, 1994), 213. My account of Bucket's regulatory and constructive powers is indebted to Thomas's description of the detective novel in general ("Detection") and of the inspector in particular (*Detective Fiction*, 131–49).

[8] On Jeremy Bentham's Panopticon and its permutations, see Michel Foucault, *Discipline and Punish: The Birth of the Prison* (1975), trans. Alan Sheridan (New York: Random House, 1977), 200–209, 216–17.

was common in the early days of the detective police in London.[9] His arrest of Hortense as the murderer is a fine piece of work, but after that seizure occurs, she unsettles the exalted image of Bucket we have built up in our minds to this point. In rapid-fire succession, the Frenchwoman asks him mockingly, "But can you restore him [Tulkinghorn] back to life?...Can you make a honourable lady of Her [Lady Dedlock]?...Or a haughty gentleman of *Him* [Sir Leicester]?" (54: 799). Of course, Bucket can do none of these things, and with these three thrusts, Hortense cuts him down to size: he is not a god, only a highly competent human being. His deflation here anticipates the larger collapse of his stature after his failure to find Lady Dedlock before she dies. The defeat in the latter case is not simply a demotion from god to man but, more crushingly given his professional pride, a decline from super-sleuth to fallible gumshoe. Although "he mounts a high tower in his mind" to locate Lady Dedlock as she flees her London residence in disguise, his panoptical powers desert him (56: 824). Ironically, he fails to see through the very kind of ruse he had penetrated earlier in the novel, when he had staged the "disguise" demonstration in Tulkinghorn's office with Hortense. Then he had been able to infer the lady beneath the uniform of a servant, but now he, a master of impersonation, fails to guess until too late that Lady Dedlock has again masked her identity beneath the clothing of a social inferior—this time a brick-maker's wife.

The reason for his failure is not immediately apparent. We could offer Lady Dedlock's cleverness as an explanation. However, given Bucket's familiarity with the "game[s]" of everyone he observes (54: 789)—games in which "there's [not] a move on the board that would surprise [him]"—this explanation seems doubtful. There is an air of inexplicability about his lapse. But perhaps we can find a reason in the sheer unprecedented nature of Lady Dedlock's flight from the family house in town. The Dickensian narrator describes her departure: "It is the figure of a woman, too; but it is miserably dressed, and no such clothes ever came through the hall, and out at the great door, of the Dedlock mansion" (56: 824). The phrase "no such clothes ever came through the hall," suggesting the absolute novelty of her "move," signals the cause of Bucket's impercipience. Her manner of flight represents not only an unforeseen move in the game of police detection, but also a gap in his social knowledge and a discontinuity in his sense of narrative design. On all three levels, and in a way that connects all three, his limitations stem from a particular commingling of novelty, contingency, and secrecy—indeed, from the idea of the new as both random and hidden.

---

[9] As W. H. Wills, in the *Household Words* article "The Modern Science of Thief-Taking," reprinted in *Hunted Down: The Detective Stories of Charles Dickens*, ed. Peter Haining (London: Peter Owen, 1996), makes clear, the detective Charles Frederick Field and his colleagues were hired "not only to counteract the machinations of every sort of rascal...but to clear up family mysteries, the investigation of which demands the utmost delicacy and tact" (62). Field, one of the first detectives of the London Metropolitan Police, was the figure after whom Bucket was probably modeled.

His simple failure to find Lady Dedlock in time points up his weakness as a detective. The damage he sustains to his reputation as a sleuth spreads, too, to his function as the epitome of a new administrative disciplinarity. Indeed, his shortcomings in this regard cast doubt on the claims that some critics have made for both Bucket's exemplarity and for the modern surveillance apparatus he represents. It has been argued that Bucket rises as Tulkinghorn falls and that, in that shift, the crisp regime of professional detection replaces the slow, ponderous rule of law.[10] However, given Bucket's stumble, it cannot be claimed that the regulatory force-field he enables, though undeniably pervasive, is all-pervading. Like the detective himself, it is too vulnerable to the contingent—the unprecedented move of a Lady Dedlock—to exercise complete mastery. Nor can it be maintained that his lapse, by the very anxiety it generates, produces further social control, whether by institutional or narrative means.[11] After leaving Esther with her dead mother, Bucket makes only one more appearance in the narrative and is missing from the general tying up of loose ends with which the novel concludes. With his absence, there is no visible sign of the new mode of discipline whose inauguration he emblematizes. In fact, the decrepit system of Chancery reasserts itself, with the story of the termination of Jarndyce & Jarndyce and Richard's ensuing death. No doubt, the efficient bureaucracy whose vanguard Bucket represents will return in strength, but the novel does not proclaim its triumph. Instead, it bows out quietly.

II

The aspect of detection upon which *Bleak House* dwells most insistently is the social. The societal dimension of the question "What connexion can there be?" concerns itself primarily with a highly stratified system of class and gender that links not only the landed aristocracy to the London poor but also men to women. The novel conceives of that class and gender connection as the interpenetration of two different "systems." The first, which is large, impersonal, widely penetrating,

---

[10] On this ideological shift, see Gordon, 240; D. A. Miller, *Novel*, 64; Jeremy Tambling, introduction to Bleak House / *Charles Dickens*, ed. Jeremy Tambling, New Casebooks (New York: St. Martin's Press, 1998), 11; and Thomas, *Detective Fiction*, 140.

[11] This is essentially D. A. Miller's position—one that is weakened, however, by his failure to consider that Bucket's detective duties extend beyond the apprehension of Tulkinghorn's murderer to include the recovery of Lady Dedlock. In neglecting this consideration, Miller misses the extent to which the novel destabilizes the twin regimes of police regulation of the bourgeois subject and narrative control of the reader. In my skepticism of readings, like Miller's, produced by a strict application of Foucault's insights, I join other critics who see in lying or secrecy a potential for disrupting disciplinary structures and thereby creating small opportunities for both individual subjects and tightly knit collectives to assert their independence and advance new social interests. On this potential, see John Kucich, *The Power of Lies: Transgression in Victorian Fiction* (Ithaca: Cornell UP, 1994), 17–20; and Albert D. Pionke, *Plots of Opportunity: Representing Conspiracy in Victorian England* (Columbus: Ohio State UP, 2004), xviii–xix.

and destructive of human happiness, joins the institutions of Chancery, Parliament, philanthropy, and business in an imbricated grid. It is the object of Gridley's wrath at Chancery—"The system! I am told, on all hands, it's the system" (15: 268)—and the subject of Esther's reservations about Mrs. Pardiggle's good works, which are "much too businesslike and systematic" for the comfort of anyone except the bustling philanthropist (8: 156). The second system is, in implicit opposition to the first, small, personal, domestic, and nurturing, centering itself in Esther Summerson, who, beginning in her home at Bleak House, sees her "circle of duty gradually and naturally expand[ing] itself" in the service of others (8: 154). The one begins on the outside and moves inexorably in; the other starts on the inside and moves slowly and organically outward. Although Esther's small kindnesses are far removed from the cruel obstructions of Chancery, her practice shares a sense of order with that of the law. As Skimpole, ever the shrewd delineator of the deep structures of English culture, exclaims, "When I see you, my dear Miss Summerson, intent upon the perfect working of the whole little orderly system of which you are the centre, I feel inclined to say to myself—in fact I do say to myself, very often—*that's* responsibility!" (37: 587). The difference between the two systems lies in their different motives: whereas institutions like Chancery concern themselves with maintaining their own oppressive power, ménages like Esther's attend to the welfare of others. Dickens himself was not opposed to order, either social or domestic, as long as it partook, as Skimpole puts it, of "responsibility." It is because the large system of Chancery is so irresponsible—both so uncaring of human happiness and so unresponsive to criticism—that it earns the wrath of the third-person narrator. Because Esther's values are the reverse of these, she elicits her author's approval, though not without some nervousness about her tendency to extreme self-abnegation.

Bucket, through his powers of social mobility and adaptability, acts frequently as the point of articulation between these macro-and micro-systems. From his vantage point between the systems, he can detect the workings of both; moreover, through his sharp eyes, readers are guided toward a comprehensive understanding of social networks. However, his detective work involves not simply monitoring society but also exerting force upon it; indeed, the act of detection is always in some way an act of deployed power. Much of the rest of my analysis of Bucket's "social" detection will examine the ways in which he *acts*, or fails to act, to bring about connection among persons.

As he moves restlessly about the social landscape, he brings his particular mode of surveillance with equal ease into the house at Chesney Wold and into Tom-all-Alone's. The secret of his ability to mediate between persons of widely different grades and professions lies in maintaining a sharp division between his public and private identities. There is a gender component to this division. If the difference between Chancery's and Esther's modes of order is partly produced by a society of separate, gendered spheres (the public Chancery being marked male and the private, domestic sphere being marked female), then the split in Bucket also represents in part a performance of those separate male and female spheres within his own person and practice.[12] Thus, he keeps compartmentalized the public, rational, conventionally male aspects of his being (the forefinger) and the private, affective, conventionally female aspects (his cozy affability). As he explains to Mr. George, "Duty is duty, and friendship is friendship. I never want the two to clash, if I can help it" (49: 734). In this way, he can befriend Mr. George in the privacy of the Bagnets' home and then take the former soldier into custody as soon as he and his companion find themselves in the street. Later, he introduces that schism into his own home; thus, he can employ his wife to act as a spy when he brings Hortense into their home and yet remain happily married.

However, the source of Bucket's great strength as a detective is also the cause of his doubtful moral and emotional fitness. His staunch unwillingness to integrate the two halves of his life makes him a figure of suspicion among those, like the Bagnets, who witness his sudden shifts between the private and public with a sense of betrayal. That same stubborn unwillingness also takes its toll on his connubial well-being. Although he and his wife appear delighted by their foray into joint detective work, he hints at their unhappiness when he mentions their childless marriage. Dickens was one of the first writers to note the mingled results of the schizoid identity that modern life imposes on its subjects, Wemmick in *Great Expectations* being the most brilliant example. The irony of this split condition is that, while it allows Bucket to form associations with many persons from diverse backgrounds, it impedes any meaningful emotional connection he might have with them and any happy integration of the two halves of his being.

An even more grievous consequence of this bifurcation concerns its larger social effects. Esther suggests, in her image of moral actions radiating outward, the ripple-effect of any personal encounter upon the wider social body. This image applies with unfortunate aptness to Bucket, particularly in his relationship with Jo. The police inspector is the person who most obviously bridges the gulf between the Dedlocks and Jo. At the behest of Tulkinghorn, the detective keeps Jo "moving on" in order to silence him. Bucket's cold-hearted attitude toward the boy—an attitude that arises from the careful sequestration of his better feelings from his professional deportment—is hard for most readers today to stomach. This may have been true for Victorian readers as well. In an illuminating essay on *Bleak House* as a condition-of-England novel, Simon Joyce points out that, given the widespread sympathy for the plight of street urchins at mid-century, "it was 'poor Jo' who most interested the novel's first readers" ("Inspector Bucket," 140). Joyce argues that, given this sympathy, "we can see Jo as Inspector Bucket's crowning failure"—and, by extension, as England's deep ineffectualness at addressing the suffering of its impoverished, abandoned children (140–41). Bucket's only response to the boy's misery is to tell him to "hook it," thus "passing the problem on to another beat or district" (141). The harm Bucket inflicts is exacerbated when

---

[12] The theater of gendered spheres takes a comical turn in the arrest scene with Hortense. There as he puts her shawl about her, Bucket explains that he has "been lady's maid to a good many before now" (54: 799).

he drives Jo into the countryside. Sick with smallpox, the boy takes refuge in Bleak House and there infects Charley and Esther, thus realizing the most horrific form of connection—communicable disease—between high and low. If an English sense of community has dissolved into Carlyle's "isolated, unrelated" monads, then, according to the novel, one way to achieve some kind of solidarity with one's fellow human beings is, grotesquely, to infect them.[13] In a strikingly direct way, the psychic cause of this malignity is Bucket's inability to integrate his domestic and professional lives. Indeed, as the contagion spreads invisibly and unpredictably from poor to rich and from male to female, its cruel success mocks the detective's failure to link these two lives efficaciously.

Bucket's inability to anticipate the consequences of chivying the feverish Jo about the land can be linked to his blindness to Lady Dedlock's final exit from her residence, since both stem from an element of the unexpected and the random that is beyond his surveillance and control. In "Tom-all-Alone's," the chapter in which the question about "connexion" appears, that query is followed in quick succession by three references to haphazard movement within the slum: that of a crowd of "vermin parasites ... that crawls in and out of gaps in walls and boards... and comes and goes, fetching and carrying fever (16: 272–3); that of Jo as he is "hustled, and jostled, and moved on" (16: 274); and that of Lady Dedlock, dressed like a servant, "going by...secretly" under Tulkinghorn's nose to meet Jo and visit for the first time the cemetery where she will later die (16: 276). In this way, Dickens juxtaposes the idea of social connection with that of a random, secret circulation of disease and human beings that disrupts the very idea of open, stable, and knowable connection.

It is tragically ironic that the "connexion" question is finally answered, if it is ever really answered, when Bucket and Esther come upon Lady Dedlock lying dead outside the gate of the cemetery where her former lover, Captain Hawdon, has been laid to rest. If for Dickens the deepest irony of social connection is that the characters who seem, because of social distance, most strange to each other are in fact most intimately allied, then no tableau in the novel more poignantly underscores this irony than that of these two bodies lying near each other in death. Yet as the linked movements of vermin, Jo, and the disguised Lady Dedlock suggest, Jo is also part of this moving tableau. He counts Hawdon as his closest friend. He brings Lady Dedlock to the cemetery for the first time to see her dead lover. It is also intimated that he catches at this noxious site the smallpox that later kills him and scars Esther. In placing the nexus of these doomed lives outside the graveyard entrance, the narrative associates the inspector's failure to find Lady Dedlock in time with his inability to foresee the working of those secret forces

[13] Thomas Carlyle, *Past and Present*, in *The Works of Thomas Carlyle*, Edinburgh Ed., 30 vols. (New York: Charles Scribner's Sons, 1903–1904), 10: 210. The story of cross-class infection in *Bleak House* echoes the story of the poor Irish widow in *Past and Present* who "prove[d] her sisterhood by dying of typhus-fever and infecting seventeen persons" (10: 211).

that vitiate healthful "connexions" among Jo and his fellow human beings. That Bucket's double failure finds its spatial correlative in the liminal space before the cemetery gate suggests that at the heart of his failure is an awful metaphysical profundity whose depths we will have to wait until the final section of this essay to plumb.

III

In an essay on Dickens and Bakhtin, Keith Easley notes suggestively about Bucket: "An artist, a director of sorts, he orchestrates and brings action to fulfillment, giving himself and his cognizance to the revelation of truth by giving it form. His art, that of detection, is framed by the author's own, with each a commentary on the other."[14] Indeed, the two do more than comment on each other. I will argue that Bucket is a stand-in for the third-person narrator and, implicitly, for Dickens himself. It has become a critical commonplace that *Bleak House* is as much an interrogation of its own strategies of interpretation as a critique of the society it interprets.[15] That self-reflexivity extends to the novel's narrative technique. In having Bucket compose a "book of fate," a monograph whose authority ultimately proves doubtful, Dickens reflects on his own risky experiment in double narrative in this novel and on the vexed enterprise of writing novels in general (53: 771). At stake in this exercise in meta-narrative are two questions: first, what brings about human connection in "the innumerable histories of this world"? and, second, to what extent does any teller of these histories have control over the telling of his or her tale? Such an exercise will pose hard questions about basic philosophical and theological issues that impinge upon the processes of fiction. Through the figure of Bucket as a sort of author, Dickens pursues the third and final kind of detection in *Bleak House*: an uncovering of the secret metaphysical underpinnings of narrative art. In this particular investigation, Bucket functions not so much as the ambiguous agent of detection as the fraught embodiment of detection gone wrong.

One of the salient details about Bucket's *modus operandi* is that he keeps a "book of fate to many" (53: 771) in which he records information about his cases. What is most striking about his fatal text from the standpoint of this argument is that, in his record-keeping, the detective becomes a kind of narrator and author. His authorial capacities are underscored by his artistic proclivities seen elsewhere. He looks at Snagsby "as if he were going to take his portrait" (22: 361). He asks Mercury if he were "ever modelled," observing him with "the expression of an artist" (53: 777). In addition, he describes the case of Tulkinghorn's murder as "a beautiful case—a beautiful case" (53: 775). As an artist, he appears to possess an awful power, as his pagan resonances throughout the novel suggest: he enfolds

---

[14] Keith Easley, "Dickens and Bakhtin: Authoring in *Bleak House*," *Dickens Studies Annual* 34 (2004): 209.

[15] J. Hillis Miller's highly influential introduction to the 1971 Penguin edition of *Bleak House* initiated this line of argument (11–34).

Hortense like "a homely Jupiter," he points his finger in the manner of the Roman Allegory that dominates Tulkinghorn's law office, and he resembles Vergil's Sybil when he guides Snagsby through the underworld of Tom-all-Alone's.[16] Indeed, given his divine or semi-divine attributes, his art seems guided by a god-like intelligence.

The seeming omniscience of Bucket as a detective-artist identifies him most closely with the third-person narrator of *Bleak House*, who is seen by many critics, as third-person narrators conventionally are, as all- knowing. However, long before Bucket arrives on the scene, Dickens has called this convention into question. Indeed, by constructing *Bleak House* as a double narrative, one comprising the third-person narrator's present-tense commentary and Esther's first-person, retrospective narrative, he has already signaled that the third-person narrator's story is only part of the total story that can be told. There are other indications, too, that the third-person narrator's story is partial. Esther's reference to "the unknown friend to whom I write" gives to the traditionally invisible third-person narrator a hint of materiality (67: 932)—a hint that takes on even greater substance when the third-person narrator unexpectedly steps into the story as a visitor to the portrait gallery at Chesney Wold and comments on it as a guest (40: 620). Here, the third-person narrator is a character like any other in the novel, with the limited vision such a character possesses. To confirm the impossibility of complete knowledge on the part of any narrator, Dickens ends Esther's "portion" with ellipses (3: 62). Even these two contributors to the story cannot say it all. *Bleak House* bears out what Audrey Jaffe has noted about all third-person would be omniscient narrators: "There are no 'third persons,' but only first persons wearing masks of invisibility." "Omniscience in general," she writes, "is a fantasy … ."[17]

In mirroring the third-person narrator, Bucket functions to embody, in abundant and concrete detail, that narrator's epistemological lack. When Bucket, from the high tower of his mind, fails to predict Lady Dedlock's use of disguise, he provides an objective correlative to the narrator's absence of full knowledge. More important, he supplies the broad metaphysical context within which to assess the novel's demystification of the fantasy of omniscient narration. When Bucket reveals his momentary blindness to Lady Dedlock's egress, the pretensions of his book to fatal knowledge grow shaky. If fate is literally "a sentence or doom of the gods" (*OED*, 2nd ed.), then Bucket has either not written or not read the "sentence" that applies to Lady Dedlock's exit. If the former is the case, then the inspector is not the author in this instance; if the latter applies, he seems to have forgotten what he wrote. In either case, we are forced to problematize not only Bucket as the incarnation of nemesis but also fate itself as the supreme mover of the novel's action.

---

16 On Bucket as Vergil's Sybil, see Marc Beckwith, "Catabasis in *Bleak House*: Bucket as Sibyl," *Dickens Quarterly* 1, no. 1 (1984): 2–6.

17 Audrey Jaffe, *Vanishing Points: Dickens, Narrative, and the Subject of Omniscience* (Berkeley: U of California P, 1991), 18, 6.

A good deal of critical commentary has dealt with the metaphysical or theological foundations of Dickens's novels and *Bleak House* in particular. I cannot go into detail about the debate that has swirled around this topic, but the parties to it might be broken down roughly in this way: (1) those who posit a providential design; (2) those who, perceiving in Dickens a skepticism about Providence, nonetheless find some kind of supernatural force at work in the novel; and (3) those who, because of the element of chance (usually in the form of coincidence), see the novel as uncertain in its attitude toward any providential or supernatural agency.[18] Plausible arguments can be made in support of all three of these positions. Readers in the first group argue that Esther's Christian belief, found in her frequent prayers "to our Father in heaven" (31: 495), preserves the concept of Providence for the novel. Critics in the second group assert that, instead of looking to a Christian God, we need to turn to a non-Christian, supernatural force—a tragic fate, for example—for an understanding of what guides this novel's narrative of human connection. It is not my aim here to analyze the providential or the supernatural argument in detail but, instead, to shed some light on the third, with its emphasis upon chance as disruptive of any totalizing metaphysical explanation. What I hope to show is, first, how a consideration of Bucket's book of fate can contribute to an understanding of the role of chance in *Bleak House*; second, how such a consideration might help us think about the problem of narration in the novel; and, third, what a study of the novel's problematical narration might say about the relation between secrecy and detection.

When the concept of fate is invoked in the novel, it is often paired with the concept of coincidence. Two passages merit attention in this regard. In the first, as Jo dies, the third-person narrator notes, "There, too, is Mr. Jarndyce many a time, and Alan Woodcourt almost always; both thinking, much, how strangely Fate has entangled this rough outcast in the web of very different lives" (47: 703). In the second, as Weevle and Snagsby meet unexpectedly after Crook's spontaneous combustion and sniff the burnt, greasy air outside his shop, they discuss the oddity of Nemo's having been a tenant in this building. "It's a curious coincidence," says Weevle, and the stationer responds, "Seems a Fate in it, don't there" (32: 501). In this second scene, the word "curious" and "Fate" are each used three times. Both these passages, in their combined use of "strangely," "curious," and "very different lives," echo the central "connexion" passage of the novel, but they also give these echoes a special resonance by introducing the figure of fate, suggesting that destiny has brought about the curious, coincidental meetings of very different

[18] For extended commentary on the themes of Providence, the supernatural, coincidence, and/or chance in *Bleak House*, see among others Neil Forsyth, "Wonderful Chains: Dickens and Coincidence," *Modern Philology* 83, no. 2 (1985): 151–65; Lawrence Frank, *Victorian Detective Fiction and the Nature of Evidence: The Scientific Investigations of Poe, Dickens, and Doyle* (Houndsmills: Palgrave-Macmillan, 2003), 71–98; Christopher Herbert, "The Occult in *Bleak House*," *Novel: A Forum on Fiction* 17, no. 2 (1984): 101–15; and Garrett Stewart, "The New Mortality of *Bleak House*," *ELH* 45, no. 3 (1978): 443–87.

lives.[19] But how, we might ask, can destiny be seen to give rise to coincidence—the chance convergence, as Aristotle saw it, of two otherwise fully determined causal sequences?[20] The answer lies in the proper alignment of points of view in time. At the precise moment of an unexpected encounter, the meeting seems random. However, in hindsight (which an interval of reflection establishes), the meeting can seem fated, entirely expected. In narrative, which is a form of verbalized hindsight, chance, particularly in the form of coincidence, is almost always rendered as some kind of fate (Monk, *Standard Deviations*, 8). In the case of the novel, even from its inception in *Robinson Crusoe*, the drive to "intrinsic coherence" of the work of art requires even more strongly that all ostensibly random events within the story be transformed into a destined, usually providential, sequence.[21]

Yet the missing "sentence" in Bucket's book of fate leaves a tear in the texture of destiny. This hitch in the working of fate is not uncommon in Dickens. When he alludes to books of fate elsewhere in his fiction, he does so, as in *Bleak House*, to ironize or parody the idea of destiny. In *Little Dorrit*, for example, when the heroine rests her head on "that sealed book of Fate," the burial volume in the three-volume Register of Saint George, she is "untroubled by its mysterious blank leaves," serenely indifferent, as Nancy Aycock Metz points out, to the defined teleology of such a narrative.[22] In *Our Mutual Friend*, the third-person narrator intones, with mock-ominousness: "it is written in the Books of the Insolvent Fates that Veneering shall make a resounding smash next week."[23] In the particular case of *Bleak House*, Bucket finds the integrity of his fatal book shaken by the very element of chance that novelistic narrative is supposed to domesticate into intrinsic design. It would be foolishly anachronistic to claim that Dickens believed in the probabilistic universe in which many of us, after Mendel and Heisenberg, believe. However, while holding both to the idea of a Christian Providence and

---

[19] According to John Forster, in *The Life of Charles Dickens* (1871–73; collected, arranged, and annotated by B. W. Matz, 2 vols., Philadelphia: B. Lippincott, 1911), Dickens was fascinated by coincidences:

> On the coincidences, resemblances, and surprises of life, Dickens liked especially to dwell, and few things moved his fancy as pleasantly. The world, he would say, was so much smaller than we thought it; we were all so connected by fate without knowing it; people supposed to be far apart were so constantly elbowing each other; and to-morrow bore so close a resemblance to nothing half so much as to yesterday. (1: 64)

Dickens, I would argue, makes the relation between coincidence and fate more ambiguous in *Bleak House* than he does in his conventional treatment of the subject here.

[20] For a discussion of Aristotle on coincidence, see Leland Monk, *Standard Deviations: Chance and the Modern British Novel* (Stanford: Stanford UP, 1993), 18.

[21] Monk, *Standard Deviations*, borrows the phrase "intrinsic coherence" from Ian Watt (41–2).

[22] Charles Dickens, *Little Dorrit* (Oxford: Oxford UP, 1979), 14: 149–50. Nancy Aycock Metz, "The Blighted Tree and the Book of Fate: Female Models of Storytelling in *Little Dorrit*," *Dickens Studies Annual* 18 (1989): 239.

[23] Charles Dickens, *Our Mutual Friend* (Harmondsworth: Penguin, 1971), 17: 886.

to its artistic corollary in the image of the artist as god-like,[24] he nonetheless opened his later works to the idea of a destabilizing contingency in ways that anticipate late Victorian and modernist experiments in realist fiction. In leaving a trace of randomness in this novel, he challenged complacent assumptions about the existence of a loving, providential God or, alternatively, an all-enveloping fate. Such a challenge had unsettling implications for his understanding not only of the possibilities of omniscient narration but also of his own aspirations, as a novelist, to an intimate, yet comprehensive knowledge of the world. In drawing Bucket as he did, he humbled himself in his own and his readers' eyes.

Dickens's implicit admission of authorial limitation also hints at a key aspect of the relation between detection and secrecy in the novel. What seems like a chance occurrence in a narrative is only an event whose significance within the plot is not yet clear—in other words, whose meaning is hidden. Within Bucket's book of fate, Lady Dedlock's unprecedented means of departure from her residence seems random, given its mysteriousness to the detective at the point that she leaves—and for a considerable length of time thereafter. That departure is also secret. We recall that, when Lady Dedlock first goes in lower-class disguise to the graveyard, she walks "secretly" by Tulkinghorn. To Bucket, the lawyer's detective successor, the nature of her later journey is equally undisclosed. On his cold, wet dash with Esther up and down the countryside, Bucket eventually uncovers her ruse, at which point detection wins out over chance and secrecy. However, his uncovering comes too late, and with his belatedness, Dickens signals something important about the temporality of secrecy.

Alexander Welsh, in distinguishing between information and knowledge (that is, between latent knowledge and knowledge itself), writes that the "value" of the former "hinges upon its release" as the later.[25] Secrets, conversely, have value for those who know them, whether for good or for ill, only *until* their "release," at which point their value as secrets dissipates. Welsh asserts elsewhere that in much Victorian fiction, including sensation fiction (of which *Bleak House* may be seen as a forerunner), "secrets must eventually and inevitably be discovered" (27). Yet although Bucket finally uncovers the secret of Lady Dedlock's flight, his discovery brings him little consolation because it comes too late to forestall her death. Put another way, the dissipation of its value as a secret for her precedes and, therefore, preempts the discovery of its value as knowledge for him. In other words, secrets do not always yield up their value at the moment of detection; some can lose it before

---

[24] In a letter to Wilkie Collins, in *The Letters of Charles Dickens*, ed. Madeline House, Graham Storey, and Kathleen Tillotson, Pilgrim Ed., 12 vols. (Oxford: Clarendon, 1969–2002), Dickens wrote, "I think the business of art is to lay all that ground carefully, but with the care that conceals itself—to show, by a backward light, what everything has been working to—but only to *suggest*, until the fulfillment comes. These are the ways of Providence, of which all art is but a little imitation" (9: 128).

[25] Alexander Welsh, *George Eliot and Blackmail* (Cambridge: Harvard UP, 1985), 44.

then if the person or persons for whom a secret has meaning have been carried, for whatever reason, beyond the force of its discovery. The timing of a secret's release, thus, has implications for the struggle over its discovery. If a secret's power lies in the control of its moment of release (or lapse, in Lady Dedlock's case), then the tormented gentlewoman can be seen to have triumphed over her pursuer.[26] Although the secret of her earlier sexual transgression may have been uncovered by Tulkinghorn and others, that of her later existential transgression—in short, her flight and suicide—remains in her keeping long enough to preserve her deadly plans: a fact that not only foils the detective's mission but also, by extension, salvages for her a scrap of personal autonomy in her confrontations with the large moral and disciplinary systems within the novel that seek to subjugate her.[27] Such an understanding of the link between secrecy and detection points up what I have emphasized throughout this essay: the ineffectuality of authoritative efforts of detection in the face of unprecedented, seemingly random, and therefore intractably secret movements.

Bucket is finally an ironic figure of detection in *Bleak House*. Although it can be persuasively claimed that he represents the advent of a new kind of police and bureaucratic discipline, what is most intriguing about this representation is its failure. Whether we look at Bucket as a detective or as a catalyst of social connections or as an embodiment of the author-function, he ends up being less successful at his business than what he initially promises to be. His most serious failure—his inability to predict Lady Dedlock's unprecedented move in her "game"—creates a series of breaches in the novel that require us to question the nature of detection in all of its aspects. Because of Bucket's lapses, *Bleak House* stands as a limit-text on the capacity of the Victorian novel to tell its deepest criminal, social, and narrational secrets.

[26] On the relation between the power of a secret and the timing of its release, see Sissela Bok, *Secrets: On the Ethics of Concealment and Revelation* (New York: Pantheon Books, 1982), 18–24; Georg Simmel, *The Sociology of George Simmel*, trans. and ed. Kurt H. Wolff (New York: Free Press, 1950), 333–4; and David Vincent, *The Culture of Secrecy: Britain, 1832–1998* (Oxford: Oxford UP, 1998), 6, 16.

[27] On the transgressive power of secrecy, see Kucich, *Power*, especially 17–33.

Chapter 5
Concealing Minds and the Case of *The Woman in White*

Maria K. Bachman

> How should I know his secrets?
>
> —Wilkie Collins, *The Woman in White*

Characterized by *Vanity Fair* as "The Novelist who invented Sensation,"[1] Wilkie Collins wrote his most successful novels in the 1860s; a decade that saw the rise of fiction featuring crime, adultery, bigamy, and, most of all, secrets. Generally regarded as the first and most influential sensation novel, *The Woman in White* is, at its very center, in its margins, between the lines, and beyond its pages, obsessed with secrecy. In addition to the novel's obsession with secret crimes, secret pasts, secret diaries and letters, secret societies, secret meetings, secret journeys, and secret selves (the list goes on), the multiple narratives draw obsessively on various forms of surveillance—spying, watching, eavesdropping. At the same time, Collins's fictional world is one in which the mind is constantly manifesting itself in conscious and unconscious revelations making the novel particularly apropos for exploring the cognitive complexities of concealment and deception.

To begin, secrecy is to be understood as the intentional concealment of information, activities, and relations. In his *Dictionary*, Samuel Johnson defined a secret as "not simply something unknown, but something deliberately, studiously hidden."[2] There is also a clear etymological connection between secrecy and discernment: the Latin *secretum*, which carries the meaning of something hidden or set apart, derives from *secernere* which "bespeaks discernment, the ability to make distinctions, to sort out and draw lines: a capacity that underlies not only secrecy but all thinking, all intention and choice."[3] Moreover, secrecy involves the control of information, whether limiting access to it, destroying it, or prohibiting or shaping its creation, and is thus intrinsic to social interaction. Certainly, one of the hallmarks of *The Woman in White* is the way in which the novel keeps its myriad secrets "hidden deep under the surface"(474)[4] and it is precisely this conscious and

---

1 "Men of the Day, No. 39" *Vanity Fair*, February 3, 1872.

2 Cited in Sissela Bok, *Secrets: On the Ethics of Concealment and Revelation* (New York: Pantheon, 1982), 9.

3 Bok, 6.

4 Wilkie Collins, *The Woman in White*, ed. Maria K. Bachman and Don Richard Cox (Peterborough, ON: Broadview, 2004). All subsequent references to the text are from this

deliberate dimension of hiding or withholding of information that presupposes a significant and unmistakable link between concealment and cognition.

My discussion is based on two premises: one, that there is a significant and productive correlation to be made in the cognitive mental functioning of both fictional and real minds, and two, that the logic of novels is analogous to the logic of disclosing secrets.[5] As Joseph Carroll points out in *Literary Darwinism*, "through literature … we recognize the elemental structures of human concerns in our own lives and in those of others." These imaginative models, moreover, "direct our behavior by entering into our motivational system at its very roots—our feelings, our ideas, and our values."[6] In fact, the "human interest" that derived from characters as "recognizable realities" was the "literary principle" that Collins claimed guided him as a novelist:

> the effect produced by any narrative of events is essentially dependent, not on the events themselves, but on the human interest which is directly connected with them. It may be possible, in novel-writing, to present characters successfully without telling a story; but it is not possible to tell a story successfully without presenting characters: their existence, as recognisable realities, being the sole condition on which the story can be effectively told. The only narrative which can hope to lay a strong hold on the attention of readers, is a narrative which interests them about men and women—for the perfectly obvious reason that they are men and women themselves.[7]

More specifically, I investigate how the novel's proliferation and unraveling of secrets engage both the story-world participants' and readers' Theory of Mind (ToM), the ability to explain people's behavior in terms of their inferred mental states.

Clinical psychologist Simon Baron-Cohen explains that ToM (or "mindreading") is an adaptive neurocognitive mechanism "that enables us to interpret the emotions, thoughts, desires, beliefs, and intentions of others."[8] Furthermore, ToM is a particularly "voracious" cognitive adaptation that is

---

edition.

5 Matei Calinescu notes that "our natural fascination with secrecy is often exploited in literary texts" (*Rereading* [New Haven and London: Yale UP, 1993], 252).

6 *Literary Darwinism: Evolution, Human Nature, and Literature* (New York and London: Routledge, 2004), 116, xxii.

7 Wilkie Collins. "Preface to the Present Edition," *The Woman in White* (London: Sampson Low, Son & Col., 1861); reprinted in Bachman and Cox, 620. In the Preface to the French edition of the novel, Collins similarly remarked, "the characters, whatever weaknesses critics might have imputed to them, had the good fortune of procuring on most readers, the same impression as living realities would have" (Wilkie Collins, "Preface," *La Femme en Blanc*, trans. E.D. Forgues [Paris: J. Hetzel, 1861]; reprinted in Bachman and Cox, 623).

8 "*Mindblindness: An Essay on Autism and Theory of Mind* (Cambridge: MIT Press, 1995), 21. The basis of ToM is found in what neurologist Antonio Damasio calls the

dependent, according to Lisa Zunshine, upon the "intensely social nature of our species" and is triggered automatically "either by direct interactions with other people" or by cultural representations ("imaginary approximations") of such interactions.[9] However, because behavioral cues are intrinsically ambiguous, and thus subject to misinterpretation (that is, we do not have direct and perfect access to other minds in real life or in fiction),[10] we must also depend on our "strategic social intelligence" (an essential component of ToM) to interact successfully in the social world. That is, no matter how adept our skills might be, if we are unable to imagine or "simulate" future scenarios and predict their possible outcomes,[11] then we are vulnerable to being deceived—this is why deception, along with empathy, self-consciousness, and the use of persuasion, have been identified as being dependent on theory of mind understanding.[12] Zunshine points out that

> … applying ToM to our study of fiction is what makes literature as we know it possible. The very process of making sense of what we read appears to be grounded in our ability to invest the flimsy verbal constructions that we generously call 'characters' with a potential for a variety of thoughts, feelings,

---

"somatic marker mechanism," the way in which cognitive representations of the external world can influence behavior, particularly reasoning and decision-making.

[9] "Theory of Mind and Fictions of Embodied Transparency," *Narrative* 16 no. 1 (2008): 66, 68. Cited hereafter as "Embodied Transparency."

[10] Zunshine points out that "even though we know that there must be a mental state behind a behavior, we don't *really* know what that state is. That is, there is always a possibility that something else is going on behind even the most seemingly transparent behavior" ("Embodied Transparency," 71).

[11] Evolutionary psychiatrist Bruce Charlton calls this "internal modeling" ("Theory of Mind Delusions and Bizarre Delusions in an Evolutionary Perspective: Psychiatry and the Social Brain" in *The Social Brain: Evolution and Pathology*, eds. Martin Brune, Hedda Ribbert, and Wulf Schiefenhovel [Chichester, UK: John Wiley & Sons, 2003], 315–38). In *Why We Lie*, philosopher and evolutionary psychologist David Livingstone Smith explains the essential role that deception has played in human evolution: "sheer social complexity compelled our prehuman ancestors to become progressively more intelligent, and as they did they also become increasingly adept at social gamesmanship …once established, the need to cope with skilled social players became a selection pressure that escalated cognitive development even further (New York: Macmillan, 2004), 2.

[12] See Patricia Howlin, Simon Baron-Cohen, and Julie Hadwin, *Teaching Children with Autism to Mind-Read: A Practical Guide*. (New York: John Wiley & Sons, 1999). Baron-Cohen explains, "By the age of 4 years old the normally developing child is showing both an interest in deception, and beginning to be more adept at it. Leaving the moral aspects aside, such signs of deception can be taken as a yardstick that the child is understanding other minds (See "Autism and Theory of Mind" in *The Applied Psychologist*, eds. James Hartley and Alan Branthwaite [Buckingham, UK: Open University Press, 2000], 181–94).

> and desires and then to look for the 'cues' that would allow us to guess at their feelings and predict their actions.[13]

While reading novels may very well exercise our ToM, reading a novel such as *The Woman in White* tests our cognitive limits.

The Fascination of Secrecy

In the Preface to the first three-volume edition of *The Woman in White*, Collins requested reviewers to refrain from "telling his story at second-hand" thus destroying what he described as "the interest of curiosity and the excitement of surprise."[14] However, one reviewer for *The Times* pointed out that because Collins's novel is constructed "as a sustained appeal to curiosity," there was no danger of the novel losing its "fascination" with readers even if the Secret was revealed in advance. "Let the cat out of the bag!" this reviewer exclaimed,

> There are in this novel about a hundred cats contained in a hundred bags, all screaming and mewing to be let out. Every new chapter contains a new cat. When we come to the end of it out goes the animal, and there is a new bag put into our hands which it is the object of the subsequent chapter to open.[15]

Indeed, from the very first page of the novel, the reader enters a densely plotted labyrinth of secrecy from which there is no turning back because the concealment and disclosure of knowledge—the operating principle of secrecy—stimulates our curiosity, our inquisitiveness, our determined and unrelenting need to know.

From the moment she mysteriously appears out of the "gap in the hedge" on the moonlit road, Anne Catherick's opacity in the narrative establishes her as the literal and figurative embodiment of Secrecy (with a capital "S"). Like the "perverse lock" in the church vestry that guards the "blank space" of Sir Percival's "Secret," the woman in white is the controlling force of the narrative, her power reverberating both within and beyond the pages of the text. According to Walter Hartright, "the way to the Secret lay through the mystery, hitherto impenetrable to all of us, of the woman in white" (459). As a kind of embodied secret—an inextricable mixture of physiological and psychic elements—the woman in white exists as a suppressed energy, a "radioactivity" in sociologist Georg Simmel's

---

13 Lisa Zunshine, *Why We Read Fiction. Theory of Mind and the Novel* (Columbus: Ohio State UP, 2006), 10. Cited hereafter as *Why We Read.*

14 Bachman and Cox, 618.

15 Unsigned review [E.S. Dallas], *The Times* [London], October 30, 1860, 6; rpt. Bachman and Cox, 634. Perhaps as an homage to Collins's wishes, a recent edition of the novel includes the following "warning" to modern readers: "Note: if you do not wish to discover the secret of *The Woman in White*, read the rest of this introduction after you have finished the novel" (Introduction to *The Woman in White*, ed. Matthew Sweet [London and New York: Penguin, 1999], xix).

figuration, who draws others toward her with the "fascination of the abyss."[16] Indeed, she is the presiding consciousness through which Hartright's experience is processed: she is "the woman, who has lived in all [his] thoughts, who has possessed herself of all [his] energies, who has become the one guiding influence that now directs the purpose of [his] life" (53).[17] Similarly, Marian Halcombe's reaction to Hartright's story of his encounter with the mysterious woman is also described as a kind of energy: "I am all aflame with curiosity, and I devote my whole energies to the business of discovery" (78).

While the kinds of secrets that people keep are far-ranging and seemingly endless, those secrets that most pique our curiosity and that compel us to pry into them are stigmatizing personal secrets, those embarrassing, disturbing, or traumatic personal experiences that people tend to hide.[18] As William Cohen has shown, the scandal story, the public dissemination of information ordinarily kept secret, was ubiquitous in the Victorian popular press.[19] Even today we need look no further than PostSecret.com, reality TV programs, Jerry Springer-type confessional talk shows, tell-all celebrity autobiographies, and supermarket tabloids to recognize our own cultural fascination with secrecy and betrayal. Scandal continues to generate powerful "affective narratives, which elicit, horror, pleasure, shame and enthrallment in its audience."[20] Indeed, part of what continues to electrify readers of *The Woman in White* is the possibility of a scandalous revelation about the "life-long terror" of Sir Percival, especially after Hartright determines what the Secret is not. It is *not* the "common story of a man's treachery and a woman's [disgrace]" (471). What we do know, however, is that Sir Percival's secret is his "weak place" which "can force him from his position of security…[and] can drag him and his villainy into the face of day" (455). Surely, we think, the uncovering of this secret will pack quite a punch, the likes of which we've never seen or

16 *The Sociology of Georg Simmel*, ed. Kurt Wolf (Glenscoe, IL: Free Press, 1950), 339. Simmel explains, "what recedes before the consciousness of the others and is hidden from them, is to be emphasized in their consciousness; that one should appear as a particularly noteworthy person precisely through what once conceals" (337).

17 Edward Fitzgerald reported that even though illness forced him to put the novel down, *The Woman in White* continued to "exert a sort of magnetism" on him (Fitzgerald to W.F. Pollock, November 11, 1867, in Norman Page, *Wilkie Collins: The Critical Heritage* [London: Routledge & Kegan Paul, 1974)], 125).

18 The secret, notes Simmel, "is the sociological expression of moral badness" (331). According to Marie Mulvey Roberts, "Secrecy is concerned above all with what human beings want to protect: the intimate, the dangerous, the profane, the fragile the sacred, the forbidden (*Secret Texts; The Literature of Secret Societies,* ed. Marie Mulvey-Roberts and Hugh Ormsby-Lennon [New York: AMS Press, 1995]).

19 William Cohen, *Sex Scandal: The Private Parts of Victorian Fiction* (Durham: Duke UP, 1996), 1.

20 Cohen, 16. According to Cohen, individuals "who frankly admit to the pleasure of witnessing someone else troubled, disgraced, or exposed…will, if they *are* truly scandalized, end up getting more than their fascination had bargained for" (16).

imagined. As Cohen points out, "the scandalousness of an act hinges upon the degree of secrecy required to its commission."[21] In fact, Collins reported that the "the Secret…connected to the existence of Sir Percival Glyde" not only was the subject of "exasperated curiosity" among an entire class of readers, but which also gave rise to "different bets that they wanted [him] to resolve."[22]

Simmel writes that "every human relation is characterized, among other things, by the amount of secrecy that is in and around it"[23] and indeed, secrecy and furtiveness are the operating principles upon which all relations are conducted in the novel. Though it is not my purpose here to exorcise the novel's dizzying array of textual secrets, a brief overview of some of the deliberate concealments, cover-ups, and confidences that occur in the first half of the novel well illustrate the "social-communicational context of secrecy."[24] Consider the following instances of when secrets are entrusted to some, but not others: Mrs. Clements tells Hartright that she wants to keep Anne Catherick's "misfortune"—her incarceration in an asylum—a "secret"; Hartright assures Anne Catherick that Laura will keep her escape from the Asylum a secret (even though everyone finds out anyway); Marian instructs Hartright not to let Laura know about the uncanny likeness she shares with Anne Catherick; Marian conceals from Laura that Hartright has gone to Central America; Laura begs Marian to keep her wedding date a secret from Hartright; Mrs. Catherick pleads with the housekeeper at Blackwater Park to not let Sir Percival know that she was there—a secret that is nevertheless given away twice; Sir Percival's keeps his financial embarrassments a secret from Laura; Marian conceals her disturbing prophetic dream from Laura; Laura keeps the tortured secrets of her marriage from Marian; and the list goes on. As psychologist Anita Kelley explains, "the existence of a secret depends on the secret keeper's awareness of another person. People work to hide their secrets only if other people who are *not* supposed to know the secrets are around."[25]

Secrets have the potential to harm others or cut others off from possible benefits, and thus outsiders to secrets who become suspicious of others' motives or intentions, may deem it a matter of vital self-interest, indeed, survival, to engage in some form of spying. This is particularly well illustrated in the novel's paradigmatic scene of surveillance where Marian sneaks out onto the verandah roof in order to listen to Sir Percival's and Fosco's "private" conversation. She explains that her conscience has

---

[21] Cohen, 5.

[22] As one reviewer noted, "the great secret never can be revealed, and the author guards himself from revealing it, prematurely—for the actors are as much in the dark as the reader on the subject" (Bachman and Cox, 630). Indeed, Collins boasted, "not one of the bettors—and apart from them, not one of the readers…succeeded in uncovering what the secret could be" (Bachman and Cox, 624–5).

[23] Simmel, 334.

[24] Calinescu, 247, 245.

[25] Indeed, "secrecy gives one person limits or destroys that of others" (*The Psychology of Secrets* [New York: Kluwer Academic/Plenum Publishers, 2002], 3).

dictated the necessity for such furtive tactics: "I wanted but one motive to sanction the act to my own conscience, and to give me courage enough for performing it; and that motive I had. Laura's honour, Laura's happiness—Laura's itself—might depend on my quick ears, and my faithful memory" (335).

The Pathology of Secrecy

While many people might assume the most crucial determinant of its effects is the *type* of secret a person is keeping, it is actually the "process of expending energy to keep information from other people that defines secrecy."[26] Simmel observes, "[t]he preservation of the secret is something so unstable; the temptations of betrayal are so manifold; the road from discretion to indiscretion is in many cases so continuous, that the unconditional trust in discretion involves an incomparable preponderance of the subjective factor."[27] Marian and Walter, for instance do not speak of the secret they share regarding Sir Percival's death, but acknowledge "it was not the less present to our minds—it was rather kept alive in them by the restraint which we had imposed on ourselves" (547). Indeed, cognitive psychologists Julie Lane and Daniel Wegner point out that "secrecy is an active process…[that] requires much deliberate behavioral and mental work."[28] It is not just Frederick Fairlie, the closeted homosexual, who is suffers from a "perpetual case of nerves." Rather, every character in the novel seems to be afflicted with generalized anxiety disorder as a result of the neurotic and destabilizing effects of concealing and/or probing secrets. Hartright, for instance, is constantly questioning his own precarious mental state. When he and Marian first puzzle over the bizarre letter warning against the marriage of Laura Fairlie and Sir Percival, Walter admits to his own "darkness and confusion" (421): "I began to doubt whether my own faculties were not in danger of losing their balance. It seemed almost like a monomania to be tracing back everything strange that happened" (118). Marian also attributes Hartright's paranoia to his obsession with uncovering the secret of woman in white: "it looks as if his one fixed idea…was becoming too much for his mind" (195).[29] Even the calm and levelheaded Marian admits more than once to the "confusion of her own thoughts" (292–3, 302, 333) and like Hartright, she becomes more paranoid, more "suspicious of everybody and everything" (287), while Anne Catherick's obsession with Sir Percival's "Secret" is described as a "fixed delusion" (534).

---

26 Kelley, 3.

27 Simmel, 348.

28 "The Cognitive Consequences of Secrecy," *Journal of Personality and Social Psychology* 69, no. 2 (1995): 237. See also Wegner and Lane, "From Secrecy to Psychopathology" in *Emotion, Disclosure, and Health*, ed. J.W. Pennebaker (Washington, DC: American Psychological Association), 1996.

29 In fact, it is only towards the end of the novel, when Hartright finally has discovered Sir Percival's secret, that he reports his mind is at last "composed" and he "feel[s] more sure of [himself]" (525).

Moreover, the conflicting pressures of concealment and disclosure increase the secret-keeper's (and secret-seeker's) vulnerability and it is this presumed loss of control that gives way to the irrational and pathological.[30] Once he is at risk for being exposed, the initially self-possessed Sir Percival becomes highly erratic, if not schizophrenic, in both temperament and action. Though he displays "a mania for order and regularity"—what we would easily diagnose today as obsessive-compulsive disorder—he frequently degenerates into being "out of his senses" and possessing "a kind of panic and frenzy of mind" (406, 318). Research has also shown that self-concealers report being "impulsive and unable to inhibit or control their behaviors…these individuals are vulnerable to engaging in acts that they will later ruminate over and regret."[31] As the housekeeper at Blackwater Park observes, Sir Percival "was very restless, that I could not help noticing it; coming and going, and wandering here and there and everywhere on the grounds…[he also] put himself on half-rations of food and a double-allowance of drinking" (380).[32] Secret-keepers also appear to be prone to an array of health problems:[33] Sir Percival Glyde suffers from a nagging, dry nervous cough; the effeminate Frederick Fairlie complains of a variety of undisclosed maladies;[34] and his fragile niece Laura Fairlie seems to be afflicted with neurasthenia. Moreover, Anne Catherick is said to resemble Laura Fairlie "after a bad illness, with a touch of something wrong in her head" (348), while her mother, Mrs. Catherick, is described as having "wasted and worn away under the Secret" for most of her life. Secrecy even takes its toll on the usually strong and resolute Marian: after eavesdropping on Sir Percival and Fosco, Marian becomes delirious with fever and subsequently develops typhus, thus preventing her from chronicling events further in the "secret pages" of her journal.

Embodied Transparency and the Betrayal of Secrets

While we believe we can control our secrets, those very private parts of ourselves, only so long as we don't speak them or put them in writing, it is often that we unconsciously betray ourselves in our dispositions and demeanor. As Fosco

---

30 Bok explains that this cognitive dissonance is the result of the conflicting (and sometimes debilitating) tensions "between concealing and revealing, and between pressing upon others what is no secret at all and refraining there from" (36).

31 Kelly, 38.

32 In another scene, Marian describes how Sir Percival "came toward us, slashing viciously at the flowers, with his riding whip. When he was near enough to see my face, he stopped, struck at his boot with the whip and burst out laughing, so harshly and violently, that the birds flew away, startled, from the tree by which he stood" (401).

33 Kelly, 38–9.

34 Marian tells Hartright, "I don't know what is the matter with him, and the doctors don't know what it the matter with him, and he doesn't know himself what is the matter with him. We all say it's on the nerves, and we none of us know what we mean when we say it" (76–7).

declares, "Mind, they say, rules the world. But what rules the mind? The Body" (594). Zunshine reminds us that "writers of fiction provide us not as much with an account of what happened as with a system of carefully organized cues that prompt us to fill in the blanks and construct a given story of social interaction by automatically deploying our own mindreading ability."[35] As a cognitive mechanism that attempts to make sense of human interactions—specifically intentionality—our ToM (as well as the characters') gets a rigorous workout when it comes to secret keeping, secret seeking, and secret sharing. Consider the farewell scene that takes place between Laura and the broken-hearted Hartright on the morning of his forced departure from Limmeridge. Though we already know that Hartright has fallen desperately in love with Laura, there has been no indication until this emotional meeting that Laura feels just as passionately about him.[36]

> She rested one trembling hand on the table to steady herself, while she gave me the other. I took it in mine—I held it fast. My head drooped over it, my tears fell on it, my lips press it—not in love; oh, not in love, at that last moment, but in the agony and the self-abandonment of despair.
>
> "For God's sake, leave me!" she said, faintly.
>
> The confession of her heart's secret burst from her in those pleading words. (158).

While the textual clues in this passage do not pose a particularly complex cognitive challenge, Hartright and the reader understand that the words Laura utters are not to be interpreted as "*Get as far away from me as possible, you psychopathic creep*" but rather, "*I am so much in love with you that the pain of your impending departure is too much too bear; please go quickly.*" That is, we can fairly accurately gauge the emotional undertones of this scene,—how Laura feels about losing the love of her life—through her body language and manner. Laura trembles, not with anger, but with despair and deep sorrow. Her agonized expression and manner thus reveal her underlying mental state and her "heart's secret": that she is in love with Hartright even though she is betrothed to Sir Percival.

The concealment of knowledge is a control mechanism, a perpetual, but always tenuous grasp for power[37] and throughout the novel we see how physiological

---

[35] "Richardson's *Clarissa* and Theory of Mind," in *The Work of Fiction: Culture, Cognition, and Complexity*, ed. Alan Richardson and Ellen Spolsky (Burlington, VT: Ashgate, 2004), 133.

[36] Had Hartright not unconsciously revealed *his* secret—that he was in love with Laura—and had Marian not read his mind accurately (as well as her sister's), he would not have been forced to leave Limmeridge House. Marian reveals that she has "discovered [his] secret—without help or hint, mind from, any one else" (109).

[37] As Bok explains, "[t]o be able to hold back some information about oneself or to channel it and thus influence how one is seen by others gives power; so does the capacity to penetrate similar defenses and strategies when used by others" (26).

expressions destabilize this power dynamic by divulging secrets that their owners would prefer to conceal. Long before we learn Sir Percival even has a Secret—the one that Anne Catherick purports to know and threatens to reveal—Marian Halcombe detects in his manner that he has something to hide.

> There was suppressed anxiety and agitation in every line of his face. The dry sharp cough, which teases him at most times, seemed to be troubling him more incessantly than ever. He sat down opposite to us at the table...he said a few unimportant words, with a visible effort to preserve his customary ease of manner. But his voice was not to be steadied, and the restless uneasiness in his eyes was not to be concealed. (195)

Though Marian's attribution of suspiciousness may not provide "perfect access"[38] to Sir Percival's mind, his observable nervous behavior reveals more about his mental state than we previously knew or surmised and provides a clue as to how we should attend to him. ToM is attuned to human body language, but mindreading (and even mis-reading) always depends on our very compulsion to spy—to watch the words and actions of others, and to make discoveries—to narrativize such embodied messages. In other words, Marian's mindreading stimulates our mind-tracking abilities, enabling us to engage in a kind of cognitive espionage.

At the same time, Marian's suspicions put her ToM, especially where Sir Percival is concerned, into hyperdrive.[39] When Laura and Sir Percival return from their wedding trip to Blackwater Park, Sir Percival attempts to trick Laura into underwriting his debts by signing a legal document that he does not allow her to see. Marian deduces that Sir Percival is not just hiding his "financial embarrassments," but is engaged in a far more sinister form of fraud. Though she has no concrete evidence to support her suspicion, she is able to make the following inference:

> My own convictions led me to believe that the hidden contents of the parchment concealed a transaction of the meanest and most fraudulent kind. I had not formed this conclusion in consequence of Sir Percival's refusal to show the writing, or to explain it...My sole motive for distrusting his honesty, sprang from the change which I had observed in his language and his manners at Blackwater Park, a change which convinced me that he had been acting a part ... (273–4)

---

38 Though our ToM is "imperfect" and "fallible," it is nevertheless what makes social interaction possible (*Why We Read*, 59).

39 Denise Cummins argues that the *selective* advantages of mind-reading must be understood within the context of a dominance hierarchy that is predicated on deceptive tactics. According to an "adaptive evolutionary arms race" theory, Cummins explains that in primitive societies survival pressures help shape our cognitive architecture: in order to have priority of access to resources, lower-ranking individuals needed to be able to deceive higher-ranking individuals, while those higher-ranking individuals similarly need to be able to detect deception and cheat to protect their share ("Social Norms and Other Minds: The Evolutionary Roots of Higher Cognition" in *The Evolution of Mind*, eds. Denise D. Cummins and C. Allen [New York: Oxford UP, 1999], 25, 59–60).

Using her mindreading abilities, Marian is able to attribute certain mental characteristics—deceptiveness and duplicitousness—to Sir Percival based on his observable behavior. At the same time, Marian's judgment about Sir Percival's dubious character deploys the reader's ToM: we may immediately assimilate this information or we may store this representation in our cognitive database as we continue to make predictions, decipher motives, and unmask deception. Our "source-monitoring" ability enables us to keep track of certain information or representations—(in this case, Marin's suspicions of Sir Percival), which then becomes a "metarepresentation."[40] Such source-monitoring occurs when Marian meets the family lawyer Mr. Gilmore to discuss Laura's reservations about her engagement to Sir Percival. Though Marian offers Gilmore no reason for Laura's change of heart other than feminine "caprice," he immediately becomes suspicious of both women's lack of candor:

> When a sensible woman has a serious question put to her, and evades it by a flippant answer, it is a sure sign, in ninety-nine cases out of a hundred, that she has something to conceal ... [I] strongly suspected that Miss Halcombe and Miss Fairlie had *a secret between them* which they were keeping from Sir Percival and keeping from me ... My doubts, or to speak more correctly, my convictions—were confirmed by Miss Halcombe's language and manner. (170, my emphasis)

This passage not only provides a glimpse of Mr. Gilmore's mindreading abilities, but also triggers our ToM, *not* however with regard to Marian's and Laura's motives but with regard to Gilmore's intentions.[41] The reader already understands why Laura is so anxious about delaying her marriage to Sir Percival and would not have sufficient cause to doubt her feelings. However because their "strange conduct" (170) has made Mr. Gilmore suspicious, we are left wondering whether he will turn out to be an ally or antagonist. We now treat the representation "Mr. Gilmore is suspicious of Marian and Laura" as a metarepresentation and any information that is presented to us about Gilmore is reassessed in terms of his possible motives and observable conduct.

According to Simmel, all secrets bear within them "a tension that is dissolved in the moment of...revelation...[The secret] is surrounded by the possibility and

---

[40] According to Zunshine, metarepresentation enables us to "discriminate among the streams of information coming at us via all this. It allows us to assign differently weighted truth-values to representations originating from different sources...under different circumstances." As the character-narrator "tags" information, the reader may hold that information "under advisement" until she learns more (*Why We Read*, 60, 50). It would appear that our "source-monitoring" ability in fiction is closely linked to the adaptive mechanism known as strategic social intelligence.

[41] Zunshine reminds us that readers generally need very little prompting in attributing states of mind to fictional characters. However, writers can exploit this readiness in "experiment[ing] with the amount and kind of interpretation of the characters' mental states that they themselves supply and that they expect us to supply" (*Why We Read*, 22).

temptation of betrayal; and the external danger of being discovered is interwoven with the internal danger, which is like the fascination of an abyss, of giving oneself away."[42] Though Marian notes that "so much depends on discretion and self control" (274), not even the most self-possessed individuals are immune to spontaneous self-betrayal.

In fact, despite Fosco's mental influence over others, despite his quasi-omniscient existence, there are moments when he spontaneously bodies forth his own vulnerabilities.[43] Zunshine describes such unintended physiological disclosures in which "brief access to a character's mental state via [his] body language stands out sharply against the relative opacity of other characters or of the same character a moment ago" as representations of "embodied transparency."[44]

When Hartright contrives to bring Fosco and Professor Pesca together at the opera house, Hartright is astonished by Fosco's strange physiological reaction to seeing Pesca:

> There was no mistaking the change that passed over the villain's face. The leaden hue that altered his yellow complexion in a moment, the sudden rigidity of his features, the furtive scrutiny of his cold grey eyes, the motionless stillness of him from head to foot, told their own tale. A mortal dread had mastered him, body and soul—and his own recognition of Pesca was the cause of it! (565)

While the Italian émigré Pesca does not recognize his fellow countryman, this moment of transparency reveals that Fosco not only knows Pesca, but that he *fears* the seemingly harmless professor as well. Fosco's observable behavior provides only brief access to his mental state,[45] but it is nevertheless a revelatory moment that galvanizes Hartright's suspicions and his ToM.

Focalization and Embedded Secrets

Ironically, the real key to Sir Percival's Secret is put under our very noses early in the novel, shortly after Hartright has arrived at Limmeridge House. In an attempt to discover the identity of the mysterious woman in white, Marian thinks that a clue might be found in the collection of private letters that were exchanged

---

[42] Simmel, 333–4.

[43] Fosco's penetrating gaze and paralyzing touch enable him to manipulate and control every character in the novel. His undue influence over Marian is apparent in her admission that he "has interested me, has attracted me, has forced me to like him" (240), despite the fact that she and Laura have come to fear and distrust him.

[44] Though these moments in which characters' bodies "spontaneously reveal their true feelings, sometimes against their wills" are entirely relative and context-dependent, they are nevertheless part of a representational tradition found within novels, genre paintings, and moving images ("Embodied Transparency," 72).

[45] That is, Fosco has revealed that he has something to hide, but what that something is—(*why* the sight of Pesca would register such terror)—is yet to be discovered.

between her late mother and her husband Mr. Philip Fairlie years earlier. After dinner one evening, Hartright observes from the drawing-room, Laura Fairlie passing back and forth on the terrace "in the full radiance of the moon" (96). As he watches her intently, Marian asks him to listen to the "concluding passages" of one of the letters that she has found to see if it "throw[s] any light upon" his strange adventure. While Marian reads these passages, Hartright half-listens, admitting that "all [his] attention was concentrated on the white gleam of Miss Fairlie's muslin dress." Suddenly he is jolted out of his slightly indecorous reverie when he recognizes the "ominous likeness between the fugitive from the asylum and the heiress from Limmeridge House" (99). What both Hartright and Marian have missed in this truly sensational moment,[46] and what has also escaped the perceptual awareness of the reader, is the all-too significant description of Mrs. Catherick embedded in the letter:

> [She] is a decent, well-behaved, respectable woman…[but] there is something in her manner and her appearance, however, which I can't make out. She is reserved about herself to the point of downright secrecy; and there is a look in her face—I can't describe it—which suggests to me that she has something on her mind. She is altogether what you would call a walking mystery. (97)

On the one hand, this passage well illustrates Mrs. Fairlie's thinking mind: based on her observations of Mrs. Catherick's "manner and appearance" she has intuited that this "decent, well-behaved, respectable woman" has something to hide. This passage is also significant because it conjoins cognition, perception, and focalization.[47] The reader's failure to notice much less ponder why Mrs. Catherick is so secretive is because we have been distracted by Walter's telescoping of Laura Fairlie. This detail—that Mrs. Catherick has "something on her mind"—as well as countless other details scattered throughout the narratives, disappears from our cognitive radar because our attention is dependent upon the object's "predominance in the mind of the focalizer."[48] We are, in other words, likely to

---

[46] In her review of the novel, Margaret Oliphant identified this particular scene (as well as the scene when the mysterious woman dressed in white suddenly appears out of the shadows of Hampstead Heath and lays her hand on Hartright's shoulder), as the two most sensational scenes in the novel where the "reader's nerves are affected like the hero's" ([Unsigned Review], "Sensation Novels" *Blackwood's Magazine* [May 1862], 565–74; reprinted in Norman Page, *Wilkie Collins: The Critical Heritage* [London: Routledge & Kegan Paul], 118–19).

[47] According to Uri Margolin, focalization involves "an external object to be attended to": "Each act of focusing one's attention on some external sensory data is also deictically anchored in a unique way, being indexed to a particular embodied mind ("Cognitive Science, The Thinking Mind, and Literary Narrative" in *Narrative Theory and the Cognitive Sciences*, ed. David Herman [Stanford: CSLI Publications, 2003], 282–3).

[48] Catherine Emmott, "Constructing Social Space: Sociocognitive Factors in the Interpretation of Character Relations" in *Narrative Theory and the Cognitive Sciences*, ed. David Herman (Stanford: CSLI Publications, 2003), 316.

neglect such details non-consciously[49] if they have little to no cognitive status for our witnesses—who do not appraise them as worthy of investigation.[50] Mrs. Fairlie's Theory of Mind, represented in her letter (her suspicion), fails to trigger the reader's ToM (our suspicion) because it does not fall within the realm of either Marian's or Hartright's perceptual awareness. Indeed, the unrelenting compulsion to uncover the secret of the woman in white paradoxically distracts us from many of the other narrative secrets as well.

For instance, despite the fact the multiple plots all revolve around the theme of wrongful incarceration, it is striking that the novel never discloses what happened to Laura Fairlie while she was falsely committed to a lunatic asylum—it is a "total blank" in her "sad story" (435).[51] We might also wonder why it is that Professor Pesca, the character who arguably sets the story in motion,[52] drops off the page (after the first installment) and off our cognitive radar, only to return some 500 pages later[53] as Hartright's necessary accomplice in defeating Fosco and restoring Laura's identity.

We might also wonder how it is that Fosco and Sir Percival—two men who are complete opposites in temperament and demeanor—came to become such close associates. When Marian initiates a series of questions to this effect, Sir Percival is reluctant to divulge any personal information revealing only that he and Fosco met "under dangerous circumstances" years earlier in Italy (245). Strangely, Marian claims that she has "alluded" to those circumstances elsewhere in her narrative, but such details remain undisclosed. Countless other secrets remain as well. Though Hartright ultimately extorts a confession from Fosco, his part in the conspiracy, the "true story of his life" (other than "his vocation in life was the vocation of a Spy"), remains an "impenetrable mystery" (558–9). Even the "Biography" of Fosco that his wife publishes after his death "throws no light whatever on the name that was

---

[49] Alan Palmer employs the term "non-conscious" to include images to which we do not attend or dispositions that are acquired through experience. He prefers this term to "unconscious" which he claims has limiting Freudian overtones and does not fully encompass unknown mental processes (*Fictional Minds* [Lincoln: U of Nebraska P, 2004], 104–5).

[50] Emmott explains that the "cognitive status" of a character is a hypothesis of the degree of prominence that a character has in a reader's mind when a referring expression is used (297).

[51] Similarly, we are not provided any retrospective account of Anne Catherick's imprisonment either.

[52] After Hartright saves Pesca from drowning, the honor-bound Italian émigré helps him obtain employment at Limmeridge House as drawing-master to the two half-sisters, Laura Fairlie and Marian Halcombe.

[53] For *All the Year Round* readers, Pesca's absence from the story would have lasted 36 weeks—from December 3, 1859 to August 11, 1860. Hartright admits however that while the Professor "has been so long absent from these pages, [and thus]…run some risk of being forgotten altogether," he has, in fact, been in contact with Pesca since he left Limmeridge.

really his own, or on the secret history of his life" (615).[54] Moreover, we don't ever find out the back story to the relationship between Sir Philip Fairlie (Laura's father) and Sir Percival Glyde, or why Laura's father promised his daughter's hand in marriage to his "friend" in the first place. What also remains secreted is the nature of the "painful and incurable" deformity that compelled Sir Percival's father to live in almost complete seclusion. In fact, at the conclusion of Hartright's process of inquiry, we are left with more blanks and gaps than we encountered at the beginning.

Narration and Secret Villainy

While the multiple plots of Collins's novel are concerned with the concealing, detecting, and divulging of myriad secrets, the method in which the story unfolds is a perpetual deferment of secrets. Collins himself acknowledged that the connection between the "substance of the novel" and its "literary form" helped to "ensnare" the attention of readers and contributed to the "augmenting intensity" of narrative events. Like witnesses at a criminal trial, various characters are called upon supposedly to offer their version of events in "a succession of individual testimonies."[55] Acting the part of the disinterested master narrator, Hartright begins the novel by explaining that

> the story presented here will be told by more than one pen, as the story of an offence against the laws is told in Court by more than one witness—with the same object, in both cases, to present the truth always in its most direct and most intelligible aspect; and to trace the course of one complete series of events, by making the persons who have been most closely connected with them, at each successive stage, relate their own experience, word for word. (50)[56]

---

[54] For a compelling investigation of Fosco's secret life, see A. D. Hutter, "Fosco Lives!" in *Reality's Dark Light: The Sensational Wilkie Collins*, ed. Maria K. Bachman and Don Richard Cox (Knoxville: U of Tennessee P, 2003), 195–238.

[55] See the Preface to the French edition of the novel (Bachman and Cox, 621–5). *The Woman in White* was first serialized in Charles Dickens's periodical *All the Year Round* from November 26, 1859 until August 25, 1860 and each weekly installment featured some kind of shock, thrill, or surprise that enticed readers to return. In addition to these "violent stimulants," Collins well understood that in order to captivate and hold his readers' attention from week to week, he had to ensure that readers would become imaginatively involved in the lives his characters.

[56] In the Preface to the 1860 edition of the novel, Collins considered his narrative innovation to be a tremendous success because "it has afforded my characters a new opportunity of expressing themselves, through the medium of written contributions which they are supposed to make to the progress of the narrative" (Preface to *The Woman in White* [London: Sampson Low, Son & Co., 1860]; reprinted in Bachman and Cox, 618).

Peter Brooks, however, reminds us that "narrative discourse is never innocent, but always presentational, a way of working on story events, that is also a way of working on the reader or the listener."[57] Indeed, just as secrecy belongs to that area of human communication that is "deliberately selective, exclusive, often elliptical, oblique, or indirect,"[58] Hartright "judiciously" presents us with a series of narratives that conceal far more than they reveal.

After Hartright finds out that his beloved drawing pupil, Laura Fairlie, is betrothed to Sir Percival Glyde, he leaves Limmeridge House broken-hearted and shortly thereafter mysteriously departs for Central America. He leaves the story—and his narrative—for quite some time, yet we never learn the details of his adventures other than cryptic hints later in the novel about certain "survival skills" he acquired during that time. Months later, Walter reappears in the narrative, and in London, only to be greeted with the shocking news of Laura's "death." When he musters enough courage to visit her grave in Limmeridge churchyard, he suffers another shock when he encounters Marian and the dead-alive Laura Fairlie (Lady Glyde) standing beside her tombstone. Hartright is so discombobulated by this astonishing meeting that he is unable to report what transpired during and after. When he finally gathers his wits, Hartright announces matter-of-factly that he has skipped a week in his narrative and has no intention of accounting for that gap: "The history of the interval, which I thus pass over *must remain unrecorded.* My heart turns faint, my mind sinks in darkness and confusion when I think of it" (421, my emphasis). How are we to account for this lapse of time? What, we *should* ask, is being suppressed or concealed?

Moreover, though the "secret pages" of Marian's diary that we read before she falls ill appear to be an accurate and thorough chronicle of the events—and indeed, Marian often boasts of the "reliability of her recollection" (304)[59]—we never have access to her full and complete statement. Instead, we are presented only with *excerpts* from her journal. Hartright explains that he has found it necessary to edit (and thus conceal) those sections of her narrative that he finds irrelevant. After Marian has transcribed the late-night conspiratorial whisperings of Sir Percival and Fosco that she overheard from the roof, she succumbs to fever and delirium, and is unable to continue with her narrative. We are then shocked to learn that while she is incapacitated and incognizant, Fosco has through "clandestine means" (592) not only read her journal, but written in it as well.[60] While D.A. Miller and other critics have described Fosco's scandalous act of inscription as

---

[57] "The Law as Narrative and Rhetoric" in *Law's Stories: Narrative and Rhetoric in the Law*, ed. Peter Brooks and Paul Gewirtz (New Haven: Yale UP, 1996), 125.

[58] Calinescu, 245.

[59] The "amazing accuracy" and "profound mental accuracy" with which Marian has represented events at Blackwater Park is also corroborated by Fosco who claims to have "accurate knowledge of the contents of her journal" (592).

[60] As Peter Brooks remarks, "[o]ur readerly intimacy with Marian is violated, our act of reading adulterated by profane eyes, made secondary to the villain's reading and indeed

a form of rape, it has escaped most readers' notice that Hartright commits a far more serious textual crime over and over again.[61] Despite his promise to let other persons "speak to the circumstances under notice from their own knowledge" (50), Hartright appropriates narrative agency from these witnesses so that he can control the dissemination of information, withholding and disclosing evidence at his discretion, thus authorizing the course of events to ultimately tell *his story*. The reader is just as much the object of violation as the witnesses in Hartright's tribunal.[62]

Even after Hartright is able to resume his narrative—following the one-week gap between the tombstone meeting and when the three fugitives (Marian, Laura, and Hartright) go into hiding in London—he does not allow either Laura or Marian to tell *their* story firsthand. Rather, Hartright explains that expedience and clarity compel him to describe in his own words (and in condensed form), the series of deceptions which brought Anne Catherick to London and Laura Fairlie (Lady Glyde) to be falsely incarcerated in a lunatic asylum:

> I shall relate both narratives, not in the words (often interrupted, often inevitably confused) of the speakers themselves, but in the words of the brief, plain, studiously simply abstract which I committed to writing for my own guidance, and for the guidance of my legal adviser. So the tangled web will be most speedily and most intelligibly unrolled. (423)

Acting as a narrative filter, Hartright boldly conceals information that he deems irrelevant to this "process of inquiry," thus completely adulterating our reading process, not to mention the purported pursuit of "truth."[63] As he liberally paraphrases Marian's and Laura's accounts—often noting their fragile mental states—Hartright not only reneges on his promise to have "the persons most closely connected" to specific events "relate their own experience, word for word" (49),

---

dependent on his permission" (*Reading for the Plot* [New York: Vintage Books, 1984], 169).

[61] See Miller, "Cage Aux Folles: Sensation and Gender in Wilkie Collins's *The Woman in White*," *Representations* 14 (1986): 117–18; and Susan Balee, "Wilkie Collins and Surplus Woman: The Case of Marian Halcombe," *Victorian Literature and Culture* 20 (1992): 203.

[62] Phelan argues that "the formal logic of character narration has consequences for our emotional responses to character narrators, and these emotional responses, in turn, have consequences for the ethical dimension of our engagement with them and with the narratives in which they appear" (*Living to Tell About It* [Ithaca: Cornell UP, 2004], 5).

[63] As a narrator, Hartright is complexly unreliable because he "underreports"—he does not fully divulge what he knows and he misrepresents what other characters know. Moreover, because Hartright is intentionally deceptive in withholding information from the reader, his unreliability exists along what Phelan terms the "axis of ethics" (See Phelan's taxonomy of unreliable narrators in *Living to Tell About It*). "Paralipsis" is the term Gerard Gennette uses for the unreliable narrator who omits or misrepresents what he knows (*Narrative Discourse: An Essay in Method* [Ithaca: Cornell UP, 1983]).

but he also violates his own mandate that "[n]o circumstances of importance from the beginning to the end of the disclosure, shall be related on hearsay evidence" (49).[64] Marian is not the only victim of censorship. Though both Anne Catherick and Laura Fairlie are the primary focus of the course of events, neither one ever has the opportunity to relate her own experiences. Countless others' narratives are expurgated or completely suppressed throughout Hartright's "process of inquiry" (49). Certainly the most manipulated testimony presented to us is Pesca's—an extensive confession that Hartright first translates (from Italian, Pesca's native tongue) and then significantly suppresses because of "its serious nature." What little we learn from this "extraordinary disclosure," is that Pesca is connected to a dangerous secret society and is clearly not the innocuous person we have assumed him to be.[65]

As Cohen notes, when "scandal recasts secret activities into a public story of exposure, it makes questions about truth almost impossible to answer."[66] Indeed, just as "the windings of the labyrinth" almost begin to make sense, when we seem to be getting closer to the truth, we are stymied by the proliferation of even more cover-ups. At end of the novel, Hartright holds "public proceedings" supposedly to make known to all Sir Percival's and Fosco's dastardly conspiracy of false incarceration, switched identities, and faked death. Ironically, the "plain account of how it had *all* happened"[67] that Hartright presents is completely withheld from the reader and it is a "plain account" that unbeknownst to its intended audience is still riddled with holes. Hartright explains how he read "the narrative of the conspiracy, describing it in clear outline, and dwelling only upon the pecuniary motive for it, in order to avoid complicating my statement by unnecessary reference to Sir Percival's secret" (609). Though "the Secret" was the driving force of the conspiracy and the narrative, Hartright does not disclose Sir Percival's illegitimacy because in his mind, to do so would "confer advantage on no one" (539). This, however, is not the only cover-up. As details of the conspiracy are patched together, the reader is completely blindsided when Hartright mentions offhandedly that his story has been told "under feigned names," offering no explanation of this

64 Hearsay evidence is to be understood as a statement presented by someone who was not a witness.

65 For an illuminating look at the "figure of the secret society" in the novel, see Albert Pionke, *Plots of Opportunity: Representing Conspiracy in Victorian England* (Columbus: Ohio State UP, 2004), 101–32.

66 *Sex Scandal*, 9.

67 Briefly, the conspiracy involves Sir Percival committing Anne Catherick years earlier to a lunatic asylum after she threatens to divulge his Secret. After she escapes, Sir Percival and Count Fosco eventually track her down and kidnap her to London where she dies shortly thereafter presumably from a chronic heart condition. Since she bears an uncanny resemblance to Laura, Anne is buried as "Lady Glyde" and the very much alive Laura is "returned" to the asylum as the severely delusional Anne Catherick. Since she is legally dead, all of Laura's property passes to Sir Percival, who as we later find out, never had a legitimate claim to a title, estate, or fortune.

stunning deception other than it was done "for Laura's sake" (539). Though Miller has identified Fosco's violation of Marian's narrative to be "the most shocking moment in the reader's drama," this revelation is the real sucker punch of the novel. This disclosure of an even more elaborate and extensive cover-up takes us completely by surprise, mocking our gullibility as members of the narrative cognoscenti. We have been duped, taken "from behind: from a place where, in the wings of the ostensible drama, the novelist disposes of a whole plot machinery whose existence—so long as it didn't oblige us by making creaking sounds—we never suspected."[68]

We are thus presented with a tangled web of deceit—an amalgam of narrative gaps, fragmentary, and at times, confusing stories, either incomplete, inconsistent, or incoherent, arranged by a master of deception masquerading as a mild-mannered drawing master. Ultimately, Hartright is the "secret" villain of the novel, the narrative conspirator whose clandestine editorial prerogative creates less "an incontrovertible chain of evidence" than a labyrinth of narrative secrecy, of "blocked communication."[69]

Narrative Secrets and Suspicious Lives

Engaging in a kind of narrative subterfuge, Hartright's edits, emendations, and even erasures of the various testimonials (including his own) have effectively undermined the stated moral premise of the novel—to represent "the truth always in its most direct and most intelligible aspect" (50). Just as the "blank space" in the church registry "told the whole story" (508) of Sir Percival's illegitimacy—that his entire life was a lie—so the blank spaces and gaps of the multiple narratives tell *a whole story* of deception.[70] Much like Anne Catherick and Laura Fairlie, we have been unwittingly held hostage in a narrative asylum, victims of our own cognitive shortcomings. Upon reflection, we wonder how we could have been so easily duped by Hartright's performed sincerity and disinterest.[71] Rather than concluding that *The Woman in White* is nothing more than an elaborate cultural representation of social gamesmanship in which we have just lost spectacularly, Collins's novel invites us rather—indeed compels us—to consider the inherent complexities of "truth," objectivity, and reliability long after the story has "ended."

Moreover, if narrative, as Brooks suggests, "is one of the large categories or systems of understanding that we use in our negotiations with reality,"[72] what

---

68 Miller, 117.

69 In *The Culture of Secrecy: Britain, 1832–1998*, David Vincent broadly defines secrecy as "blocked communication" (New York: Oxford UP, 1999), 20.

70 As Philip O'Neill notes, "the written word conceals reality" (*Wilkie Collins: Women, Property, and Propriety* [Totowa, NJ: Barnes and Noble, 1988], 123).

71 Hartright's name has also been a clever disguise, a form of moral camouflage; his "heart" was never in the "right" place.

72 *Reading for the Plot*, xi.

are the cognitive implications of reading novels that deliberately provoke a "fascination of secrecy"? While reading novels may both reflect and trigger our voracious need to attribute minds, it also points to the inherent instabilities of the mind-reading process. Indeed, Zunshine notes that "works of fiction magnify and vivify various points on the continuum of our imperfect mutual knowledge: Spectacular feats and failures of mind-reading are the hinges on which many a fictional plot turns."[73] To be sure, *The Woman in White* engages its readers in a kind of ToM marathon, pushing our mind-reading ability to its limits and making us all embarrassingly aware of our cognitive weaknesses. Ultimately, however, we emerge from the rigorous "windings of the labyrinth" more discerning than when we first began. No matter how we "finish" the course—(and indeed, no matter how many times we "go around" or reread)—each reading experience promises the rich reward of a more finely-nuanced, if not astute, strategic social intelligence. In fact, cognitive anthropologist Dan Sperber reminds us that in "our everyday striving to understand others, we make do with partial and speculative interpretations…for all their incompleteness and uncertainty, these interpretations help us—us individuals, us peoples—to live with one another."[74]

As a cultural representation of the complexities of social interaction, particularly with regard to detecting and unmasking deception, our reading experience of *The Woman in White*, however fallible and imperfect, nevertheless enhances our ability to "read" the real world—to look beneath the surface, to question motives, to doubt what is spoken. Indeed, if "all human being and doing, to be sure, flows from enigmatic forces,"[75] then the novel's myriad indeterminacies—the uncertainties of perception, the unanswered questions, the secrets never uncovered, the deceptions never unmasked—remind us that people have lives and minds that ultimately are not entirely accessible to others.

[73] "Embodied Transparency," 72.

[74] *Explaining Culture: A Naturalistic Approach* (Oxford: Blackwell, 1997), 38.

[75] Simmel, 333.

Chapter 6
A Victorian Picture Puzzle: Richard Dadd's *The Fairy Feller's Masterstroke*

Eleanor Fraser Stansbie

The pursuit of a richer perspective on issues of secrecy within Victorian culture and society is an important project, one that involves paying close attention to the historical settings within which various deceptions and dissimulations may (or may not) have taken place and one that calls also for carefully considered interpretive approaches. My contribution to this endeavor is an investigation into the strategies of concealment as employed by Victorian painter and parricide Richard Dadd through his well-practised medium of artistic expression, arguing that these were his means of reclaiming individual agency and of confounding the apparently all-encompassing clinical gaze of the Victorian asylum authorities, during a period that saw an increasing focus on uncovering the secrets of both mind and body. In producing the enigmatic puzzle of a picture known as *The Fairy Feller's Masterstroke*, and casting himself as the major protagonist of his own story in paint, it is my contention that Dadd mounted a surreptitious defence of his secret self, thus alerting us to the possibilities of subtly subverting panoptical power.

We can begin to comprehend the circumstances that led to Dadd's elaborate subterfuge by looking at this photograph of him at work, which itself does not immediately reveal its true nature, for this image was captured not within an artist's studio, but inside Bethlem Asylum in 1854, where Dadd had been committed for life ten years earlier, after being judged insane following the brutal murder of his father (Fig. 6.1).

Dadd's portrait depicts a unique historical moment; a Victorian asylum inmate, who also happened to be a Royal Academy trained artist, practicing his former profession within the inhospitable confines of Bethlem's Criminal Insanity Ward. This compelling image also, however, provides a valuable insight into Dadd's technique. The painting on which we see him working is entitled *Contradiction. Oberon and Titania* (1854–8, Collection of Lord Lloyd Webber) and we can clearly observe how he produced this picture and undoubtedly, due to its striking similarity in style, *The Fairy Feller's Masterstroke* (1855–64, Tate Britain, London), the subject of this essay (Fig. 6.2), by drawing the majority of the design in outline before adding color and modulation.

Fig. 6.1 Henry Hering, *Richard Dadd at his easel painting Contradiction—Oberon and Titania*, c 1857–1859, photograph, 240 x 170 mm, photograph reproduced by permission of the Bethlem Art and History Collections Trust

Fig. 6.2 Richard Dadd, *The Fairy Feller's Masterstroke*, 1855–64, Oil on canvas, 540 x 394 mm ©Tate, London 2009

Dadd offered his own, rather different, account of how the latter picture came to be, in a poem entitled *Elimination of a Picture and Its Subject – Called the Feller's Master Stroke*,[1] which he wrote after completing the painting. The artist describes how he smeared paint onto the canvas and stared at these cloudy forms intently until the fantastical shapes that would comprise the final painting emerged, as though by magic:

> And nuzzling the cloth, on which
> The cloudy shades not rich,
> Indefinite almost unseen
> Lay vacant entities of chance,
> Lent forms unto my careless glance
> Without intent, pure fancy 't'is *[sic]* I mean
> Design and composition thus –
> Now minus and just here perhaps – plus –
> Grew in this way – and so – or thus,
> That fairly wrought they stand in view
> A Fairy band, much as I say, just so 'tis true.

The linearity of form and the immensely complex composition of *The Fairy Feller's Masterstroke*, however, render the idea of such a nebulous approach deeply incredible. Looking again at the photograph of him at work on *Contradiction*, this can be nothing less than a deliberately disingenuous account of the painting's origin that belies his working method, which was to produce a complicated and minutely detailed line drawing which he then, at length, proceeded to fill in. The idea that *The Fairy Feller's Masterstroke* is simply an impulsive outpouring of imagination, or even the embodiment of insane hallucinations in paint, is also undermined by other factors, including the length of time it took him to complete—almost nine years. Indeed, his work on that painting was interspersed with approximately forty-eight further pictures produced within that time span, in a widely differing array of styles, subject matter and media, including the equally complex *Contradiction*.[2]

The Fairy Feller's Masterstroke is Richard Dadd's most celebrated work; it hangs in one of the UK's most prestigious galleries, Tate Britain, and its reputation rests not only on the complexity and skill of its execution, but also on its unusual contexts of production, which have lent it an air of romantic notoriety. Critical reception of the painting has frequently adopted this romantic approach, characterizing the picture as the result of a creative imagination heightened by insanity and freed from any commercial constraints. Or, the painting has been consistently pathologized, and used as evidence of Dadd's inability to produce

---

1 Richard Dadd, *Elimination of a Picture and its Subject – Called the Feller's Master Stroke* (Beckenham, Kent: Bethlem Royal Hospital and Maudsley Hospital Archives and Museum,1865).

2 See Patricia Allderidge, *The Late Richard Dadd 1817–1886* (London: Tate Gallery, 1974), the catalogue to the 1974 exhibition and, to date, the most comprehensive, illustrated resource of the majority of Richard Dadd's oeuvre.

any coherent, comprehensible work.[3] Predominantly, the picture has been denied any meanings outside Dadd's disturbed psyche and this perplexing image, with its apparently impenetrable iconography, its elusive symbolism, and its unconventional spatial composition is thus consigned to the historiography of the art of the insane; a move that places it outside mainstream art and its explanatory methodologies.

I suggest that a consideration of its unusual conditions of production, that is, Bethlem in 1854, will provide a firmer foundation from which to investigate Dadd's puzzle of a picture. This was a significant historical moment when profound changes in the care of the insane had been implemented within that institution, and Dadd's return to painting was closely connected to those nineteenth-century asylum reforms and their guiding principle, moral treatment. Indeed, his work on *The Fairy Feller's Masterstroke* began shortly after Bethlem's management had been recently severely censured for its regime and forced sharply into line with what were considered to be more effective and humane asylum practices.[4] Reforms within Bethlem comprised part of a much wider movement of radical transformations in the care of the insane that had begun earlier in the nineteenth century, due to newly emerging and evolving theories of the causes, classification and possible cures for insanity.

By the mid-century, almost all insane asylums, both private and public, had modified their regimes by eschewing punitive treatments and mechanical restraints such as manacles, straitjackets and even the infamous scold's bridle, in favor of the system known as moral treatment. Broadly, moral treatment was the rejection of the perceived cruelty of these methods of physical containment and their

---

3 See in particular J. B. L. Allen, "Mad Robin: Richard Dadd," *Art Quarterly* 30, no. 1 (1967): 19–30; Peter Fuller, "Richard Dadd: A Psychological Interpretation," *Connoisseur* 186, no. 749 (July 1974): 170–77; David Greysmith, *Richard Dadd, The Rock and Castle of Seclusion* (London: Studio Vista,1973); Peter Jones, "A Painter Possessed," *Observer Magazine* (London: June 16, 1974): 28–9, 31, 33–5; Christopher Neve, "The Lost World of Richard Dadd," *Country Life* 156 (London: July 4, 1974): 16–17; Helen Smailes, *Method in Madness* (exh. cat Edinburgh: Scottish National Portrait Gallery, 1981); Allen Staley, "Richard Dadd of Bethlem," *Art In America* 62, no. 6 (Nov/Dec 1974): 80–82; Alexander Theroux, "Artists who Kill and Other Acts of Creative Mayhem," *Art & Antiques* Summer (1988): 95–103. The only recent work that offers more sophisticated and historically contextualized analyses of Dadd's work can be found in: Louise Lippincott, "Murder and the Fine Arts; or, a Reassessment of Richard Dadd," *The J Paul Getty Museum Journal* 16 (1988): 75–94; Nicola Bown, *Fairies in Nineteenth Century Art & Literature* (Cambridge: Cambridge UP, 2001); and John M Macgregor *The Discovery of the Art of the Insane* (Princeton: Princeton UP, 1989).

4 A series of complaints of abuse and neglect within Bethlem had prompted the Home Secretary to make an order for inspection by the Commissioners in Lunacy in 1852, who subsequently recommended a complete change of regime at the hospital. See Jonathan Andrews et al., *The History of Bethlem* (London & New York: Routledge, 1997), 83–113 for a comprehensive account of these events and others in Bethlem Hospital in 1852. See also "The Commissioners in Lunacy's Report on Bethlem Hospital," and "The Report of Bethlem Hospital," *Journal of Psychological Medicine and Mental Pathology* 6 (1853): 129–45 and 595–8.

replacement with a system that would enable patients to exercise and re-establish self-control over their own wayward psyches. The aim of moral treatment, also known as moral management, was to restore sanity from within, rather than through external, physical means of control and this meant involving the patient in his or her cure. The idea was to inculcate self-control and self-restraint within the asylum population, and one method that was held to be of great therapeutic value within this scheme was engaging patients in some form of productive employment or rational amusement.[5] Drawing and painting, for example, were pursuits that were actively encouraged and several asylum superintendents became avid collectors of such works, not only for the truths they might yield about their patients' mental condition, but also for their aesthetic and collectable qualities.[6]

In Dadd's case, there is evidence that his doctors actively commissioned his work. For example, the inscription on the reverse of *Contradiction* states that it was painted for Bethlem's Chief Superintendent William Charles Hood and *The Fairy Feller's Masterstroke*, bears a similar dedication to Bethlem's chief steward Thomas Haydon. In addition, the manuscript of the poem *Elimination of a Picture and Its Subject—Called the Feller's Master Stroke,* was found in Haydon's effects after his death and suggests very strongly that Dadd produced it in response to Haydon's specific request for a fairy painting, a genre with which he had formerly, in his pre-asylum career, achieved notable success.[7] There is further confirmation that supports the suggestion that Dadd's doctors were significant patrons of

---

[5] Moral treatment was not, however, a simple or straightforward concept. See Vieda Skultans, *Madness and Morals, Ideas on Insanity in the Nineteenth Century* (London: Routledge & Kegan Paul, 1975): 2–11, who indicates that in nineteenth-century terms "moral" was roughly equal to our term "psychological," although its meaning also retained a strong ethical element. In other words, it referred not only to an individual's mental or emotional state, but also denoted his or her physical and social conduct and behavior. These two different definitions inevitably caused a certain ambiguity in terms of the purpose of moral therapy; overtly it proposed to treat the patient through the emotions, but, less obviously, it was also aimed at modifying inappropriate behavior. See also Andrew Scull, *Museums of Madness, The Social Organization of Insanity in Nineteenth-century England* (London: Allen Lane, 1979) who makes a direct connection between this particular strategy and emerging capitalism's need to encourage rational thought and self-discipline in order to create an efficient and compliant workforce. In deploying the same ideas of self-discipline and the work ethic, moral treatment could be used to reform the insane and restore them to a civilized, manageable and ultimately productive condition.

[6] See Maureen Park, "Early Examples of Art in Scottish Hospitals, 2: Crichton Royal Hospital, Dumfries," *Journal of Audiovisual Media in Medicine* 26, no. 4 (December 2003): 142, for one important example of this in W A F Browne, renowned Scottish alienist and superintendent of the Crichton Royal Institution in Dumfries, who widely encouraged and collected art work by his patients.

[7] Dadd produced a series of critically acclaimed fairy paintings before his incarceration, which he exhibited at prestigious exhibitions such as the Royal Academy. In keeping with contemporary trends, these were based on Shakespearean themes: *Titania Sleeping*, c. 1841 (Louvre, Paris), *Puck*, 1841 (Private Collection) and *Come unto these Yellow Sands*, c. 1841–42 (Collection of John Rickett).

his art.[8] After Hood's death, thirty-three of Dadd's works previously belonging to him were sold at Christie's in 1870, as part of his estate, along with over fifty engravings and prints after artists such as Landseer, Millais, Turner, Faed, Maclise and Bonheur. Indeed, the only original works in Hood's collection were by Dadd's hand, indicating his importance to Hood as a source of original art.[9]

Both Hood and Haydon were central to the newly-instituted changes at Bethlem, having been appointed in 1853 as, respectively, medical superintendent and resident physician, specifically to instigate the philosophies and practices of moral treatment.[10] Hood, in particular, was keen from the start to establish a new regime and immediately set out his agenda in his *Statistics of Insanity*, the report he produced for the Governors of Bethlem as a condition of his employment, and which echoed the general sentiments of moral management; advocating exercise and amusements, and emphasizing the need for productive employment. As he wrote, "occupation is of even greater importance than amusement; indeed systematic employment, in various forms, is now a duly recognized essential to successful treatment in all properly conducted asylums."[11] Hood's ideas on moral management also extended to "criminal lunatics," such as Dadd, whom he believed would also benefit from being encouraged to take up useful employment relating, if possible, to their previous occupations. Significantly, Hood also stated his opinion that these particular patients offered the most interesting opportunities for clinical observation in terms of the effects of moral treatment on their condition.[12]

Joel Eigen argues that at that particular historical point, the early to mid-nineteenth century, asylum keepers began to surpass mere custodial roles in order to perform the function of "scientific observers and chroniclers of the essence of insanity."[13] As he further writes, "never before had there converged a confined

---

[8] See Macgregor (1989): 127–33, who argues, it is not a manipulation of the facts to describe Dadd's physicians as the major patrons of his career, in the sense that they did not merely collect, but actively commissioned, significant portions of Dadd's asylum art. It is also worth noting that not only was Haydon himself interested in art, having been trained and continuing to practice as a draughtsman, but he even had several illustrations published in *Punch* magazine, belonged to the Langham Sketching Club, and had contact with many professional artists, not least his brother Samuel B Haydon, who shared a studio with William Rossetti. Haydon's involvement with art was crucial. It is highly probable that he provided Dadd with current exhibition catalogues and art periodicals as well as providing him with new developments and ideas from the London art world, in the form of texts and reproduced images.

[9] See Christies catalogue of 1870 in the archives department of Christies Auctioneers, 8 King Street, St James, London, SW1.

[10] See "The Report of Bethlem Hospital," *Journal of Psychological Medicine and Mental Pathology* 6 (1853): 129–45.

[11] See W Charles Hood, *Statistics of Insanity, Being a Decennial Report of Bethlem Hospital from 1846–1855 Inclusive* (London: Batten, 1862), 102.

[12] Hood, 147–50.

[13] Joel Peter Eigen, *Witnessing Insanity, Madness and Mad-Doctors in the English Court* (New Haven & London: Yale UP, 1995), 132.

community *and* a generation of keepers eager to delineate distinct classifications and categories of derangement."[14] Eigen is expressing here, of course, a recognizably Foucauldian view of nineteenth-century asylum reforms. Firstly, in the idea that this move towards more intensive medical scrutiny was part of the zeal during the period to classify, scientifically, diseases and also a power strategy through which the medical profession claimed authority to diagnose, treat, and ultimately cure illness. Foucault conceptualizes this intense scientific scrutiny as the "clinical" and the "observing" gaze, claiming that physicians actively promoted the idea that clinical practice, that is, intense observation and the construction of patients as individual cases, permitted doctors to uncover hidden truths about the causes and progress of illness, something that was not possible through mere theorizing. Secondly, and equally importantly, Foucault derided moral treatment as intrinsically controlling, arguing that it merely masked paternalistic practices of surveillance and coercion.[15] There have been more recent revisions of Foucault's own revisionist history of madness which, whilst acknowledging Foucault's powerful influence on new asylum studies, searchingly critique his methodology, mainly for its monolithic viewpoint and lack of coherent and accurate historical contextualization. There is still consensus, though, across both earlier and more recent scholarship on asylum reforms that the nineteenth century marked a change in the ways in which insanity was both recognized and treated and that there was a definite increase in asylum population and asylum building. Moreover, it is generally agreed that this paradigmatic change in the treatment of the insane contributed to the rise and consolidation of the profession of psychiatry. The main distinction between early and later research, however, is a tendency to be more cautious in constructing a homogeneous account and to emphasize the complexity and contingency of the many and varied institutional agendas.[16]

---

[14] Eigen, 131.

[15] See Michel Foucault (tr. R Howard), *Madness and Civilisation: A History of Insanity in the Age of Reason* (New York: Vintage, 1988), 241–78, first published in France as *Folie et déraison: Histoire de la folie à l'âge classique* (Paris: Gallimard, 1961) and first published in English in 1967. Foucault proposes that the birth of the asylum and the concomitant rise of the psychiatric profession were far from being part of the progressive drive towards a humane system of care and cure of the insane that has been suggested in earlier histories. Rather, he argues that the apparently transparent benignity of that approach masked the efficacy of psychiatry as a powerful instrument of social control. See also Michel Foucault (tr. A. M. Sheridan Smith), *The Birth of the Clinic: an Archaeology of Medical Perception* (New York: Vintage, 1975).

[16] For a comprehensive re-consideration of these issues see: Arthur Still & Irving Velody eds., *Rewriting the History of Madness, Studies in Foucault's 'Histoire de la Folie'* (London & New York: Routledge, 1992); Colin Jones & Roy Porter eds., *Reassessing Foucault, Power, Medicine and the Body* (London & New York: Routledge, 1994); Joseph Melling, 'Accommodating Madness, New Research in the Social History of Insanity and Institutions' in Joseph Melling & Bill Forsythe eds., *Insanity, Institutions and Society, 1800 – 1914: A Social History of Madness in Comparative Perspective* (London & New York: Routledge, 1999), 1–4.

A study of patients' records, nevertheless, has proved that there was indeed an increase in clinical observation at Bethlem from 1853 onwards, the beginning of Hood's tenure. These findings support the idea that Hood increased observation on taking up his new post in 1853, calling it his "new game." Furthermore, patient records from Bethlem during that precise period also show that Hood involved the patient in this observational scheme far more than previous Bethlem doctors, thus suggesting not just an increase in surveillance, but a rise in interaction between patient and doctor, a phenomenon I will explore further in this essay.[17] Significantly, the mode of narrative that Hood inculcated was confessional, in an attempt to uncover the innermost, the most private, workings of his patients' minds, their secret life, so to speak. Hood encouraged his patients to tell their own stories of their descent into madness, in their own voices. When these patient narratives were successfully drawn out, they were then institutionalized and included as part of their hospital records, becoming part of the drive towards classifying and determining the causes of, and eventually cures for insanity.[18] I suggest that, prompted by Hood to reveal his innermost secrets, Dadd chose a mode of storytelling wherein he could retain the most confessional control—paint on canvas.

In his study of the social history of madness, Roy Porter considers many examples of the narratives of the insane and argues that it is a mistake to dismiss them as mere incoherent ravings. Indeed, Porter sees these liminal accounts as valuable as mainstream texts in offering great insights about the times in which these individuals lived. The stories that the insane recounted, he argues, were attempts to explain and make sense of their actions, to themselves as well as others and although the language and idioms they used may have been unconventional and obscure, many of the concerns and ideas they expressed were the same as their saner contemporaries. Thus, Porter challenges the idea that valid historical accounts emerge only from normal society, and that the voices of those outside those boundaries, in this case asylum inmates, should not be heard and can never be comprehended. The autobiographical narratives of the mad, Porter further suggests, acted not only as a defense of individuality, but were also a form of critique.[19] As he writes, "It should be no surprise then that those who have felt profoundly threatened by devils or mad-doctors should have wanted to leave their own testament in order to achieve justice temporal or eternal, or simply as the only

[17] See Akihito Suzuki, "Framing Psychiatric Subjectivity: Doctor, Patient and Record-keeping at Bethlem in the Nineteenth Century," in *Insanity, Institutions and Society, 1800–1914,* ed. Joseph Melling & Bill Forsythe (London & New York: Routledge, 1999), 128. Suzuki strongly suggests that Hood took advantage of his newly-gained, and unprecedented, power in his drive to detect the secrets of his inmates' insanity. In addition, Bethlem's smaller size, and Hood's status as sole Medical Superintendent made observation and classification much easier than in the much larger county asylums.

[18] Suzuki, 122–32.

[19] Roy Porter, *A Social History of Madness* (New York: Weidenfeld and Nicolson, 1987), 2–3, 230–32.

way to answer back."[20] I suggest that *The Fairy Feller's Masterstroke* although couched in an artistic, rather than textual, idiom is just such a story about the self, and Dadd's comment on life inside nineteenth-century Bethlem. Thus, the picture can be construed as Dadd's personal retort to the threat to his identity posed by the clinical and observing gaze of his physicians and a covert critique of the institution in which he was held captive.

If we look at *The Fairy Feller's Masterstroke* in this autobiographical light, and at the eponymous central figure as a symbolic self-representation of the artist, this picture can be seen as Dadd's deeply personal, artistic response to the conditions of his captivity and, to some degree, an elaborate riddle that conveys, in coded symbolic form, some of the secrets of the world of the Victorian asylum. That does not imply that the picture is entirely the result of conscious and deliberate intentions. The painting was constructed over a period of almost a decade and must, therefore, contain unconscious, even oblique, symbols and allusions some of which will always remain irrecoverable. The result is a tightly-knit and complicated compositional tapestry which I am not going to attempt to unpick, stitch by stitch here, but will, instead, concentrate on what I believe are some of its most telling iconographical elements.

In his explanatory poem *Elimination*, Dadd identifies and describes the actions of almost all of the figures in the painting, the majority of whom are mythological, literary or supernatural figures. As Dadd writes in this poem, they are in the main "fays, gnomes and elves and suchlike" and include such figures as Queen Mab in a carriage drawn by centaurs, with a gnat as coachman and Cupid and Psyche as pages; the childhood favourites of tinker, tailor, soldier, sailor, beggar and thief and other fantastical figures such as the dragonfly trumpeter on the top left of the composition.[21]

This miscellany of magical characters also includes the figures of Oberon and Titania, who are perched upon a leaf above the Patriarch, the white-bearded and crowned figure in the centre of the painting (Fig. 6.3). Indeed, he is the most significant figure, other than the Fairy Feller himself, the leather-clad figure who stands with his axe raised with his back towards the viewers. He is without doubt the wizard-like Patriarch, whom Dadd describes as the "arch magician," with his "triple crown of subtle might" and who is both compositionally and conceptually central to the meaning of the picture. He occupies an elevated position of surveillance, as befits the ultimate authority figure he represents, and the Fairy Feller is in the direct sight line of his probing and controlling gaze. The Patriarch's power is further suggested by the following line from the poem, an utterance which is directly aimed at the figure of the Fairy Feller, "Except I tell you, strike if you dare," he declaims, indicating that the Feller cannot proceed in his task without a direct command from the Patriarch's raised right hand.

---

20 Porter, 30. I do not believe that Porter means to suggest a simplistic model of victimization, although he does concede that within the asylum system the psychiatrist was, unsurprisingly, the dominant figure. However, his model does, unequivocally, allow a level of reciprocity, if not outright dissidence.

21 Allderidge, 125.

Fig. 6.3 Detail – Richard Dadd, *The Fairy Feller's Masterstroke*, 1855–64, Oil on canvas, 540 x 394 mm © Tate, London 2009

Concurrently, the Patriarch's left hand stretches out to grasp what Dadd, in his poem, describes as "a large little club" with which the Patriarch threatens to hit the smaller fairies about the head. Rather than grasping this "club," however, in a manner which suggests it is a potential weapon, the Patriarch's hand firmly covers the tip in a controlling gesture, whilst his gaze continues to fall relentlessly on the Fairy Feller. Moreover, the form of this weapon is so explicitly phallic that we are fully justified in interpreting it as a powerful signifier of Dadd's suppressed masculinity and sexuality and as a symbol of his disempowerment and personal and sexual frustration. This libidinal theme is echoed by the small figural group pictured to the left of the Patriarch, which can also be read as an expression of enforced celibacy. It consists of two female fairies, both of whom are depicted with an exaggerated and highly eroticized femininity, with prominent breasts and exaggerated calves balanced on impossibly tiny, delicate feet. On closer inspection, one can also see an almost invisible satyr who is peeping up the skirt of one of them. Dadd provides a poetic explanation of this part of his composition that reveals his dissatisfaction with the celibate terms of his incarceration and his banishment forever from the garden of earthly delights:

> A satyr peeps; at what, it doth not lack
> An explanation. At such a book,
> His right to look,
> I care not to dispute
> Such secrets surely some must know.
> All are not saints on earth below.
> Or if they are they know the same.
> Or are shut out from nature's game,
> Banished from nature's book of life

The narrative of the picture so far, then, is redolent with the themes of captivity and control, mediated through the two main characters:,the Fairy Feller as sign for the mental patient caught in the full glare of the penetrating gaze of the Patriarch, who represents the inescapable scrutiny of the newly-reformed asylum. In Foucauldian terms, the aim of this method of close observation of the patient was to read the mind and body, to make it "entirely legible for the clinician's gaze: that is, recognizable by its signs."[22]

Moreover, these further lines from "Elimination"—"T'unlock the secret cells of dark abyss / The power which never doth its victims miss"—seem to express Dadd's feeling that, as the captive object of his doctors' scrutiny, their aim is not merely to fathom the meaning and source of his madness, but also to uncover the very essence of his individuality. Indeed, Roy Porter has highlighted the importance of doctor/patient dynamics as a means of further understanding the history of nineteenth-century psychiatry, writing that, "The history of psychiatric ideas and practices has conventionally been written as a saga of good versus

---

[22] Foucault, *The Birth of the Clinic*, 159.

bad psychiatry. It is rarely sufficiently acknowledged that the real protagonists are the doctors and patients, and the real subject the complex range of their encounters."[23] Foucault has gone even further in constructing an intriguing model of a doctor/patient relationship, which sees them caught in a deeply paternalistic dynamic wherein the doctor's authority is based not only on his power to punish transgression and restore social and moral order, but also on his claims to cure. According to Foucault, the patient is complicit in his own domination, and finally becomes increasingly convinced of the doctor's almost miraculous powers:

> the doctor-patient couple sinks even deeper into a strange world. In the patient's eyes, the doctor becomes a thaumaturge [wizard, conjuror or magician]; the authority he has borrowed from order, morality, and the family now seems to derive from himself … it was thought, and by the patient first of all, that it was in the esotericism of his knowledge, in some almost daemonic secret of knowledge, that the doctor had found the power to unravel insanity; and increasingly the patient would accept this self-surrender to a doctor both divine and satanic, beyond human measure in any case; increasingly he would alienate himself in the physician, accepting entirely and in advance all his prestige, submitting from the very first to a will he experienced as magic.[24]

Of course I am not suggesting that either Foucault's flamboyant rhetoric or that Dadd's pictorial language were literal translations of asylum authority into a wizard-like Patriarch figure; they are obviously symbolic in essence. It is, nevertheless, intriguing that both the name and the white-bearded, sage-like appearance of Dadd's Patriarch figure should not only connote the paternalistic attitudes that underpinned nineteenth-century asylum reforms,[25] but also align itself so uncannily with Foucault's occult imagery.

The next few lines of *Elimination*, however, when coupled with Dadd's compositional technique, reveal a desire to deflect the scrutiny that Foucault prescribes as unavoidable:

> 'Tis so – no doubt, but even Almighty Power
> Suffers defeat each day & every hour
> As unforeseen some little trifling thing
> Cheats of a stave, another song we sing

In order to cheat the "Almighty Power" of its authority, Dadd's defensive strategy was simply to pose the figure of the Fairy Feller with his back towards his intended viewers, Dadd's doctors, so that his face, the most telling, or legible, aspect of his person, is concealed from their gaze (Fig. 6.4).

---

23 Porter, 231.

24 Foucault, *Madness and Civilization*, 274–5.

25 See Anne Digby, *Madness, Morality and Medicine, A Study of the York Retreat, 1796–1914* (Cambridge: Cambridge UP, 1985), 57–61.

Fig. 6.4 Detail – Richard Dadd, *The Fairy Feller's Masterstroke*, 1855–64, Oil on canvas, 540 x 394 mm ©Tate, London 2009

This is Dadd's explicit assertion that physiognomy, particularly the analysis of facial expressions and features, had, during the nineteenth century, become an instrument of social and cultural investigation; capable of accessing and analyzing an individual's interiority through the decoding of his or her exterior appearance. During this period, physiognomy existed as a wide-ranging cultural phenomenon that offered a seemingly uncomplicated route to decoding character through physical signs, and the artist's use of these systems was understood to be a means of achieving a similar legibility of human character and emotions—

in paint. Physiognomic practices in the arena of fine art in the nineteenth century were deeply influenced by the work of Charles Bell (1774–1842). Bell was a surgeon and anatomist who produced, in 1806, what was in effect the first textbook of anatomy for painters, *Essays on the Anatomy of Expression in Painting*.[26] His treatise proved such a fundamental aspect of art education that it went on to be published in numerous editions throughout the century and would, thus, definitely have been an important resource within Dadd's academic studies.[27] As Ludmilla Jordanova observes, Bell made explicit the representation of the human body as an emphatic point of convergence between medicine and the fine arts.[28] Without doubt, exposure to Bell's theories influenced Dadd's own approach to the visual representation of the human body, alerting him, moreover, not only to the aesthetic importance of physiognomy, but also to its social and cultural significance. Dadd would have clearly understood that physiognomy involved the close observation of the physical exterior of an individual, especially the face, as a way of exposing human emotions and character. In addition, either consciously or unconsciously, Bell's work must have raised in Dadd an awareness of physiognomy as a vital connection between art and medicine.

Physiognomy was thus not only an intrinsic component of institutionalized artistic education, but also permeated Victorian culture and society on many levels. Physiognomy was predicated on the basic notion that the external characteristics of the body, especially the face, stood as markers for an individual's morality, intellect, social status, and more. The further belief was that these outwards signs could be read and interpreted systematically, thereby rendering the human body legible. It was not merely, however, a simplistic taxonomy: a means of attaining legibility of face and body and the reading of character. Rather, the ideologies underpinning nineteenth-century physiognomy proposed that the outward human form mirrored the inner human condition, morally, psychically, and, more insidiously, in terms of race, class and any other form that separated the normative from the transgressive, the simply different, or the potentially socially disruptive.

Indeed, the emerging psychiatric profession drew heavily upon these social and cultural physiognomic notions in its drive to classify and cure insanity. Physiognomy proved, in fact, to be an irresistible concept for emergent nineteenth-century psychiatric philosophies and practices, which held that insanity was a medical condition that could be diagnosed and treated by studying its external,

---

[26] Charles Bell, *Essays on the Anatomy of Expression in Painting* (London: J Murray, 1824), 104.

[27] See Lucy Hartley, *Physiognomy and the Meaning of Expression in Nineteenth-Century Culture* (Cambridge: Cambridge UP, 2001), 63–9.

[28] Ludmilla Jordanova, "The Representation of the Human Body: Art and Medicine in the Work of Charles Bell," in *Towards a Modern Art World*, ed. Brian Allen (New Haven & London: the Paul Mellon Centre for Studies in British Art and the Yale Center for Art, Yale UP, 1995), 70–94. See also Hartley (2001), 47–64.

physical effects, particularly the facial expressions.[29] The concept of physiognomy seemed to offer an apparently unproblematic means of categorizing and ordering the inner turmoil of insanity through observation and analysis of the disordered outward form. And, by the mid-century the illustrated treatises and atlases, with their physiognomic visualizations of madness, was firmly embedded in nineteenth-century psychiatry.[30] There were, thus, undeniable connections between the use of physiognomic theories in art and science, particularly in visual representations of madness.

As established above, for Foucault, the clinical gaze, based as it was on the close observation of the patient, was a means of uncovering the mysteries of the diseased body, or in this case, mind, as to some extent insanity was seen at that time as somatic in origin.[31] These secrets, Foucault proposes, had formerly remained hidden and invisible, until "suddenly offered to the brightness of the gaze."[32] Returning to Dadd's painting, we see how the figure of the Fairy Feller, which we can now understand as a sign of Dadd's subjectivity, stands bathed in the full glare of the searching, probing scrutiny of the figure who symbolizes the paternalistic authority of the asylum, but stands concealed from the gaze of the actual intended viewers of his art: his doctors. The Fairy Feller's face, the most telling, or legible aspect of his person, is turned away from the gaze of the picture's viewer; a recognition of the importance of reading the expressions of the face as a key to the inner-self. As I have argued, physiognomy in the nineteenth century was seen as crucial in its revelatory capacity in art, science and popular culture. Thus, hiding the facial features of the central, eponymous and autobiographical figure implies Dadd's comprehensive knowledge of the power of physiognomy to expose individuality and attests to his wish to preserve some semblance of selfhood from the prying eyes of his psychiatrist-patrons.

The picture's perspective also resonates with a sense of surveillance and a feeling of voyeurism, which is achieved by the obscuring strands of timothy grass that sweep across the picture, through which the viewer must peer in order to access a tiny, secret, hidden world. The picture surface is far from flat or highly finished, rather it has a raised, embroidered-like texture, attesting not least to the strata of paint that must have been applied and re-applied over the long years of its execution. The mesh-like configuration of grass is the topmost and the most

29 See Janet Browne, "Darwin and the Face of Madness," in *The Anatomy of Madness: Essays in the History of Psychiatry, Vol. 1, People and Ideas*, ed. W F Bynum, Roy Porter & Michael Shepherd (London: Tavistock, 1985), 151–65.

30 Significant examples can be found in Jean–Etienne Dominique Esquirol, *Des maladies mentales, considerées sous les rapports médical, hygiénique et medico-légal* (Paris: J B Baillière, 1838) and Alexander Morison, *Outlines of Lectures on Mental Diseases* (London: Longman et al, 1826) and Alexander Morison, *The Physiognomy of Mental Disease* (London: Longman & Co, 1840).

31 L S Jacyna, "Somatic Theories of Mind and the Interests of Medicine in Britain, 1850–1879," *Medical History* 26 (1982): 233; Scull (1979), 132–63.

32 Foucault, *The Birth of the Clinic*, 195.

physically prominent layer of paint on the canvas and is an essential element of subtle symbolic subversions. They can be read as representing the bars of captivity, but they also they provide a tangible screen against unwelcome intrusion, thus operating as a sign of protection as much as punishment. Furthermore, the picture lacks a conventional perspective; in Dadd's imaginary, miniaturized and claustrophobic landscape, there is no deep recession of space, and there are no instantly recognizable vanishing points. The result is no firm path, or clear trajectory, for the eye to follow to a logical conclusion of the narrative. The viewer's gaze is forced to range randomly over the picture plane, preventing any easy reading of the picture's elements or decoding of its symbolism, all of which seems only to add to its apparent impenetrability and illegibility.

Through his academic training, Richard Dadd was thoroughly schooled in the techniques of mathematical perspective and compositional techniques. A glance at many of his asylum pictures demonstrates that he had never abandoned or forgotten these skills. So why is this picture so rife with these perspectival incongruities and spacial disunities? Was it that Dadd's technical skills were somehow overridden by his insanity in this particular instance? James Elkins, in his work on perspective as a cultural practice, suggests that 'correct' perspective practice has been seen, since its inception in the Renaissance, as the solution to creating a legible view of the world. It is fundamentally a mode of representation that is used to create an ordered, rational and clearly comprehensible pictorial space. Whilst this may be true, it does not preclude the idea that from the Renaissance onwards, artists have experimented with perspective and manipulated pictorial space in order to produce effects which are more complex, and more deliberately playful, than hitherto considered. Disruptions of perspective may be used, Elkins argues, in order to achieve either a particular dramatic effect, or to be intentionally iconoclastic. Although they might not explicitly add to or create narratives within the picture frame, there are meanings to be found in these deliberate distortions.[33] Perspectival correctness may, thus, be absent in *The Fairy Feller's Masterstroke,* but in the light of Elkins's theories, coupled with the other evidence accumulated here, it would not be beyond the bounds of probability to suggest that these were compositional principles chosen in part to perplex the viewer's response and delay or disrupt the decoding of its hidden meanings.

One further idea to consider is the picture's possible location within the genre of Victorian fairy painting, indicated by not only its title, but also suggested by Dadd's previous interest in this subject matter. The context from which Victorian fairy painting emerged was an increasingly industrial, urban and mechanized world, within which the cultural authority of science, especially the advent of Darwinism, began to displace that of religion. The Victorians' preoccupation with folklore, fairies and all things supernatural was a reaction to their disenchantment

---

[33] James Elkins *The Poetics of Perspective* (Ithaca & London: Cornell UP, 1994), 145–79. Elkins cites Holbeins's *The Ambassadors* (1533, National Gallery, London), and his use of anamorphosis to embed a 'secret' message within the image as a case in point.

with those, and other, more unsettling and unpalatable aspects of modernity. Fairies offered a comforting vision to the Victorians, an alternative, magical world where they could imagine themselves free from all constraints and anxieties.[34] If fairyland could function as a consolatory substitute for a pre-industrial Arcadia outside the asylum, could not Dadd have devised his very own personal dreamworld in order to escape the reality of his surroundings? If fairy painting was the modern world re-imagined in order to provide solace and reassurance, does Dadd's version of fairyland work in the same way, as a means of escape from his bleak asylum existence? Possibly, but fairy painting was never universally sugary or sentimental; it also possessed cruel and sinister aspects, and the *Fairy Feller's Masterstroke* is a distinctly darker vision of a magical otherworld, one that can be said to be both grotesque and gothic in style.

Victorian art was widely influenced by early nineteenth-century art in the grotesque style such as neo-gothic German illustration, which drew heavily on myth and the supernatural for its subject matter. Engaging with grotesque aesthetics provided Victorian artists a means "of embodying or realizing experience as dense, chaotic, contradictory, deforming, overpowering, disorientating,"[35] and thereby "generates interpretations of the marginal, the aberrant, the uncanny, the liminal, the vital and the excessive."[36] These are all categories that can account for both the form and the meanings of *The Fairy Feller's Masterstroke*; uniting the occult and fragmentary aspects of its visual field with its slyly subversive message. Sarah Burns, in her study of the darker, more irrational elements of nineteenth-century American painting, elucidates the grotesque's capacity for dissent, proposing that this was not simply a mode of pictorial self-expression but was also a visual form of anti-Enlightenment critique; one which questioned assumptions that the American Republic was unproblematically harmonious and progressive. Burns has defined American nineteenth-century gothic painting as "the art of haunting, using that term as a container for a constellation of themes and moods: horror, fear, mystery, strangeness, fantasy, perversion, monstrosity, insanity."[37] In order to express those concepts, she suggests, many of these gothic artists shared a common pictorial style of dark and gloomy tones, grotesque figures and compressed and oppressive spatial compositions. In addition to their function as expressions of a painter's individual psyche, however, they had a possibly ideological function. As such, gothic pictures can be characterized as dissident in that they "trade on terror, ambiguity, and excess while inverting or subverting the status quo."[38] Similarly, Nicholas Royle has argued that cultural expressions of the uncanny are "often to

---

[34] Bown, 1–6; 82–4, 96–7.

[35] See Colin Trodd , Paul Barlow & David Amigoni, ed. *Victorian Culture and the Idea of the Grotesque* (Aldershot & Vermont: Ashgate, 1999), 17.

[36] Trodd, 1.

[37] Sarah Burns, *Painting the Dark Side. Art and the Gothic Imagination in Nineteenth-Century America* (Berkeley: U of California P, 2004), xix.

[38] Burns, xix.

be associated with an experience of the threshold, liminality, margins, borders, frontiers."[39] If, as I argue, Dadd's vision of a fairy world is to some extent his perspective on life in the asylum, it is a much more "unheimlich," or uncanny, version inasmuch as it peels away and unmasks the civilizing, domesticating veneer of moral treatment and replaces it with a much more dystopic, much less benign, representation of asylum reforms. The presence of a grotesque or gothic aesthetic in an artist's work can, then, suggest a notable level of personal and political subversion, which provides an important consideration for viewing the production of this picture as Dadd's subtle and covert act of resistance to his captive situation.

So, as a somewhat grim glimpse of certain aspects of Dadd's life in the asylum and as Dadd's artistic response to the clinical gaze, *The Fairy Feller's Masterstroke* is a complex image that reflects and deflects that invasive scrutiny. The picture conveys the idea of an oppositional gaze; a scenario where the surveyor and the surveyed did not necessarily, or constantly, occupy static, hierarchical positions. This image suggests that, to some extent, these positions could be reversed, and the authority of the dominant presence might be subtly usurped by the subordinate figure. The idea that these Foucauldian theories of surveillance could, maybe should, admit the possibility of inverting the power dynamics of looking has been explored by bell hooks in her essay on black women film spectators' interrogative response to stereotypical racial representations:

> all attempts to repress our/black peoples' right to gaze had produced in us an overwhelming longing to look, a rebellious desire, an oppositional gaze … Even in the worst circumstances of domination, the ability to manipulate one's gaze, in the face of structures of domination that would contain it, opens up the possibility of agency.[40]

Exposing the idea of the "possibility of agency" has been central to my reading of Dadd's picture puzzle as an oppositional artistic response to his captive situation. This painting represents and resists the operation of the clinical, observing gaze within the Victorian asylum. Whilst acknowledging that particular power balance was necessarily weighted towards the doctor as a figure of authority, I have refuted the idea that the patient was so completely disempowered that he or she had no means to either reciprocate, or even deflect, that invasive observation. For Dadd, his artistic vision offered recourse to reply to that omnipresent gaze. Indeed, as both the title of the painting and the significant space he occupies suggest, the figure of the Fairy Feller is the focus of this elusive visual narrative. He is depicted with his back to the viewer, his axe lifted in the act of striking the hazelnut. This is an arrested moment, however, never to be realized, forever frozen within the picture's tableau-like composition. The splitting of the shell is an act of revelation,

---

[39] Nicholas Royle, *The Uncanny* (Manchester: Manchester UP, 2003), vii.

[40] bell hooks, "The Oppositional Gaze: Black Female Spectators," in *Reading Images*, Julia Thomas ed. (Basingstoke & New York: Palgrave, 2001), 123.

and to cleave the nut would be to expose its secret centre, which is symbolic of the themes of disclosure and concealment that lie at the heart of this picture.

In my discussion of *The Fairy Feller's Masterstroke*, I have attributed an unprecedented level of agency to Dadd, as both mental patient and painter, in the construction of meanings in his asylum art. Rather than incoherent and unintelligible, the picture can be more easily comprehended when attending closely to its contexts of production, rather than solely on the psychopathology of its creator. This beguiling example of Victorian artistic virtuosity is deliberately secretive, ambiguous and playful. Moreover, his deliberately puzzling pictorial strategies were a manifestation of Dadd's resistance to and subversion of the intense clinical scrutiny to which he was subjected as a mental patient in a Victorian asylum at the height of the moral reform movement.

Chapter 7
Detecting Business Fraud at Home: White-Collar Crime and the Sensational Clergyman in Victorian Domestic Fiction

Tamara S. Wagner

White-collar crimes committed or concealed within the confines of the Victorian home propel some of the most complex narratives of detection. The sensation novel's Domestic Gothic notoriously capitalizes on such incursions of the public into the private, of business into the intimacies of the family, quickly establishing plotlines that realist domestic novels of the mid-century then critically revaluate. This intertextual rewriting, I argue, addresses the narrative functions of secrecy with an important self-reflexivity. It is not only that the exposure of a central secret can no longer work as the driving force of the narrative. Instead, individual accountability and responsibility outweigh the excitement of detective work. The question of punishment, or atonement, as well as of moral culpability, is often lost sight of in sensational plots of detection as the outcome itself becomes submerged in the sensationalized pleasure of reconnaissance and often also of personal revenge. By contrast, the reworking of these new plots within domestic realism hinges on the investigation of these very issues. This complicates the narrativization of public exposure—and its opposite, secrecy—through what can be seen as an increasingly self-reflexive engagement with literary sensationalism. As it adapts the narrative potential of detective plots, domestic novels produced during the "sensational sixties" thus help facilitate a reconsideration of the development, more generally, of popular fiction at the time.

While drawing on various mid-nineteenth-century novels to illustrate the changing narrative functions of both domestic and business secrets, I shall concentrate on Charlotte Yonge's *The Clever Woman of the Family* (1865), a domestic novel written at the height of the sensation genre's popularity. In its adaptation of sensational devices, it employs the figure of a fake clergyman to address issues both of social indeterminacy and of personal accountability through the sensational trope of the double life, while situating the construction of secret identities within a set of crimes generated by modern finance capitalism. Not only fake, but fraudulent, this new villain speculates on the intimate spaces of domesticity as he does on large-scale financial ventures. At the same time, the impersonation of business truthfulness, domestic trustworthiness, and reliability in matters of religion or spirituality as embodied by the doubly false clergyman, discloses parallel alignments that draw the integrity, or at the very least separateness, of all three categories—business, domesticity, and religion—into doubt.

In order to do full justice to the representational strategies evoked and redirected as part of Yonge's take on business crime and its impact on domestic settings that indisputably remain her prime focus of interest, a close reading of *Clever Woman* needs to be situated within the ongoing rewritings—sensational and anti-sensational—of domestic as well as of business ideals and the various threats to both. Yonge's novel works out established sensational clichés in an intriguing merging of an importantly inverted sensational anti-Catholicism and a likewise reassessed emplotment of business crimes imported into the home. The redirection of narrative strategies in Victorian popular fiction, in fact, was by no means a one-way infiltration of sensationalism into domestic fiction. Literary influences went significantly beyond either hostile reactions or imitative attempts to break into a sensationally popular book market. White-collar criminals at home acquired a new fascination especially for realist, even emphatically anti-sensational, novelists writing in the wake of the "sensational sixties." It is not merely that issues of confidentiality could be differently addressed and weighed against demands for privacy. In a process of intertextual interchanges pivoting on the sensation novel's central interest in secrecy, the public spectacle of exposure marked the moment of most intensive sensationalization in an important number of popular novels of the mid-century, but became transformed into an impetus for moral catharsis when rewritten in domestic fiction.

When it comes to a public trial in *Clever Woman*, the shamefaced heroine, victim as much of her own inflated sense of self-importance as of the fraudulent clergyman's schemes, is forced into the spectacle of public confession in the witness box. As the family lawyer uncompromisingly puts it, Rachel Curtis, the "clever woman" of the title, is personally accountable for the fraudulent transactions she has inadvertently supported. By engaging in charitable schemes for which she has "been getting subscriptions from all the world, making [her]self answerable to them," she has rendered the villain's embezzlement and fraud possible in the first place, and hence "it does not simply lie between [her] and him—a silly girl who has let herself be taken in by a sharper."[1] The court scenes act as part of her punishment and ultimately of her personal, emotional, religious, and hence salutary, trials. Literary sensationalism is adapted for a specific agenda that preaches the pre-eminence of domestic moral economies underpinned by religious doctrine. The exposed culpability's redemptive power lies in its proclamation in public, whereas concealment leads to criminality at home as well as in business. It is such adaptations of the sensational secret's narrative functions that an analysis of Victorian domestic fiction promises to bring to light.

The central aim of this discussion of secret fraudulent business is therefore threefold: firstly, a close look at the "re-presentation" of secrecy in domestic

[1] Charlotte Yonge, *The Clever Woman of the Family* (Peterborough, OT: Broadview, 2001), 346. Hereafter cited parenthetically in the text.

fiction discloses its intricately complex engagement with sensationalism at the mid-century. Secondly, the consequent reworking of detective plots the more probingly addresses the central ambiguities in the notion of secrecy at home and in business because domestic fiction's main concern is with moral economies, with a reordering of confidences, of privacy, and reliability, and not with the titillations of reconnaissance or exposure. Trials that are at once legal and, through metaphorical extension, emotional, moral, and physical, function as an act of confession, while detective work serves chiefly to testify to personal loyalties. Thirdly, the figure of the bogus clergyman additionally helps to locate some of the least explored shifts in domesticity's sensationalization. A fraudulent figure of trust, he abuses his access to the intimacies of the home, and as he does so within the structures of business enterprises, an often curiously aborted sensationalism operates in a dual projection of the allure and fear of secrecy. Before interrogating the clergyman as a white-collar criminal in Yonge's novel, I shall begin by discussing the significance of this dual fascination for the redirection of secrecy's narrative potential.

Rethinking Victorian Sensational Secrets

Anticipating detective and crime fiction, the sensation genre pivoted on the suspended exposure of secrets. This unravelling was regularly accompanied by various red herrings, concealed by false clues, and further obfuscated by a proliferation of interconnected secrets. While this is clearly not the place to trace the remarkably diverse working out of sensational elements within the confines of domestic realism throughout the nineteenth century nor, conversely, the fictionalization of the various slippages in its definition within the Victorian sensation novel itself, I believe that it is vital first to highlight secrecy's centrality for debates on literary sensationalism. Mary Elizabeth Braddon's *Lady Audley's Secret* (1862), one of the most influential exponents of an emergent genre, provides a revealing point-of-entry into this discussion as it plays with a series of mysteries in the villainess's past, some of which are openly declared early on in the narrative, while the slow revelation of others adds ever-new plot twists until they are all safely locked away in an asylum abroad. Lady Audley's secret—her bigamy, her misrepresented origins, her concealed child, her attempted murder of her first husband, or her fear of hereditary insanity—is rendered deliberately ambiguous. Most importantly, while the revelation of private scandal may constitute the desirable climax, the Audleys' desire to keep the lady's crimes secret necessitates an alternative closure. The avoidance of scandal, "to save the *esclandre* of a Chancery suit," as an obliging doctor puts it before he signs the papers that consign the fake (for bigamous) Lady Audley into a "home" abroad, successfully precludes public disclosure. Such containment was to become a standard feature of Victorian sensation fiction.[2]

---

[2] Mary Elizabeth Braddon, *Lady Audley's Secret* (Ware: Wordsworth), 299.

After the publication of the first seminal sensation novels—now regularly evoked as the trinity of Braddon's *Lady Audley's Secret*, Ellen Wood's *East Lynne* (1861), and Wilkie Collins's *The Woman in White* (1860), which followed his experiments with sensational secrets in the 1850s—the concealed mystery indeed became so characteristic of the genre that a sensation novel without a secret was soon considered a contradiction in terms.[3] An anonymous reviewer of Braddon's *John Marchmont's Legacy* (1863) even questioned whether the novel could be said to belong to the genre at all since it contained "no grim secret vaguely hinted at," and this despite the fact that the novel sported the usual reliance "for effect on startling positions, sudden surprises, and a series of incidents rousing painful emotions," which allowed it to "be fairly classified with the author's preceding works."[4] This form of classification has persisted as a paradigmatic definition of the mid-Victorian sensation genre. Lyn Pykett has already stressed that "the sensation novel habitually focuses on the secrets and secret histories of women. All of Mary Elizabeth Braddon's early novels are structured around women with a concealed past."[5] Fashionable fiction of the "sensational sixties," in other words, was expected to sport a skeleton in the closet. Simultaneously evincing a growing self-reflexivity, it is in a tongue-in-cheek evocation of the desire for this proverbial family skeleton's dissection that Braddon's *Aurora Floyd* (1863) shows a would-be amateur detective compelled by "that ravenous curiosity common to people who live in other people's houses": "There were mysteries and secrets afloat, and she was not to be allowed to discover them; there was a skeleton in the house, and she was not to anatomize the bony horror."[6] If this anatomization formed a main driving force in narratives of detection, precisely such an experience of frustrated curiosity (on part of the reader as well as of would-be detective figures in the novel itself) could increasingly serve a narrative turning point.

The classic exponents of mid-Victorian sensation fiction, after all, allow the reader to partake of a fictional scandal that is revealed in the course of the narrative. It is thus that the secret, in all its slippages, drives the plot. When anti-sensational, domestic novelists combine interest in the new narrative structures of

---

[3] Sensation novels that promise a mystery in their titles range from Wilkie Collins's *Mr Wray's Cash Box; Or, the Mask and the Mystery* (1851), *Hide and Seek* (1854), and *The Dead Secret* (1857), to Mrs Henry (Ellen) Wood's later tales of detection such as "The Mystery at Number 7" (1877), and also Braddon's first full-scale novel, which had initially been serialized as *Three Times Dead; Or, The Secret of the Heath* in 1860 before its publication in book-form as *The Trail of the Serpent*.

[4] Review of *John Marchmont's Legacy*, by Mary Elizabeth Braddon. *Athenaeum* (December 12, 1863): 792.

[5] Lyn Pykett, *The "Improper" Feminine: The Women's Sensation Novel and the New Woman Writing* (London: Routledge, 1992), 84. Compare Tamar Heller, *Dead Secrets: Wilkie Collins and the Female Gothic* (New Haven: Yale UP, 1992) on the "paradigmatic instance" (1) of the intricate fraud that underpins the eponymous secret of Wilkie Collins's *The Dead Secret* (1857).

[6] Mary Elizabeth Braddon, *Aurora Floyd* (Oxford: Oxford UP, 1999), 177.

secrecy and detection with a rejection of quickly typecast sensational formulae, their rewriting of issues of secrecy, trust, and confidentiality perhaps expectedly become extended to discussions of the structuring of popular fiction itself. Taking the reader into their confidence, omniscient narrators of realist fiction increasingly eschew the usage of the sensational secret explicitly. In one of Trollope repeated stabs at the persistent popularity of the sensation craze in his late novel *Dr Wortle's School* (1881), suggests that, given his intention to concentrate entirely on characters' reactions to the moral dilemma of unwittingly committed bigamy, readers in need of an elusive secret to keep them interested should simply go elsewhere: "Therefore, put the book down if the revelation of some future secret be necessary for your enjoyment. Our mystery is going to be revealed in the next paragraph,—in the next half-dozen words. Mr and Mrs Peacocke were not man and wife."[7] Such an outright rejection of what the sensation genre had come to stand for had admittedly become easier thirty years after its heyday. Reactions during the sixties were necessarily more complicated. Yet it was their intrinsic ambiguity that was to generate some of the most revealing engagements with the narrative potential of Victorian sensationalism.

Recent criticism has begun to draw more attention to the changing adaptation of sensational elements in nineteenth-century domestic fiction. Winifred Hughes has already suggested that even though "in theory sensationalism was routinely denounced ... even Trollope and Eliot began to incorporate recognizably sensational elements into their own portrayals of everyday life."[8] The "craving for the genre," Deborah Wynne adds, was "so overwhelming that even the staunch practitioners and defenders of the domestic novel, Margaret Oliphant and Charlotte M. Yonge, were forced at the height of the craze to offer their readers sensational novels featuring murders and mysteries."[9] That Oliphant felt compelled to introduce a sensational subplot into *Salem Chapel* (1863) with the purpose to boost her sinking sales figures, for example, has almost become a critical commonplace in discussions of the nineteenth-century book market and the influences and instances of intertextuality it fostered.[10] Trollope's *The Eustace Diamonds* (1873) has similarly been read as a parody of the emergent detective fiction of the time in general, and the structures of Wilkie Collins's *The Moonstone* (1868) in particular.[11] Patrick

---

7 Anthony Trollope, *Dr Wortle's School* (London: Penguin, 1999), 25.

8 Winifred Hughes, *The Maniac in the Cellar: Sensation Novels of the 1860s* (Princeton: Princeton UP, 1980), 9.

9 Deborah Wynne, *The Sensation Novel and the Victorian Family Magazine* (Houndmills, Basingstoke: Palgrave, 2001), 3.

10 See Marlene Tromp's *The Private Rod: Marital Violence, Sensation, and the Law in Victorian Britain* (Charlottesville and London: UP of Virginia, 2000), especially on the prefiguring or reworking of sensation elements in Dickens's *Oliver Twist*, George Eliot's *Daniel Deronda*, and also Margaret Oliphant's venture into literary sensationalism in *Salem Chapel*. Tromp speaks of "generic boundaries slippages, the blurring of sensation and realism" (18).

11 Hughes, 168.

Brantlinger has termed it "a sort of inside-out 'sensation novel,' whose plot seems to reverse the mysteries or secrets involved in Wilkie Collins's *The Moonstone* or Mary Elizabeth Braddon's *Lady Audley's Secret*."[12] Trollope's most pointed invocations of detective plots, however, are already to be found in *He Knew He Was Right* (1869). With its obtrusive "private detective," Trollope's emphatically anti-sensational take on lurid descriptions of an often heavily sensationalized, if not idealized, madness simultaneously rejects the attractiveness of the emergent genre's detective figures most directly.[13] As a former policeman is employed by a pitiful monomaniac to spy on a wrongly suspected wife, he is guilty first and foremost of meddling in private affairs. The sanctioning of such interference is in itself a symptom of the husband's insanity.[14]

In negotiating such ongoing re-engagements with the sensational and the problems of its attempted containment, the various ways of, and reasons for, exposing secrets fascinatingly surface as a complicated narrative strategy in Victorian domestic fiction. What is of most interest here is that when secrets are unfolded—rather than shared from the beginning—even this disclosure is chiefly anticlimactic, with the emphasis often resting on a reassertion of moral values or domestic ideals. Conversely, especially didactic, religious domestic fiction such as Yonge's renders exposure the more necessary for the full acknowledgement of (moral) failure, whereas sensation fiction remains more interested in the perpetuation of secrecy, of the fissures in the social fabric, in the network that Jane Austen had so pointedly termed "a neighbourhood of voluntary spies … where novels and newspapers lay every thing open," as the most effective prevention of the Gothic at home.[15] To an extent, keeping home affairs private even (or especially) after the secrets have been revealed to the reader admittedly forms a common plot-twist in nineteenth-century fiction. Thus, a compromise is struck with Oliver's half-brother Monks in *Oliver Twist* (1839), and Tom Gradgrind's escape is triumphantly facilitated at the end of *Hard Times* (1854). These examples

---

[12] Patrick Brantlinger, *The Reading Lesson: The Threat of Mass Literacy in Nineteenth-Century British Fiction* (Bloomington: Indiana UP, 1998), 136.

[13] Mutual allegations of madness propel the plots of various sensation novels. Lady Audley's dismissal of the detective work undertaken by her husband's nephew as a symptom of monomania exemplifies this most clearly, but there is never any doubt about the monomaniac's delusions in Trollope's novel.

[14] Looking back at decades of sensation fiction's impact on the book market in his *Autobiography* (1883), Trollope eventually eschewed artificial lines of demarcation between "sensational and anti-sensational [or] realistic" novels and writers ([London: Trollope Society, 1999], 140). His engagement with new detective plots during the 1860s was directed particularly against the meddling in private affairs that is already presented as a complex, ambiguous, and hence perhaps easily misread problem in *The Moonstone*. Compare D.A. Miller, "From *roman-policier* to *roman-police*: Wilkie Collins's *The Moonstone*," *Novel* 13, no. 2 (1980), 156.

[15] Jane Austen, *Northanger Abbey, Lady Susan, The Watsons, Sanditon* (Oxford: Oxford UP, 2003), 145.

all predate the sensation craze and hence also its dramatization of what could be done with such domestic or familial self-policing. The ultimate expulsion of Lady Audley shows the dual power with which concealment becomes invested in the "sensational sixties." What Karen Chase and Michael Levenson have diagnosed as a "spectacle of intimacy" created by a demand for the publication—the rendering public—of the private is thereby imbued with additional titillations. Chase and Levenson suggest that in a climate of publicized scandal, "the Victorian investment in family life unfolds in the awareness that at any moment it can turn into the antifamily of popular sensation."[16] The secret's very containment trades on an intimacy with the reader: it is shared to be contained once more. As disclosure is refused to a general public, the novel's readership is proffered the semblance of an exclusive spectacle of revealed intimacy.

In order to reconsider the representations of secrecy and public exposure both as providing a popular narrative structure and as centrally engaging with a concept that becomes invested with moral ambiguities in the popular culture of the time, I shall therefore direct attention specifically to the different narrative uses of trial scenes in mid-century domestic and sensational fiction. Recent studies that read developments in nineteenth-century literature and law side by side have repeatedly stressed the connections between their epistemological and representational issues. The matter of influence was by no means limited to one-way traffic. Fiction preceded the legal defence of the accused so that "the comparatively late appearance of defence lawyers in trials for felony may have afforded authors the imaginative space to explore narratives of exculpation."[17] Novelists, therefore, "experimented with the inclusion or exclusion of different voices and different types of evidence whilst criticizing the law's methods of representing reality."[18] Alexander Welsh has already suggested that the novel genre as it developed in the course of the eighteenth and nineteenth centuries "may be seen to come to the aid of its subjects a couple of generations before the criminal law afforded much of a defence."[19] What is more, as alternative arrangements of evidence (external facts and witness accounts) in narrative forms, novels registered the loss of confidence in circumstantial evidence. This awareness of incongruities in legal

---

[16] Karen Chase and Michael Levenson, *The Spectacle of Intimacy: A Public Life for the Victorian Family* (Princeton: Princeton UP, 2000), 7.

[17] Jan-Melissa Schramm, *Testimony and Advocacy in Victorian Law, Literature, and Theology* (Cambridge: Cambridge UP, 2000), 6. Although Schramm cautions against all too easy alignments between literary and legal texts, she argues that it was not simply that the criminal trial became "an important fact-finding model for authors" (23).

[18] Schramm, 66.

[19] Alexander Welsh, *Strong Representations: Narrative and Circumstantial Evidence in England* (Baltimore: John Hopkins UP, 1992), 11.

procedures opened up a new, even more self-reflexive, approach to the accusation and specifically the exculpation of criminals in fiction.[20]

The alignments of the criminal trial with the revaluation of fictional narrative were premised on the concept of their substitution of each other. They constituted alternative forms of the same development. In a detailed study of these interactions between law and literature, Jan-Melissa Schramm has suggested that fictional representation was evoked as replacing, while replicating, legal methods.[21] Neither, legal trials, like the incompetent professional (as opposed to more successful amateur) detective figures, are often incapable of arriving at the right conclusion. Nor is the delineation of public exposure necessarily in the interest of sensational writing. On the contrary, it is often deliberately avoided. The containment of concealed crimes hence becomes part of the resolution, frequently leaving novels open-ended or fissured by uncertainties about questionable legal institutions. In its place, retribution is exacted through a *dues-ex-machina* realization of poetic justice. Braddon's Lady Audley is not the only criminal character who receives the most appropriate, albeit not lawful, punishment by being turned into a family secret. In Wilkie Collins's *The Woman in White*, Sir Percival burns to death in the attempt to destroy the records of his illegitimacy and fraud; in *The Moonstone*, the real thief of the eponymous Indian diamond is murdered by the three nameless Indians who have come to retrieve it from the domestic space of the English Great House. Bringing the criminal to justice is not the issue at hand in this first fully-fledged detective novel. Instead, it engages with the processes of truth-finding, replicating in its juxtaposition of witness accounts a trial that never takes place. Yet spying at home therein often features as a threat rather than an investigating or even corrective force.[22] This casts an ambiguous light on the detective figure's own reconnaissance work, which symptomatically becomes thematized in popular fiction at large. In sensational narratives of detection, competing forms of exposure regularly lay open the intimacies of the Victorian family, including the seemingly

---

20 Schramm, 61. Compare Welsh, *Representations*, 17. Dickens's *Bleak House* (1853) perhaps most memorably attacks legal procedures beyond the more sensational interest of criminal cases. Compare Schramm on the fictional commentary on legal reform in the works of Dickens and George Eliot (104). See also Tromp on the "conversation between sensation and the law" in mid-nineteenth-century discourses (4).

21 As Schramm emphasizes, it is "a common fictional device for an author to explain why his or her tale could not be heard in a court of law or why the protagonists were seeking literary recognition rather than a judicial remedy" (11). Schramm mentions Richardson's classic epistolary novel Clarissa as well as Wilkie Collins's *The Woman in White*.

22 Lisa Surridge suggests that the confusion between private and political spying in *The Woman in White*, for example, indicates that the intruder at home at once replicates and outdoes the figure of the political traitor (as both embodied by that sensational arch-villain, Count Fosco): in this "drama of domestic secrets and revelations, the political spy causes nothing like the frisson of the domestic spy or court witness, from whom private conduct is never secure" (*Bleak Houses: Marital Violence in Victorian Fiction* [Athens: Ohio UP, 2005], 146).

inviolable spaces of the Great House. And yet, they become encapsulated once more, framed by narratives that seek to contain family secrets.

What renders this containment additionally problematic is the fact that it frequently remains premised on an obfuscation of legal justice. Public exposure, whether at a trial, through the press, or in the course of an official arrest, becomes displaced by an exacting of personal revenge and thereby impels further concealment often even for the sake of protecting the guilty protagonists or of circumventing a lack of legally acknowledged evidence. Hence "the *telos* of the plot is generated by its very dissimilarity to a trial; the conception of law as foil in turn liberates fiction to pursue its own idea of justice."[23] When it comes to the involvement of business secrets, of large-scale financial crime, or of the infiltration of the home through such criminal actions, this disengagement from the power of the law is complicated further. As an illustrative example, Sir Percival's exposed illegitimacy in *The Woman in White* proves him to be a fraud in more senses than one, however who exactly has been defrauded by the forgery of his parents' marriage record is not an issue. What the fraud's exposure re-establishes is the identity of the eponymous Women in White. It remains a private affair. If the law is partly instrumental in restoring Laura Fairlie's claims, it does so quietly, not as part of a public spectacle. In this, it is significant to note that the dispute about her fortune has nothing to do with the invalidated baronetcy. In other words, fraud at home is taken care of privately. Lawyers, like the physician in *Lady Audley's Secret*, operate as convenient tools, largely behind closed doors, in the homes of those who pay them. It is this protection of family secrets through an economizing on truth values, more even than the laying bare of the private, that is taken up as an issue for renewed investigation in anti-sensational fiction.

Sensationalizing the Clergyman's Business

Since they extend across the porous boundaries of the domestic and the marketplace, narratives of fraud lend themselves particularly well to such a reinvestigation of moral economies. The abuse of the clergyman's position and credentials is in itself an intrinsically sensational device, yet the fraudulent clergyman combines the threat of finance capitalism with the power of the clergy. The new financial plots that take precedence in the fiction of the second half of the century move away from issues of inheritance to explore instead "matters involving personal agency and individual will, like financial temptation and fiscal responsibility."[24] The fake clergyman functions within this shift as the insider fraudster *par excellence*. The duality of business and domesticity as colliding, or mutually infiltrating, spheres of life that the Victorians would rather have had separate, thereby becomes newly interrogated as financial exploitation of religion can be seen to converge with

---

[23] Schramm, 12.

[24] Mary Poovey, "Writing about Finance in Victorian England: Disclosure and Secrecy in the Culture of Investment," *Victorian Studies* 45, no. 1 (2002): 33.

the plotting of white-collar crime. What Yonge's fiction additionally helps to focus as it exemplifies the intricacies of literary sensationalism's adaptation, or domestication, is this fusion of traditional and new figures associated with both secrecy and conspiracy. More than a simple importation of material of sensational potential, the consequent reactivation of anti-Catholic typecasting not only operates through an eerily apposite projection on a seemingly transparent, but to the layman (and, in Yonge's novels, in particular the laywoman) opaque financial system. This system is shrouded not so much in acknowledged secrecy than in misleading incomprehensibility.[25] Introducing an additional level of complication, this updating of a cultural stereotype is embedded in narratives that seek to propose a newly forming Anglo-Catholicism.

In a recent study of anti-Catholic topoi in Victorian literature, Susan Griffin has linked the traditional figure of the infiltrating Jesuitical priest to the emergent "figure of the Confidence Man." Both reflect "uneasiness about identity and authenticity" that is rampant in a newly mobile, urban, society.[26] This linkage between financial and religious institutionalization mystifies the workings of finance capitalism, while underscoring the micropolitics of power in institutionalized religion. This also explains the reappearance of what Griffin terms "the Confidence Man's iconographic ancestor, the Jesuit" in popular fiction, just at a time when white-collar criminals seemed to be taking center-stage as some of the Victorian novel's most memorable villains.[27] In a pointed critique of social institutions, the infiltration of the home could be embodied by the speculator as a promulgator of Mammonism and hence as the prevailing religion of modern society. Exploited trust and (exploited) confession became the crux of this fusion.

Debates on the introduction of the confessional in Tractarianism, or Anglo-Catholicism, played a particularly ambiguous role within such revivals of the Jesuit as a stock-figure of traditional Gothic. On the one hand, it reinforced the sensationalization of the clergyman in Domestic Gothic. As Mark Knight and Emma Mason have shown, fears of "male confessors cajoling female penitents to betray their sins and sexual secrets" were not only central to anti-Catholic propaganda, but connected Tractarianism as well "to the gothic, grotesque, and supernatural."[28] Confession was considered a particularly disturbing, even invidious, form of infiltration in that it presupposed willing participation in disclosing family secrets.

---

[25] Although David Vincent focuses exclusively on official, or state, secrecy, he also emphasizes that "[n]either the development nor the significance of government controls can be properly understood without a parallel examination of professional, commercial, welfare, and domestic secrecy, and what Harriet Martineau in a famous attack [1859] called the 'Secret Organisation of Trades'" (*The Culture of Secrecy: Britain 1832–1998* [Oxford: Oxford UP, 1998], 17–18).

[26] Susan Griffin, *Anti-Catholicism and Nineteenth-Century Fiction* (Cambridge: Cambridge UP, 2004), 8.

[27] Griffin, 8.

[28] Mark Knight and Emma Mason, *Nineteenth-Century Religion and Literature* (Oxford: Oxford UP, 2006), 97.

Hence, it pinpointed the widening fissures in the boundaries between Roman and Anglo-Catholicism as part of a larger cultural interpenetration. As Patrick O'Malley has pointed out, "the particular contours of eighteenth- and early nineteenth-century Gothic literary tropes and narratives provided a language for a *specific* cultural epistemology during and after the Oxford Movement; *both* Protestant and Catholic writers relied on Gothic resonances for powerful rhetorical support."[29] In addition, in mid-Victorian Britain, the growing attraction of ritual and a reliance on the power of the priest-figure were seen as specifically anti-domestic and anti-familial. Fear of the disclosure of secrets in the confessional came to rival anxieties about public spectacle as authorized by the law or exploited by the press. On the other hand, confession became a particularly controversial issue in Anglo-Catholic discourse because of a twofold "exposure" that might moreover facilitate an infiltration of "Romanism." Confession continued to be feared as a violation of privacy, and it meant a form of infection through the confessor's influence.

The clergyman exposed as a fraud and a fraudster consequently did more than simply export these topoi into a modern world ruled by finance capitalism. Through projection onto financial temptation, the feared eroticism and anti-familial propaganda associated with the confessional became replaced by what was considered exerting a much larger and more disruptive impact on society. In popular fiction, both the Jesuit and the confidence trickster were shown to trade on duplicity, and on the usefulness of the double life. But if this may seem a revived traditional Gothic structure, it was specifically the mobility and instability of modern society that was felt to generate the ease with which secret identities could be created, perpetuated, and made to disappear just as quickly. As Welsh has pointed out in his study of blackmail, the new transportation and communication technologies created a social and geographical mobility that provided new opportunities for secrecy and thereby also the very preconditions for blackmail as "an opportunity afforded to everyone by communication of knowledge at a distance."[30] Railroad travel, for example, likewise rendered the bigamist's simultaneous maintenance of two households all the more feasible. In other words, a double life exploded social order and yet was also feared as a natural outgrowth of modernity. This marked it out as one of the most ambiguous aspects of the Victorian sensation novel's definitional—Domestic Gothic.

The fake clergyman in Yonge's *Clever Woman*, Mauleverer *alias* Maddox, tops this oscillation between two households, as he trades on a High Anglican

---

[29] Patrick O'Malley, Catholicism, *Sexual Deviance, and Victorian Gothic Culture* (Cambridge: Cambridge UP, 2006), 6.

[30] Alexander Welsh, *George Eliot and Blackmail* (Cambridge, MA: Harvard UP, 1985), 58. Secrecy became a refuge from the growing prevalence of information (and surveillance) technologies. Following Welsh in suggesting that social mobility compelled individuals to conceal information about their past, John Kucich speaks of the new forms of concealment as "a counteruse of knowledge" (*The Power of Lies: Transgression in Victorian Fiction* [Ithaca: Cornell UP, 1994], 20).

community in one part of the country, while setting himself up "as a popular lecturer upon philanthropical subjects" (390) in another. These "haunts [where] it seems that he plays the philanthropical lecturer" (364) for the benefit of a respectable widow and a dissenting minister whose "faith in him was genuine" (390) are to serve as his backup as he negotiates two identities, neither of which are genuine. That this twofold disguise imposes on divergent religious communities at once exonerates both and illuminates the dangers of his camouflage. At one point, the town's gossip symptomatically alleges that Rachel Curtis is "fostering a Jesuit in disguise" (321). If this is in part a stab at sensationalizing circulation of scandal that capitalizes on the absurdity of the suggestion, it also ominously foreshadows the fatal repercussions this modern-day Jesuitical swindler has on the community. Although double lives recur in sensation fiction under various guises, most often perhaps as part of bigamy plots, the counterfeit clergyman also stands in a tradition of religious hypocrites, a tradition that Maddox takes to its extremes.

The promulgation of a specific religious doctrine under an assumed name therein literalizes the religious hypocrisy that "sermonizing" characters embody in Victorian fiction. Prefigured by oily Chadband in Dickens's *Bleak House* and Obadiah Slope in Trollope's *Barchester Towers* (both 1853), deceitful or manipulative preachers range from the philanthropist who turns out to be the real thief of the eponymous diamond in *The Moonstone* to the converted priest in Collins's later *The Black Robe* (1881), a blatantly anti-Catholic work, in which the untransformed Gothic figure of the Jesuit seems a curious anachronism. Slope, moreover, is anticipated by an equally obnoxious character in *The Vicar of Wrexhill* (1837) by Fanny Trollope, Anthony's mother. In Amelia Edwards's *Hand and Glove* (1858), a counterfeit clergyman is exposed as an absconded speculator. He is revealingly taken for "a Jesuit in disguise."[31] With pointed stabs at the emergent detective genre, Trollope's *The Eustace Diamonds* introduces the fraudulent Rev. Emilius alias Yosef Mealyus, a bigamous bogus preacher of indeterminate origins, who is said to be a converted "Bohemian Jew … an impostor who has come over here to make a fortune," and who has "a wife in Prague, and probably two or three elsewhere."[32] *Phineas Redux* (1873–4) sees him convicted of murder, committed with the help of a "Bohemian key" (an English latchkey duplicated abroad) and a "foreign bludgeon."[33] This excess of foreignness is counterpoised by the equally indeterminate amateur detective, Madame Max, an English-born businesswoman from Vienna, and widow of a Jewish banker.[34] In Yonge's adaptation of these plot devices as part of her intricately embedded religious agenda, a counterfeit clergyman with a history of white-collar crimes is brought to trial at the turning-

[31] Amelia Edwards, *Hand and Glove* (London: Rubicon, 2000), 122.

[32] Anthony Trollope, *The Eustace Diamonds* (London: Penguin, 2004), 767.

[33] Anthony Trollope, *Phineas Redux* (Oxford: Oxford UP, 2000), vol.2, 238.

[34] Later examples include the suspiciously charming Rev. Miles Mirabel in Collins's *I Say No* (1884) and the pairing of fake and real clergymen in G. K. Chesterton's "The Blue Cross" (1910).

point of the heroine's maturation. Via the tripartite progression of failure, suffering, and redemption the linear structure of detective plots is counteracted. It is a progression that works through moral failure and atonement. It manifests itself as an emotional and religious crisis that is mapped on Rachel's body to climax in physical suffering that allows her redemption.

Yonge more than once describes trials in her novels, but *Clever Woman* is of significance precisely as it pivots on the moral value of exposure. By setting the salutary effects of the very humiliation brought about by public disclosure into the foreground, it utilizes sensationalism for a religious agenda, promoting the latter while adapting the former to an emphatically domestic, moral structure. Although John Keble, one of the founders of the Oxford Movement, and Yonge's literary as well as religious mentor, had cautioned her not to revert to explicit preaching in her fiction, it has been remarked that Yonge saw herself as a "self-appointed popularizer of Tractarianism."[35] Her religious orientation and her antifeminism have consequently not only obstructed her inclusion in the ongoing reassessments of "forgotten" popular women writers. They have also been identified as specifically anti-sensational. It has only been recently, within a more encompassing reconsideration of the integration of sensational elements into domestic realism, that her often pointed use of literary sensationalism has begun to be reassessed.[36] The bibliography of Victorian sensational fiction compiled by Andrew Maunder thus spans works from the mid-1850s into the 1890s. It comprises writers so far not commonly associated with the genre, including a number of Yonge's novels.[37]

The suggestively titled *The Trial* (1864), the sequel to Yonge's immensely popular family chronicle, *The Daisy Chain* (1856), has thus recently received more attention because of its strikingly sensational plot developments. Although one of

---

[35] Kim Wheatley, "Death and Domestication in Charlotte M. Yonge's *The Clever Woman of the Family*," *Studies in English Literature* 36, no. 4 (1996): 895.

[36] Although Yonge has until recently been marginalized even in discussions of "rediscovered" women writers, critics have begun to remark on ambiguities in her representation of institutionalized religion and women. As Catherine Sandbach-Dahlstrom has put it, "[a]t an imaginative level Charlotte Yonge, as implied author, has access to patterns of thought and feeling that do not accord with the ideology she sets out to preach" (*Be Good Sweet Maid: Charlotte Yonge's Domestic Fiction: A Study in Dogmatic Purpose and Fictional Form* [Stockholm: Almqvist & Wiksell International, 1984], 107). Still, Valerie Sanders speaks of the "unease" Yonge causes "in the modern reader—even in those not immune to her appeal—because of her apparent endorsement of conservative, anti-feminist values, and her distrust of ambition" ("'All-sufficient to one another'? Charlotte Yonge and the family chronicle," in *Popular Victorian Women Writers*, ed. Kay Boardman and Shirley Jones [Manchester: Manchester UP, 2004], 90). Compare also Talia Schaffer, "The Mysterious *Magnum Bonum*: Fighting to Read Charlotte Yonge," *Nineteenth-Century Literature* 55, no. 2 (2000): 245.

[37] Andrew Maunder, ed. *Varieties of Women's Sensation Fiction: 1855-1890. Vol.1: Sensationalism and The Sensation Debate* (London: Pickering & Chatto, 2004). Maunder lists *The Trial* (1864), *The Dove in the Eagle's Nest* (1866), and *Lady Hester* (1873).

its central plotlines revolves on a wrongful conviction for murder, critics agree that the evocation of sensationalism is not only deliberately subdued, but also self-reflexively integrated in order to be worked out anew. Gavin Budge has stressed that even when they "incorporate incidents which might find a place in a sensation novel," Yonge's works in general "resolutely downplay such elements in favour of a concentration on [domestic detail]."[38] June Sturrock notably refers to *The Trial* as a "quasi-sensation" novel that operates through "the uneasy intermeshing of public and private—family chronicle as sensation novel, domestic drama as national news."[39] In confining the murder, the trial, and the incipient detective plot to male protagonists, Sturrock suggests, the novel circumvents sensation fiction's focus on female transgression.[40] The wrongful conviction occurs early on in the plot and is lifted in a vaguely evoked, offstage, procedure after the real culprit's death abroad. The main interest instead rests on the reactions of the legal system's victim and further on his relationships with other members of the community. Even his release, after three years of penal servitude, is poignantly anticlimactic. So far from offering a prison break, it is a release to confusion and slow recovery by the means of "grace," of religious consolation that counterpoises both the damage the legal system has done to the wrongly convicted hero and any easy dismissal of his emotional, or spiritual, trials as the symptoms of insanity. Whereas sensation novels notoriously trade on the exposure of clinical diagnoses of madness, Yonge has one of the strikingly few positively presented physicians of Victorian literature freely acknowledge "the temptation to us doctors to ascribe too much to the physical and too little to the moral."[41] In short, the trial itself unearths nothing; legal justice cannot be trusted; the medical profession is as incompetent as the legal. What remains is, in accordance with Yonge's religious vision, the redemptive potential of suffering and, above all, the power of "grace" to provide the necessary strength: "I do verily believe that all the anguish you describe could and would have been insanity if grace had not been given you to conquer it."[42]

If suffering is likewise salutary in *Clever Woman*, exposure in public through a juxtaposed series of trials plays a crucial role in facilitating it. In *The Trial*, failed legal procedure helps to create the circumstances of suffering, and a

---

[38] Gavin Budge, "Realism and Typology in Charlotte M. Yonge's The Heir of Redclyffe," *Victorian Literature and Culture* 31 (2003): 204.

[39] June Sturrock, "Murder, Gender, and Popular Fiction by Women in the 1860s: Braddon, Oliphant, Yonge," in *Victorian Crime, Madness and Sensation*, ed. Andrew Maunder and Grace Moore (Aldershot: Ashgate, 2004), 79.

[40] In carefully differentiating between the sensational elements the novel takes up (murder, trials) and those it rejects (female dissidence), Sturrock suggests that the novel "masculinises" its central murder trial by avoiding putting women in the dock: "Reluctant to address commonplace female fictional delinquency (bigamy, adultery), Yonge turns to violent crime, and keeps herself in the current market with a brutal murder" (75).

[41] Charlotte Yonge, *The Trial; Or, More Links of the Daisy Chain* (Doylestown: Wildside, n.d.), 371.

[42] Yonge, *Trial*, 371.

clinical approach exacerbates its effects by being just as incapable of proffering any solution. In this, the novel ironically becomes more akin to the fully-fledged sensational representation of wrongful incarceration (of suspected criminals or the allegedly insane) in the fiction of the time.[43] What is of vital importance to the reworking of the trial as a sensational formula, however, is the failure of a cursorily evoked detective plot, which deliberately undercuts the familiar substitution of amateur reconnaissance for professional police work and criminal justice. Despite the protagonists' suspicions, speculations, and systematic research, involving even the use of a microscope to analyze blood samples, their investigations remain as fruitless as the lawyers' attempts until a providential disclosure of the much-needed evidence three years later.

Published a year after *The Trial*, *Clever Woman* redresses the resigned denunciation of the failed legal system in the earlier novel; also significant is the investigation of personally involved amateur detectives that brings the real culprit to justice. Although the law serves as a workable instrument, it needs to be carefully deployed to be of any use. The trial scenes' dual function effectively welds together the novel's main plots. The degree of Rachel's unwitting culpability prevents the villain's conviction, yet his exposure in the process makes possible his conviction for past crimes. Since their disclosure sets to right a web of characters, the publicity of the heroine's confession doubly supplies a catalyst. In the context of Yonge's religious vision, Rachel's trials (in all its connotations) therein appositely operate as a cleansing experience. At the same time, the exploitation which her "self-sufficient" enterprises are shown to have invited brings an absconded fraudster to justice. This lifts suspicion from the wrongfully accused brother of the novel's second heroine, Ermine Williams, Rachel's less opinionated, more selfless, "clever woman." The fake clergyman, it transpires, has a history as a white-collar criminal, having impoverished the Williamses through risky speculation and fraudulent transactions, so that he can, years later, be convicted of "very extensive frauds upon Miss Williams's brother" (406). Having fled the country "under some terrible suspicion of dishonesty" (57), Edward Williams has left his sisters as well as his young daughter to a life of poverty, social obscurity, and illness—to a range of distresses, in fact. This foreshadows the salutary effect suffering will have on the eponymous clever woman of the family.

Like Rachel, Edward Williams has facilitated, to an extent impelled, fraud at home and in business. His agent, Maddox, "knew the state of the business; Edward did not" (123). So if Maddox's first trial exposes the self-satisfied way in which Rachel has set out "to battle every suggestion with principles picked up from every catch-penny periodical, things she does not half understand" (167), his second trial

---

[43] As I have shown in more detail elsewhere, the novel thereby posits an alternative—spiritual—approach as a counterpoise to the threats of clinical simplifications and consequent policing of emotional distress. Compare Tamara S. Wagner, "Depressed Spirits and Failed Crisis Management: Charlotte Yonge's Sensationalization of the Religious Family," *Victorians Institute Journal* 36 (2008): 275–302.

similarly reveals "a good deal about culpable negligence almost inviting fraud" (497) on Edward's part. It is in a partly parodic invocation of the sensation novel's clever villain that the convicted fraudster, standing exposed with "a meanness and vulgarity in his appearance" now he "has entirely dropped his *alias*" (494), takes "a kind of pleasure in explaining the whole web … with vanity at his own ingenuity" (500), both with reference to the elaborate deception he practiced in Edward's business and to its almost comically domesticated version in Rachel's homemade journal and plans for charity institutions: "he really could hardly have helped himself; he had only to stand still and let poor Rachel deceive herself, and the whole concern was in a manner thrust upon him" (501).

Further linking different forms of fraud the counterfeit clergyman and the white-collar criminal are merged to create a doubly sensationalized figure. The twofold exposure of Maddox's fraudulence and Rachel's misguided self-publication is appropriately achieved through his plagiarized contribution to her "prospectuses of a Journal of Female Industry" (311). In an attempt to cover up his abuse of the charity school he has set up with funds raised by Rachel, he forges woodcuts to pass them off as the children's work. Furthermore, this is to cover up the fact that he has really been exploiting them by forcing children ostensibly liberated from arduous lace-making to produce even more in secret. Pasted prints, these pictures become exposed as "mere fabrications to deceive Rachel" (335). This exposure leads to an unannounced inspection of the "school," which contrasts pointedly with an earlier visit during which its real function is carefully concealed. For one of the overworked girls, this liberation comes too late. She dies of diphtheria, which Rachel contracts at the child's deathbed. As Robert Lee Wolff summarizes, "[a] clever swindler in pseudoclerical dress deceives [Rachel], misappropriates her money, and starves and mistreats the poor girls, one of whom must die before Rachel begins to think that she may have been wrong in her goals and methods."[44]

Yet as the first trial reveals, Maddox cannot be convicted either for embezzlement or child abuse "because of the looseness of the arrangements" (387). This adds another layer to Rachel's public humiliation: "Here was she, the Clever Woman of the family, shown in open court to have been so egregious a dupe that the deceiver could not even be punished" (387). Similarly, she cannot take credit for the retrieval of the title-deeds of the property on which the institution is erected. They are only safe because, as her future husband puts it with pointed irony, "[l]awyers don't put people's title-deeds into such dangerous keeping; the true cheese is safe locked up in a tin box in Mr Martin's chambers in London" (432). Rachel, therefore, has not been able to hand over important papers because she has only a copy. The obscurity of unexamined institutions, both of business regulations and of doctrinal orthodoxies, makes such deception all too easy, although in both cases, it is chiefly Rachel's self-satisfied refusal to seek any guidance from professionals—lawyers

[44] Robert Lee Wolff, *Gains and Losses: Novels of Faith and Doubt in Victorian England* (New York: Garland, 1977), 137.

and priests—that has facilitated it. The fake priest's series of false identities, in other words, aligns various forms of fraud, while it assists in the exposure of degrees of individual accountability.

What becomes crucial in the context of Yonge's religious agenda, in fact, is that the sensationalized counterfeit clergyman also acts as a manifestation of Rachel's doctrinal confusion. That "there may have been much disturbance of her opinions" (417) is a euphemism of doctrinal carelessness rather than of religious doubt. It is the same carelessness that renders her open to abuse in financial projects. The untrustworthiness of this indeterminate stranger is established clearly from his first appearance onwards: clad in "a sort of easy clerical-looking dress ... his dress that of a clergyman at large, his face keen" (206–7). His assumed name is as fanciful as it is misleading: "The card was written, not engraved, the name 'Rd. R.H.C.L. Mauleverer;' and a discussion ensued whether the first letters stood for Richard or for Reverend, and if he could be unconscionable enough to have five initials" (210). The first warning sign is his use of unorthodoxy as camouflage. Although he admits that he is "unhappily not in orders" (228), as he puts it, he also makes it understood that he is "a clerical gentleman who had opinions" (211). His letters of reference are glaringly obscure, including "some testimonials from a German university, and letters from German professors in a compromise between English and German hand, looking impossible to read, also the neat writing and wavy-marked paper of American professors and philanthropists," as well as "some distinguished names of persons interested in Social Science" (230). Indeterminacy of origins is a common characterization device of Victorian villains, yet that Rachel fails to question his identity or agenda is pointedly connected to her wilful dismissal of doctrinal uncertainties: "Modern research has introduced so many variations of thought, that no good work would be done at all if we required of our fellow-labourers perfect similarity of speculative belief" (226). Embedded in Yonge's unfaltering loyalty to the Anglican Church, this is a dangerous belief. The villain's euphemistically described unorthodoxy at once masks and reveals a larger duplicity.

It is therefore particularly significant that the clearest warning about undue, even dangerous, confidence is articulated by Ermine as the daughter of a clergyman as well as the sister of an ingenuous inventor exploited and abused by a fraudulent speculator. Her comment on the suffering caused by "trusting too implicitly ... without thorough knowledge of a person's antecedents" (226), foreshadows the later identification of the bogus clergyman Mauleverer with the speculator Maddox. Ermine, moreover, is a quietly resigned, yet intellectually alert, sofa-bound young woman, whose anonymous contributions to well-reviewed journals provide an important counterpoise to Rachel's own bungling attempts to place her articles or to edit her own magazine. This juxtaposition indeed clarifies one of the central ambiguities in Yonge's representation of writing women. What distinguishes Rachel from Ermine is not only her inexperience, but her self-satisfaction. So far from agreeing with what is termed conservative society's "instinctive avoidance of an intellectual woman," the novel endorses "the simple manner that goes with real superiority," "genuine humbleness and gentleness … The very word humility presupposes depth" (175). Ermine's fiancé revealingly considers Rachel "so intolerable" exactly because "she is a grotesque caricature of what [Ermine] used to be" (167). Rachel needs the public humiliation at the trial to teach her such humility so that she can then proceed with her work.

This indisputably evinces an antifeminist condemnation of unguided women engaging in business ventures as Rachel is handed over into the care of a husband who moreover conveniently impels her experience of moral conversion by discussing the specificities of the Anglican faith at her sickbed. In the Ermine-subplot, however, female protagonists are central to the reworked detective plot. Ermine herself leads one of the most fulfilled and active lives of disabled characters in Victorian literature. It is the ignominy of her brother's wrongful accusation and, to an extent, their consequent poverty that barred her from marrying, not the fact that she is lame after a domestic accident. Enabled to marry after the villain's successful conviction, she continues writing and acts as adoptive mother both to Rose, her brother's practically abandoned daughter, and to an orphaned infant.[45] In addition, Rose is the one who first identifies Maddox as her father's fraudulent partner. Acting inadvertently as the perhaps youngest female detective figure of Victorian fiction, this otherwise dreamy, quiet, eight-year-old girl also displays a useful form of strong-mindedness in court that contrasts pointedly with Rachel's confusion. Additionally testifying to the simultaneity of Maddox's break of trust in domestic and business arrangements, it transpires that he has, with the assistance of a nursery maid he seduces, frightened the child with threats written in phosphorescent letters so that she will not mention his violation of his business partner's domesticity.

What remains the most striking, however, is that the child's clear, calm, witness account both at the first, locally held, trial and at the pageantry of the county assizes condemns Maddox the most decisively. By contrast, Rachel's "evidence broke down completely," rendering "the absurdity of her whole conduct … palpable" (400). In the novel's most moralizing moment, sandwiched between detailed accounts of court procedures, it is hoped that it will be "a lesson" (400) to her. Rachel's real trial consists of having to come to terms with its humbling effects. Chapter 22, "The After-Clap," details Rachel's lingering nightmares of "tiers of gazing faces, and curious looks turned on her" (401). In what forms Yonge's most effective and persistent reworking of sensationalism, in fact, her representation of various "trials" focus on their lasting repercussions, on the aftershocks, and the distress caused by lingering trauma. Rachel suffers most from her emotional reactions to public exposure: "The crush of public censure was not at the moment so overwhelming as the strange morbid effect of having been the focus of those

[45] This child's fashionable mother has died of carelessness in falling, while pregnant, over a croquet hoop that symbolizes her social entanglement. This subplot additionally underlines the novel's exploration of intersecting domestic carelessness and social self-importance.

many, many, glances" (401). Rachel's interlinked emotional, physical, and spiritual trials are climactic in the novel. Her participation in a legal trial, moreover, culminates in a fainting fit (of which she is very much ashamed) and temporarily enfeebles her in order to prepare for a traditional sickbed conversion supervised by her husband.

This assertion of the helpfulness of institutional, professional, and indeed patriarchal authorities whose business it is to advise the layman (and perhaps especially the laywoman) indisputably cuts short the transgressive potential associated with sensation fiction. Yet the adoption of elements of literary sensationalism to articulate a specific doctrine the more effectively testifies to their adaptability. The sensational secret is realized with a particular poignancy through the fusion of white-collar crime and doctrinal misrepresentation. It contains a dual warning that links together the demands of business and of institutionalized religion in the exposure of the abused charity project. Although professional advice and its institutionalization stand triumphant in a pointed generalization of the Tractarian emphasis on official guidance, this reliance needs to be met with a transparency in business that extends to charitable organizations. It is therein of particular significance that the exposure of business crimes rids the community of the fraudulent would-be clergyman. The trial scenes work together with Rachel's familial "confession" to her future husband to bring out both the narrative significance and the moral evaluation of exposure. In Yonge's domestic novel, safety (especially from willful misrepresentation) can be found in community networks. Secrecy is the fraudster's weapon publicly exploded. In their redeployment, sensational detective plots serve a different function, as the domestic is ironically preserved best through public exposure that at the same time forms a personal trial. Although secrecy is unambiguously valorized as a ploy, it doubles up with exposure as an interlinked threat that may help reorder domestic, social, and business relations while simultaneously providing a revealing purging process for the private individual. Concealment is the mark of the villain, but the reassertion of privacy—a purged privacy that is above the need for exerting secrecy and embedded within familial, communal structures built on the acknowledgment of mutual reliance as well as trust—constitutes the desired closure.

Chapter 8
George Eliot's *Felix Holt, The Radical* and Byronic Secrets

Denise Tischler Millstein

Andrew Elfenbein's *Byron and the Victorians* (1995) is the first book to open discussions of Byron and the Victorians, addressing the particular examples of Carlyle, Emily Brontë, Tennyson, Bulwer Lytton, Disraeli, and Wilde. Elfenbein treats Byron as a cultural institution and a known marketplace commodity, which encouraged these authors to assert their own Victorianism.[1] Elfenbein and I agree on Byron's function as a cultural touchstone in the Victorian era, furthermore, I apply some of his findings to George Eliot, an author left out of his study. In this essay, I posit that Eliot used Byron as a code to maintain certain secrets that characters in *Felix Holt, The Radical* would like to keep hidden; however, Byron's cultural cache ironically reveals these secrets to the reading audience. It should be remembered that like many late Victorians, George Eliot did not particularly like Byron, whom she thought sexually immoral. Similarly, she disapproved of Byron's works generally because she found them vulgar. Despite these personal views, however, Eliot's works, especially *Felix Holt, The Radical*, often invoke both Byron the man and his poetic works to reveal the threatening overlap of political and sexual secrets.

Byron was initially extremely popular after his death in Greece in 1824, when several young Victorians were first imagining themselves as writers. One oft repeated story is that the fifteen-year-old Alfred Lord Tennyson, then living at Somersby, ran from his home distraught, and somewhere in the woods near the rectory, carved into a sandstone rock the phrase "Byron is dead." At first, reaction to Byron's death seems to have been personal and intense. However, the public's overall interest in Byron dwindled from the years 1840–68. No more than twelve works that discuss or contain references to Byron were produced annually during this time. This shifted dramatically in 1869, which opened with some sixty-eight pieces published about him, keenly demonstrating that a Byronic revival was taking place.[2]

---

1 Andrew Elfenbein, *Byron and the Victorians* (Cambridge: Cambridge UP, 1995), 10.

2 Oscar Jose Santucho, *George Gordon, Lord Byron: A Comprehensive Bibliography of Secondary Material in English 1807–1974, With a Critical Review of Research By Clement Tyson Goode, Jr.* (Metuchen, NJ: Scarecrow, 1977), 24–5.

The chief cause of this sudden interest is not hard to find; the epicenter was a re-examination and confirmation of Byron's incestuous sex scandal, produced by Harriet Beecher Stowe, in cooperation with Byron's widow Annabella Milbanke. Stowe's article "The True Story of Lady Byron's Life" was published in September of 1869, simultaneously in the *Atlantic* in America and *MacMillan's* in England. According to Jennifer Cognard-Black, the piece "initiated a transatlantic media blitz so virulent and wild that Oliver Wendell Holmes called it the 'Byron whirlwind.'"[3] Stowe apparently believed that, in tarnishing the memory of Byron, she could weaken the influence of his immoral writing and permanently destroy the last of his reputation. In less than six months, Stowe rewrote the article into the book-length *Lady Byron Vindicated* (1870).

The nucleus of Stowe's argument was an unsupported conversation with Annabella Milbanke. The story goes that, on a trip to England in 1856, Annabella requested a meeting with Stowe, in which she shared the secret of her marital estrangement, claiming that Byron fathered a child with his half-sister Augusta and maintained their incestuous relationship even after his marriage. Byron is said to have blamed his dissipation on Annabella's frigidity. Stowe decided to share this information with the public thirteen years after the event due to a memoir written by the Countess Teresa Guiccioli, Byron's last mistress. Guiccioli portrayed Annabella as a "'narrow-minded, cold-hearted precisian' who stifled Byron's art and drove him to seek solace in other women."[4] Stowe said she was angered by the blatantly one-sided attack on an innocent victim and frustrated that English writers lacked the compunction to come to Annabella's defense; thus, she decided to attempt it herself. The result of "The True Story" for Byron studies was extraordinary, as dozens jumped to Byron's defense. Even Medora Leigh, the supposed product of Byron and Augusta's affair, published an account of her parentage in an attempt to acquit her uncle. Most found that Medora's memoir actually corroborated Stowe's case.

For stirring up such controversy, Stowe herself was viciously attacked in the press; Algernon Swinburne actually took to calling her "Harriet Bitcher Spew." In the words of Donald Thomas, "Byron's posthumous enemies were precisely the sort of people Swinburne detested."[5] Swinburne was attracted to Byron as the epitome of a social rebel. He thoroughly enjoyed stories of how Byron ignored prevailing sexual mores, reveling with "shrill enthusiasm [in] the details of Byron's sexual eccentricities, particularly with regard to the charge of incest with Augusta Leigh, which eventually wearied even his closest friends."[6] Swinburne's outrage

---

[3] Jennifer Cognard-Black, *Narrative in the Professional Age: Transatlantic Readings of Harriet Beecher Stowe, George Eliot, and Elizabeth Stuart Phelps* (New York: Routledge, 2004), 63–4.

[4] Cognard-Black, 65–6.

[5] Donald Thomas, *Swinburne: The Poet in His World* (New York: Oxford UP, 1979), 81.

[6] Thomas, 81.

at Stowe's accusations became a force behind why he chose to write a "Preface" on Byron when his publishers, Moxon's, began a series of selections of major English poets of the past with selections by Victorian critics. Swinburne later reprinted his piece in *Essays and Studies* (1875). Other critics denounced Stowe's impropriety as a woman, Christian, and American: her gender and self-claimed piety was the basis for accusations that she was behaving in an "unwomanly and ungodly manner by spreading sexual scandal and breaking feminine confidence."[7] Just as Stowe's book portrayed Byron as a liar, mid-Victorian critics retaliated so that not even the fantastic reception of *Uncle Tom's Cabin* eighteen years before could guarantee her standing as a credible author.

Of the sixty-eight items published on Byron in 1869, roughly forty deal with the controversy, with nearly all the material expressing disapproval of Stowe's revelation in favor of Byron's defense. Almost every reviewer denounced Stowe's article for lack of proof. Theodore Tilton of *The Independent* wrote, "Startling in accusation, barren in proof, inaccurate in dates, infelicitous in style, and altogether ill-advised in publication, her strange article will travel around the whole literary world and everywhere evoke against its author the spontaneous disapprobation of her life-long friends."[8]

When Stowe expanded her article into a book, she dramatically altered her approach to the subject, adding the kind of evidence that so many felt was missing—specific names, dates, documents, and other data. Stowe added layers of hard proof in every chapter of her book, except for the "confession scene" itself, which still sounded more like a novel than objective reporting. Stowe returned to the familiar conventions of novel writing for Annabella's confession, pitting Stowe's word, as a woman and worse an American, against Byron's male and aristocratic silence. According to Cognard-Black, while Stowe seemed to comprehend "the import of speaking out on such a topic and against such a favorite as Byron ... she couldn't have foreseen the universal wrath she would incur."[9] As Stowe says in the book, "The world may finally forgive the man of genius anything ... but for the woman there is no mercy and no redemption."[10] Stowe was accused of smearing Byron's name in the pursuit of notoriety and personal financial gain. Even almost fifty years after his death, taking on Byron's myth, as a totem of male Englishness, proved detrimental to Stowe's career; her book failed miserably on both sides of the Atlantic.

The end result of the Stowe controversy was the opposite of what she ultimately sought; it created a movement that established Byron's rightful place in literary history. However, it bears noting that even during the darkest of times, Byron's

---

[7] Cognard-Black, 66.

[8] Cognard-Black, 69.

[9] Cognard-Black, 80–81.

[10] Harriet Beecher Stowe, *Lady Byron Vindicated: A History of the Byron Controversy, From Its Beginning in 1816 to the Present Time* (Boston: Osgood, Fields, & Co., 1870), 74.

poetry never ceased to be read; the personal scandals of his biography, as they had in life, only made him that much more attractive. As a result, in 1881 Matthew Arnold and John Ruskin published discussions of Byron's merits that ensured his lasting reputation; these were, respectively, an essay entitled "Byron," which enrolled him with acknowledgments of his deficiencies, along with Goethe and Wordsworth as the three greatest poets of the century, and *Fiction, Fair and Foul;* Ruskin later expanded his observations in *Praeterita* (1885–9). Rounding out the close of the nineteenth century and published simultaneously in England and America was *The Works of Lord Byron* (1898), the first thoughtfully completed collected works and letters, edited by Ernest Hartley Coleridge, the poet's son, and Rowland Prothero Ernle.

George Eliot was disgusted by the nature of the sexual scandal itself rather than by Stowe's attacks on Byron's reputation. As Rosemarie Bodenheimer says, the "revival of public attention to the connection between Byron and his half sister Augusta Leigh shocked and enraged Marian, who could not bring herself to refer to it except as 'the Byron subject' or 'the Byron question.'"[11] Eliot once wrote that "the fashion of being 'titilated [sic] by the worst is like the uncovering of the dead Lord Byron's club foot.'"[12] And, Eliot's letters of the time discuss the topic in some detail. Writing to the largely forgotten novelist Sara Hennell on 21 September 1869, Eliot remarked on the dangers of publicly discussing the scandal: "As to the Byron subject, nothing can outweigh to my mind the heavy social injury of familiarizing young minds with the desecration of family ties. The discussion of the subject in the newspapers, periodicals, and pamphlets, is simply odious to me, and I think it a pestilence likely to leave very ugly marks."[13] Eliot claimed that she was divorced from Byron defenses. In fact, in the same letter to Hennell, Eliot wrote, "As to the high-flown stuff which is being reproduced about Byron and his poetry, I am utterly out of sympathy with it. He seems to me the most *vulgar-minded* genius that ever produced a great effect in literature."[14]

Interestingly, Eliot was on very friendly terms with Harriet Beecher Stowe and even wrote to her about "The True Story." However, her letter only hints at the depth of her own judgments concerning the article's immoral subject. Rather than chastise Stowe, Eliot focused her attention on how women authors often experienced "harsh and unfair judgments" in the press. Eliot says, "with regard to yourself, dear friend, I have felt sure that in acting on a different basis of impression, you were impelled by pure, generous feeling. Do not think that I would have written to you on this point to express judgment; I am anxious only to convey to you a sense of my sympathy and confidence."[15] Of the Byron controversy

---

[11] Rosemarie Bodenheimer, *The Real Life of Mary Ann Evans: George Eliot, Her Letters and Fiction* (Ithaca: Cornell UP, 1994), 237.

[12] Bodenheimer, 238.

[13] George Eliot, *Selections From George Eliot's Letters*, Ed. Gordon S. Haight (New Haven: Yale UP, 1985), 366. Hereafter cited as *GEL*.

[14] Eliot, *GEL*, 366.

[15] Eliot, *GEL*, 369.

specifically, Eliot gently admonishes, "For my own part, I should have preferred that the 'Byron question' should not have been brought before the public, because I think the discussion of such subjects is injurious socially."

Eliot's own life, it should be remembered, was also not without its sexual scandal. She created a storm of controversy after eloping from England to Germany with the married father of six George Henry Lewes in July 1854. On returning, Eliot took Lewes' name and they lived openly together as husband and wife despite being shunned socially. Eliot's brother Isaac showed his disapproval by cutting off communication with his sister. The *Brother and Sister* sonnets, written in 1869, the year the Stowe controversy ensued, record Eliot's desire to be reunited with Isaac and are "loaded with autobiographical regret."[16] The sonnet sequence, which reads like a letter from a cast-off sister to her brother, is a mirror version of Byron's "Epistle to Augusta," *from* a beloved brother *to* his cast-off sister. It is almost as if the two poems create a whole when read together, with Eliot as the sister of her poem responding to Byron as the brother of his. The sonnets echo Byron's "Epistle" in the first-person confession of the closeness felt by the siblings, and more importantly, in detailing the after effects of losing that connection.[17] But, Eliot also responds to Byron in her novels.

Due to Eliot's malleable opinion on Byron's usefulness, which may have been influenced by the evolving literary taste for him as just discussed, her canon, especially works written in the 1860s and 70s, contain two conflicting judgments on the poet. It is interesting to note that *Felix Holt*, first published in 1866, three years before the Stowe controversy began, and thus produced within the scope of the virtual Byronic wasteland, seems largely to denounce Byron, although it can be seem as simultaneously questioning the value of his works and demonstrating the depths of his mythic importance. *Felix Holt, The Radical* is a useful example that reveals the nature of Eliot's complex responses to Byron, which were shared by many Victorian authors before the accepted establishment of his literary reputation.[18]

---

[16] Angela Leighton and Margaret Reynolds, eds., *Victorian Women Poets: An Anthology* (Oxford: Blackwell, 1995), 221.

[17] While much has been made of Eliot's responses to William Wordsworth in these sonnets, attention to the details of "Tintern Abbey" (1798) reveals how different Eliot's subject is. In "Tintern Abbey," Wordsworth mentions his relationship with his sister, but does not foreground that discussion. Even the end of the poem, which includes some details of the relationship, differs from Byron's and Eliot's in that there is no estrangement between the brother and sister. Rather, Wordsworth employs Dorothy as tool to explore how his mind has grown since he first contemplated the scene; they have not experienced the break in connection that Eliot and Byron focus their thoughts on in the *Brother and Sister* sonnets and "Epistle to Augusta."

[18] For a discussion of Eliot's uses of Byron later in her career, please see Denise Tischler Millstein, "Lord Byron and George Eliot: Embracing National Consciousness in *Daniel Deronda*" *Forum: The University of Edinburgh Postgraduate Journal of Culture and the Arts* (2005), which argues that by 1876, Eliot was able to offer a reformed Byronic hero as the messianic hope for the Jewish people and a catalyst to social reform in England.

My argument about Eliot's thoughts on Byron stems from a six-page sequence in *Felix Holt,The Radical*, the first introduction of Esther to the title character. The encounter begins with Felix's physical clumsiness as tea commences; he accidentally upsets Esther's sewing basket, revealing a hidden copy of Byron's works within. Eliot writes, "In the act of rising, Felix pushed back his chair too suddenly against the rickety table close by him, and down went the blue-frilled work-basket … dispersing on the floor reels, thimble, muslin work … and something heavier than these—a duodecimo volume which fell close to him between the table and the fender."[19] Embarrassed by his error, Felix exclaims, "'O my stars! ...I beg your pardon.' Esther had already started up, and with wonderful quickness had picked up half the small rolling things while Felix was lifting the basket and book" (59). On examining the book more closely, the conversation takes a dramatic turn: "'Byron's Poems!' he said, in a tone of disgust, while Esther was recovering all the other articles. 'The Dream'—he'd better have been asleep and snoring. What do you stuff your memory with Byron, Miss Lyon?'" (59). As he asks this, Felix at last looks "straight at Esther … with a strong denunciatory and pedagogic intention." Felix's intention, his aim as Esther's self-appointed teacher, is to instruct her on how Byron should be viewed, with "denunciatory," of course, indicating his disapprobation. Commonly, males of the period, as Andrew Elfenbein tells us, treat "female reactions to Byron as naïve" so that they would "appear more refined in contrast. The passionate female admirer of Byron became a convenient image" onto which they could "demonstrate their superior morality and judgment by scorning the female reader's supposed naiveté."[20] The situation leads to Felix's next internal observation: "Of course, he saw more clearly than ever that she was a fine lady" (59). Being a "fine lady" is not a positive attribute to Felix; fine ladies are like Byron.

In response to Felix's questioning, Esther "reddened, drew up her long neck, and said, as she retreated to her chair again, 'I have a great admiration for Byron'" (59). Elfenbein has observed that such esteem in a female reader became a cliché of Victorian literature, and cites many novels in which women are criticized for admiring Byron.[21] Because of this tendency, we notice Esther's reaction all the more as she blushes, and then raises her neck, perhaps in an effort to disguise her blush. It also becomes very telling that Esther keeps her copy of Byron hidden from view; for, it seems to betray that she is ashamed of owning it. Eliot indicates Esther's guilt about reading Byron: "Esther would not have wished [her father] to know anything about the volume of Byron, but she was too proud to show any concern" (59). However, Esther has already demonstrated this. One can assume that Esther is somewhat embarrassed about being discovered and so unceremoniously exposed. This could be perhaps in part because she reads Byron as a guilty pleasure; it is something that she apparently knows she should not do,

---

[19] George Eliot, *Felix Holt, The Radical* (London: Penguin, 1995), 58–9.

[20] Elfenbein, 67.

[21] Elfenbein, 66–7.

but it is something she enjoys anyway, perhaps even *because* it is generally not condoned. We might assume this based on the objections to it that Felix raises.

What is more interesting is that Esther hides her copy of Byron's poetry in her sewing basket, a container she is likely to keep close by and readily available. It is also a symbol of Esther's position in the household and society in general; it is a gendered personal item and thus an extension of Esther's identity. Stowing Byron securely into a standard symbol of femininity, Eliot seems to be indicating the intimate connection between Byron's poetry and some Victorian female readers like Esther. His poetry is being constantly read by women, but not openly. It could be that women felt keenly both a simultaneous attraction to and repulsion of Bryon's poetry. Or, they feared reprisals for reading it, which would require hiding the fact from view—all in order to escape the judgments of others, especially the men in their lives.

On witnessing this exchange, Mr. Lyon is oddly silent. Eliot writes, "Mr Lyon had paused in the act of drawing his chair to the tea-table, and was looking on at this scene, wrinkling the corners of his eyes with a perplexed smile" (59). Eliot's description of Lyon's smile implies that he does not know what to make of the rising tension inherent in the situation, the ensuing argument between his daughter and his guest. When he does finally speak, Eliot tells us that Mr. Lyon "knew scarcely anything of the poet," and yet, his judgments on him are quite sure. When Mr. Lyon claims that Byron "'is a worldly and vain writer,'" one can assume that he does not openly approve of his daughter reading Byron anymore than Felix does.

At the same time, however, Mr. Lyon admits to the importance of Byron to the younger generation. He says that Byron's "books embodied the faith and ritual of many young ladies and gentlemen" (59). Eliot thus reveals one of the double consciousnesses inherent in reading Byron in Victorian culture: while Byron is considered egotistical, his works have become foundational of the young. Byron is a powerfully influential writer, despite his personal flaws. The reverence of him is not without its religious component. The young, it seems read him as a rite of passage. It's almost as if Eliot is suggesting that Byronism is a phase in the maturation process of English adolescents, as so many Victorian writers would later describe themselves. As *Felix Holt* seems to indicate, women like Esther are reading Byron secretly for good reason.

Felix's opinions on Byron are much harsher than Mr. Lyon's and require a closer investigation. Byron is proclaimed as "'A misanthropic debauchee,'" by Felix as he "lift[ed] a chair with one hand, and [held] the book open in the other" (59). By continuing to hold the volume open, Felix accomplishes two things: he lengthens the duration of Esther's mortification, and he seems to hope to reveal the hidden nature of Byron's immoral writing. Felix feels justified in exposing the hidden shame Esther is so obviously attempting to deny. It is also almost as if Felix expects the open book, the text of the poetry itself, to testify to its own immorality. When this does not happen, Felix supplies his own denunciations, by saying that Byron's notion of a hero was "'that he should disorder his stomach and despise mankind. His corsairs and renegades, his Alps and Manfreds, are the most paltry puppets that were ever pulled by the string of lust and pride'" (59).

Like Lyon, Felix recognizes Byron's personal flaws. Calling him a "misanthropic debauchee," Felix reveals his own disgust at Byron's sexual past. Even more telling is that Felix sees that Byron's heroes are "paltry puppets" for the poet's identity. Because Byron's characters are morally corrupt, Byron himself must have been even more so. What is worse is that Byron's heroes become merely expressions of the poet's "lust and pride," the first connection in the text between Bryon's sexual cache and his ego. Ignoring this latest indictment, Esther says, "'Let me beg of you to put [the book] aside till after tea, father … However objectionable Mr Holt may find its pages, they would certainly be made worse by being greased with bread-and-butter'" (59). Esther separates herself and Felix's views rather sharply, both changing the subject and retaliating indirectly against Felix's abuse.

In reference to Lyon's observations on the exchange, Eliot tells us, "He saw his daughter was angry" (59). His spirited daughter has not missed Felix's pedagogical inclination, and she resents it as well as his comments on one of her favorite poets. All the while, Felix has continued his mental observations, noting with a "'Ho, ho!' … her father is frightened of her. How came he to have such a nice-stepping, long-necked peacock for his daughter? but she shall see that I am not frightened'" (59). The conversation about Byron at this point has become a miniature contest of wills between Esther and Felix, which is perhaps why Felix wants her to see that he is unafraid of her. Surely, Felix wants Esther to note that although her father likes to avoid provoking her displeasure, he will not shrink from it. At the same time, of course, these comments demonstrate that Felix is taking stock of Esther's refinements and that he may even be somewhat attracted to her "long-neck," which he references several times in the sequence.

Having thus revealed his distaste for Byron and eager to continue his didactic instruction, Felix wonders how Esther could stomach reading him. He interrogates: "'I should like to know how you will justify your admiration for such a writer, Miss Lyon'" (59). Felix's accusations are almost impossible for Esther to counter, as she is aware of Byron's reputation. She only replies, "'I should not attempt it with you, Mr Holt.'" Perhaps in an effort to restore the peace, or even to excuse his daughter's outbursts, Mr. Lyon tells Felix, "'My daughter is a critic of words, Mr Holt … and often corrects mine on the ground of niceties'" (60). In response, Felix works himself to a near fever pitch, turning his denunciatory intentions now on Mr. Lyon, who obviously also needs correction. "'O, your niceties—I know what they are," said Felix, in his usual *fortissimo*. 'They all go on your system of make-believe. "Rottenness" may suggest what is unpleasant, so you'd better say "sugar-plums," or something else such a long way off the fact that nobody is obliged to think of it … I hate your gentlemanly speakers'" (60). We may assume that this comment is directed more pointedly at Byron.

The subject of conversation then shifts to local social and political concerns only to return to Bryon a page later. The connections between Byron and politics are not made coincidentally. This time, Eliot discusses Byron in connection with fashion. Speaking of young ladies, Esther remarks, "'A real fine-lady does not wear clothes that flare in people's eyes, or use importunate scents, or make a noise as she moves: she is something refined, and graceful, and charming, and never obtrusive'" (61). Esther cites all that is expected of women of her class and she seems to think that she typifies them. Seeing his chance to call Esther out on her reading Byron, which, apparently, to him means that she is quite unlike the feminine ideal, Felix contemptuously retorts, "'And she reads Byron also, and admires Childe Harold—gentlemen of unspeakable woes, who employ a hairdresser, and look seriously at themselves in the glass.'"

Felix admits that while Byron is standard reading for young ladies, the devotion they exhibit for him is misplaced, echoing the pronouncements of Matthew Arnold that "the man, in Byron, is of a nature even less sincere than the poet [in him]. This beautiful and blighted being at bottom is a coxcomb. He posed all his life long."[22] According to Felix, women who read Byron must be as frivolous as he was. While Childe Harold is a gentleman of "unspeakable woes," he also "employ[s] a hairdresser." While Byron did not actually keep a hairdresser on staff, Lady Blessington observed that he vainly "smothered [his hair] with oil to disguise the grey" as he aged.[23] Obviously, Felix feels that these two inclinations are mutually exclusive. Serious men and real heroes do not care what they look like: they certainly do not "look seriously at themselves in the glass." According to Lord Sligo, who befriended Byron in Athens, he once found Byron, "admiring himself in front of a looking-glass. Byron remarked he should like to die of consumption" due to the slimming effects of the disease.[24] Women more commonly exhibit these attributes; thus, Felix is casting doubt on Byron's masculinity. In response to this tirade, Eliot indicates, "Esther reddened, and gave a little toss [of her head]" (61). Here Eliot portrays Esther much like a spirited horse, which refuses to be easily broken. Just as Felix is not afraid of rousing her anger, Esther is not frightened to resist his attempts to reform her opinions. It is this rebellious spirit among other things that indicates Esther's investment in the cult of ego so often associated with Byron.

Having made his comparison rather explicit, Felix further insults both women and Byron by suggesting that "'A fine-lady is a squirrel-headed thing, with small airs and small notions, about as applicable to the business of life as a pair of tweezers to the clearing of a forest'" (61). What women and Byron seem to have in common is their lack of usefulness; neither fine ladies nor Byron are suitable for "the business of life." They are too wrapped up in the superficial. Felix continues his attack on Esther, who, to most observers, would seem like the epitome of a fine lady; he does so by adopting the voice of Medora, the murdered wife of

22 Matthew Arnold, "Byron." *Essays in Criticism: Second Series* (London: MacMillan, 1935), 123.

23 Phyllis Grosskurth, *Byron: The Flawed Angel* (Boston: Houghton Mifflin, 1997), 423.

24 Grosskurth, 120–21.

Byron's protagonist in *The Corsair.* Incidentally Medora was also the name of the daughter Byron supposedly fathered with his half-sister. According to Felix, who paraphrases the Medora of the poem, she: "'wouldn't have minded if they had all been put into the pillory and lost their ears. She would have said, 'Their ears did stick out so'" (61). Again, Byron and his works are unsuitable for the harsh realities of the world because they belong to the superficial, and here associated with the feminine. The only reason Medora would have justified cutting off the ears of "fine-ladies" was because they were unattractive.

Felix, as a working-class and utilitarian somewhat stereotypical Victorian man, believes in all that is simple and sincere; Mr. Lyon observes, after Felix has left their home, "'That is a singular young man, Esther … I discern in him a love for whatsoever things are honest and true'" (62). In this light, Felix feels obliged to express his doubts about those above him. Of course, Byron, and to a lesser extent, Esther, are both members of the upper class and are therefore guilty of useless vanity. The animal most quintessentially connected with such vulgarity is the peacock, and also generally associated with the figure of the dandy, a category to which Byron obviously belongs. The truth is, he was a bit of a coxcomb and rather proud of his dandyism, which he claimed garnered him much female companionship. Byron was known to be extravagant in his personal dress. According to Christine Kenyon Jones, between January 1812 and September 1813 Byron spent almost 900 pounds with "one tailor alone, while in three months in 1812, he bought no less than 24 fine white quilted waistcoats."[25] To Felix, Byron, as a poet, lacks substance, and as man, Byron is hardly the epitome of the masculine, both fairly common complaints about Byron by the middle of the Victorian period. And yet, as Felix knows, proper ladies and gentlemen were raised reading Byron. Felix believes, as Eliot may have, that the cult of Byron is a fashion to be purged.

If Esther enjoys reading Byron, she must share in his frivolity; she too must be a peacock, which Felix alludes to several times in this short scene. "'A peacock!' thought Felix. 'I should like to come and scold her every day, and make her cry and cut her fine hair off'" (62). It is difficult to miss the sadomasochistic overtones of this internal monologue. Certainly, Felix admits that he wants to correct Esther, even "make her cry," telling readers that in fact he should enjoy such activities. However, he also wants to make her feel that she is wrong in being trivial to such an extent that, to make amends, she should want to "cut her hair off." This action, surely, would stunt her egotism and vanity. However unintentionally he may deliver it, Felix also admits that her hair gives Esther reason to feel proud. This, of course, also indicates that he is aware of her attractiveness in the very moment that he appears to be the most repulsed by her egotistical characteristics.

Felix considers this after he leaves the Lyon's home, concluding this thoughts on Esther thusly: "I could grind my teeth at such self-satisfied minxes, who think they can tell everybody what is the correct thing, and the utmost stretch of their

---

[25] Christine Kenyon Jones, "Fantasy and Transfiguration: Byron and His Portraits," *Byromania*, ed. Frances Wilson. (New York: St. Martin's, 1999), 112.

ideas will not place them on a level with the intelligent fleas. I should like to see if she could be made ashamed of herself" (63). Employing "self-satisfied" demonstrates the main objection Felix has to Esther: she is proud, too proud; he sees her egotism as her most salient feature. Another aspect of her personality that he dislikes and would like to dispense with is her confidence in her own beliefs, when, according to him, she is so obviously mistaken in them. Included in these beliefs, of course, is her admiration of Byron. This places her not on "a level with the intelligent fleas." Felix resents the fact that she has corrected his taste, especially when she needs to correct her entire life-stance including the Byronic egotism that is so evident in her behavior. He wants to make her feel so "ashamed of herself" and her Byronism that she wishes to purge it.

Esther must learn to put her Byronism behind her before she can wholeheartedly choose to live a worthwhile life. As a reader and defender of Byron, Felix sees that Esther needs to be reformed, believing that he is the one to teach her how to transform her engrained Byronism. Esther needs to be taught how the egotistical forces in her can be "sublimated rather than expressed in negative form"[26] as they are in this particular scene. Though Felix possesses, according to K. M. Newton, "similar egotistic tendencies," he has been able to control them, or so he thinks, since this scene, of course, simply reveals them. In the example of his own life, Felix had hoped to demonstrate how self-interested behavior can be redirected beyond mere self-gratification, which Byron represents. Newton argues that the Romantic aspects of egotism, which feature so prominently in Eliot's characters, are linked to the cult of the ego associated with Byron, and her rejection of them seems to indicate that this needed to be reformulated.[27]

There are two central ironies revealed in these brief exchanges between Felix and his future spouse. The first is the secretive nature of the sexual, which Byron embodies. This works in many ways. First, Esther hides her copy of Byron in her sewing basket, a symbol of her femininity, which no man would dare to defile. And yet, because of his reputation as a sexual libertine, Esther's hiding his poetry in such a place seems to tempt such defiling. Moreover, Felix hides his own lust and sexual attraction to Esther by couching it as distaste for the Byronic. As we know, Felix is interested in Esther; he is sexually attracted to her as evidenced in their marriage later in the novel. However, in these two scenes, he denies and attempts to hide his sexual interest and instead focuses on the disgust he feels for a notorious womanizer.

Perhaps, Felix feels guilty about his own lust for Esther and wonders if he has too much in common with Byron. Or, it could be that Felix sees him as a rival for Esther's affections. Felix has realized the position that the poet holds in Esther's estimation; the volume of Byron's poetry is almost equated with secretive love letters from another man, one who holds the position of a sexual mate, a space

[26] K. M. Newton, *George Eliot: Romantic Humanist* (New York: Barnes & Nobel, 1981), 44.

[27] Newton, 49.

that Felix would like to fill. And, Felix can only express his outrage by attacking his rival, in an attempt to lower him in Esther's estimation. At the same time, Felix makes Esther equally guilty in the affair with Byron, hardly the best way to secure her lasting affection—unless it is to demonstrate that Felix is the better man, and thus able to save Esther from the lascivious clutches of one who would only like to debauch her. Perhaps, Felix wishes to rescue her from her own lustful impulses. Or, it could simply be that Felix is using Byron as a subconscious code, a signifier that admits his own sexual interest in Esther by way of displacement. In this way, Byron becomes the voice for sexual desire that characters do not want to admit. As Elfenbein indicates, the image of Byron's female admirers "had its uses ... If Byron was what respectable women wanted, the cultured heterosexual Englishman could take his cue accordingly. Although women were supposed to keep their admiration for Byron purely ideal, men might dare them to cross the line by imitating Byron. Byron's success at least influenced the way they had to perform erotic roles."[28] Byron, then, could easily function as a kind of sexual scapegoat. This is due to the fact that in his own life he was known for keeping his sexual secrets, rather notoriously—in the open.

At the time that *Felix Holt* was written, there was no public confirmation of Byron's debauched sexual past, though he had been tried in the court of public opinion as early as 1816, when rumors of his homosexual and incestuous liaisons came to light and he was forced to leave England for self-imposed exile. Critics like Elfenbein, remind us how the infamous life of Byron was used as a double-edged sword that both risked and insured his position in the marketplace. The scandals of Byron's life were valuable to his position in the market because they reinforced a transgressive thrill. In order to correct this, it is common that Victorian treatments of him censored or censured him, therefore allowing his poetry to become respectable reading.[29] This created a paradox in the Byron market such that efforts to make him acceptable only served to keep alive his scandalousness, "since his excesses had to mentioned in order to be deplored." This is essentially what Felix is accomplishing in this scene, intentionally or otherwise. However, the situation offers Eliot a slightly different opportunity, providing a chance to have "conventional norms reinforced by learning about Byron's departures from them." In relation to the Stowe controversy, which began this discussion, we are presented with a extraordinarily vivid example of the extent to which Byron's marginal respectability depended upon scandal and how his debauched past was necessarily retold in the very effort to keep it quiet.

Another irony central to these exchanges is more political in nature. Felix Holt, as the novel's subtitle reminds us, is a "radical." Yet, Felix rejects Byron as a personal and political hero; despite the fact that Byron might have been a good role model for political liberalism, due to Byron's support of the Luddite Rebellion, on which he composed his maiden speech in the House of Lords, his

---

[28] Elfenbein, 67.

[29] Elfenbein, 83.

conspiring with the Carbonari in Italy, and his eventual financing of the Greek war for independence from the Turk. Felix refuses to accept that Byron was at the heart of sincerely held liberal politics in England and on the continent during the beginning of the century. Or, perhaps Byron's positive, political concerns are overwhelmed by his negative, personal ones. As R. W. Chambers reminds us, "mid-Victorian Liberalism was nothing if not proper: and Byron was nothing if not shocking."[30] What Eliot does, through Felix's judgments, is to remind us of why Byron is not an acceptable political role model. Ironically, Felix denies that Byron was more sincere in his politics, which giving his life for Greece shows, than Felix is, as Eliot proves at the end of the novel.

It is worthwhile to pause for a moment and consider how Eliot employs the term "radical" in referring to Felix, especially considering that he only proposes modest reforms; he is certainly not interested in leading any revolutions in the style of Byron. Hao Li points out that "radical" refers less to the political type of reform than it suggests "the scope of the reform needed."[31] Li reminds that radical, can mean "going to the root or origin ... what is essential and fundamental."[32] This definition of the term characterizes Felix's focus, which is to question inherited tradition, which Byron can be seen to represent. Thus, Felix deserves the epithet, despite his conservative political reforms.

Instead of focusing his attention on the inclination to agree with Byron's politics at least on the surface, Felix rather harps on the fact that Byron is a self-confirmed sexual libertine. Felix only focuses his attack on part of Byron's myth; he conflates the political with the sexual, which was not all that unusual at the time. In fact, Byron's own poetry establishes their connection in *Don Juan*. That is, the mock-epic extols staunchly-critical political satire amid raunchy sexual escapades. Felix's logic appears to be that, since Byron's life was morally corrupt, his politics must have been insincere. Certainly, his politics could not have been an outward sign of an inner altruism, as presumably that kind of selflessness would have been destroyed by Byron's egotistical sexuality.

Felix seems to believe that the debauched liberal sexuality of Byron could contaminate nobler political aims, making it dangerous to test the theory, since following the typical Byronic egotist can lead inevitably only to corruption. Again, we find that Byron offers a convenient scapegoat for such discussions. This could be because Byron was the product of a corrupt society, which rejected him in part due to its own guilt in having created him.[33] Moreover, Byron as well as his poetic heroes are figures of rebellion, and revolutions can be dangerous. Eliot argues for

---

30 R. W. Chambers, *Man's Unconquerable Mind* (London: Jonathan Cape, 1939), 315.

31 Hao Li, *Memory and History in George Eliot: Transfiguring the Past* (New York: St. Martin's, 2000), 100.

32 Li, 99.

33 Malcolm Kelsall, "The Byronic Hero and Revolution in Ireland: The Politics of *Glenarvon*," *The Byron Journal* 9 (1981): 14.

modest reforms through Felix, so that she might applaud equality and freedom, without putting her own elevated social and political rank at risk. Byron's example inspires and explores both political and sexual rebellion. Many of Byron's sexual conquests, like Teresa Guicciolo, for instance, may have been attracted to him in the first place precisely because of his radical political and sexual views. It was the married Teresa, after all, who introduced Byron to the secret society, the Carbonari, after he became her Anglo *cavalier servente.* As Malcolm Kelsall has called it, Byron's *libido dominandi,* is fully capable of debauching both political and sexual aims.[34] Thus, he embodies both the fundamental human drive toward revolution as necessary to challenge the evils of the world as well as and the practical fear of the disastrous consequences of insurrection in the world they might produce.

As *Felix Holt* demonstrates, in 1866, Eliot was hardly at the forefront of Byronic defenses, which only begs the question of why she would include direct references to him at two important times: first, during the wasteland of Byron texts, and secondly, at such a crucial point in the novel, the first introduction of the title character to his future wife. As a testament to Eliot's and other Victorian authors thoughts before the scandal broke, *Felix Holt, The Radical,* demonstrates that Eliot was aware of Byron's lingering influence on Victorian culture, even at the height of his most virulent unpopularity. And, because he was a cultural touchstone, Eliot could easily use the public's knowledge of Byron to explore her own agenda, part of which may well have been a warning about the dangers inherent in both excessive political and sexual liberty, with Byron serving simply as a well-known example. Ironically, in using Byron as a secret code for such discussions, Eliot actually relies on the public knowledge of these secrets to prove her point.

---

[34] Kelsall, 14.

Chapter 9
The Perverse Secrets of Masculinity in Augusta Webster's Dramatic Poetry

Robert P. Fletcher

Introduction

In recent years, study of dramatic monologues by male poets of the Victorian period such as Browning and Swinburne has often focused on their function as portraits of masculinity in the era. Speakers formerly analyzed as insane individuals—such as Porphyria's lover, the Duke of Ferrara, or the speaker of "The Leper"—now seem to be representative, symptomatic of strains in Victorian culture. Rather than simply monomaniacs driven to reveal their secrets in their monologues, in other words, these speakers are prisms through which the various colors of the Victorian rhetoric of gender are revealed (to use one of Browning's figures of speech). When one looks to Browning's fellow aficionado of the dramatic monologue, Augusta Webster, one finds similar interests in monomania and secrets. The telling therefore functions to revealing the relations between violence, heterosexual and dissident masculinities, and the poet's subjectivity.

Although in her influential book *Victorian Women Poets* Angela Leighton claimed that "the element of morbid criminality, which fascinates Tennyson and Browning, gives way [in Webster] to more ordinary inconsistencies of self," because the latter's speakers are "real men and women, with altogether smaller sins and guilts,"[1] in actuality Webster also wrote with some frequency in the voices of those obsessed with awful secrets. Although famously skeptical, she composed monologues with speakers haunted by visions ("Jeanne D'Arc," "Sister Annunciata") and troubled by revelations ("An Inventor"). Her portraits of secretive monomaniacs, like Browning's or Swinburne's, allow the poet to explore the discursive contradictions about gender and sexuality in Victorian culture, especially as demonstrated in the links between eros and aggression. However, as both a female poet who holds a Keatsian view of the poet's neutrality and an advocate of women's right not to be dominated, Webster's relationship to that voice of monomaniacal masculinity is deeply ambivalent, poised, as it is, between an ethical identification with its humanity and a moral imperative to expose its secrets and offer alternative versions of masculinity. As Albert Pionke notes in "Victorian Secrecy: An Introduction," "the complex of motives behind the

---

1 Angela Leighton, *Victorian Women Poets: Writing Against the Heart* (Charlottesville: U of Virginia P, 1992), 178.

Victorians' secrets" is often wed, so to speak, to the period's vexed gender politics, with male and female gender positions exploiting secrecy differently at times, either to shore up social controls or subvert them.[2] As we'll see, like the "self-reflexive and self-critical" Christina Rossetti, Webster is strikingly conscious of the mysterious risks and potential behind the lyric or dramatic "I" for both asserting and undermining such controls.[3] The three dramatic monologues I will discuss here involve secrets that undermine normative definitions of both masculinity and heterosexuality while at the same time revealing this woman poet's uneasy relation to self revelation.

"The most closely-knit minds [are] still in so many workings a secret to each other."

In her discussion of the nineteenth-century diagnosis of monomania, Maria Van Zuylen focuses repeatedly on the monomaniac's rejection of the arbitrary, the random, or the unstable in the world around him and on the strategies he uses to control such incoherence—strategies that can resemble the artist's attempts to create order. Indeed, artists provide Van Zuylen with prime examples of the monomaniac, since in their art they do "everything in their power to stabilize their universes and expel indeterminacy from their worlds."[4] In a pair of articles published in the *Examiner* and later collected in *A Housewife's Opinions*, Webster discusses the work of the novelist and the poet in what I take to be analogous terms. The poet, she emphasizes in "Poets and Personal Pronouns," takes the idiosyncratic or the quirky and transforms it into the familiar and the necessary and thereby, paradoxically, the distinctive or memorable. In her essay on the novel entitled "Lay Figures," while arguing against the wisdom of using real people as the basis for fictional characters, Webster conveys her sense of character as frustratingly inexplicable or even arbitrary, basing its mysteriousness in our merely relative understanding of other people: "because of the differences of perceptions and sympathies which make each man's mental vision in some way differently tinged from every other man's, no two human beings form exactly the same conception

[2] See especially his discussions of Anthony Trollope, Christina Rossetti, and Elizabeth Barrett Browning in the Introduction to this volume.

[3] On the subject of the ambiguously gendered and sexualized identity of the lyric "I" in Victorian women's poetry, see Virginia Blain, "Sexual Politics of the (Victorian) Closet; *or*, No Sex, Please—We're Poets," and Robert P. Fletcher, "'I leave a page half-writ': Narrative Discoherence in Michael Field's *Underneath the Bough*," both in *Women's Poetry, Late Romantic to Late Victorian: Gender and Genre, 1830–1890*, eds. Isobel Armstrong and Virginia Blain, (London and New York: Macmillan and St. Martin's, 1999).

[4] Maria Van Zuylen, *Monomania: The Flight from Everyday Life in Literature and Art* (Ithaca: Cornell UP, 2005), 2.

of any third human being."[5] Moreover, human beings are unpredictable even to those who know them well:

> Everybody does things which, as coming from him, are quite unaccountable to his most intimate friends—more unaccountable to them the more intimate they are … even sympathy will not overcome that inevitable separation of self from self which makes the most closely-knit minds still in so many workings a secret to each other. (147)

This arbitrariness of character and the resulting pervasive secrecy of human beings one to another is even more of a challenge for the poet than the novelist. Whereas the novelist can get away with drawing characters whose singularities are tied to history, the poet must aim for "a suitability not so much to a given epoch and theatre as to always and everywhere, no matter under what disguise of date and story" (150). Even more than the painter and novelist, the poet must fictionalize to make the random seem the necessary, the idiosyncratic seem the typical. For, argues Webster,

> [w]e look to the poet for feelings, thoughts, actions if need be, represented in a way which shall affect us as the manifest expression of what our very selves must have felt and thought and done if we had been those he puts before us and in their cases. He must make us feel this is not only what we ourselves, being ourselves, could come to think and feel and do in like circumstances, but of what no circumstances could possibly call out in us. (151)

Not only does the poet make the most improbable seem natural, she triggers in the reader an analogous "assimilative consciousness"—in a phrase from one of her *Athenaeum* reviews—which signifies again not only an understanding of the ideas but the feeling that they are one's own.[6] Here again is a link to the monomaniac, who also owns what might be called an assimilative consciousness capable of transforming the foreign into the familiar, of bringing the other into the self.

However, if the poet creates characters whose secrets seem plain, she does so without revealing her own secrets. Webster's is, like Browning's, a strictly anti-confessional poetic: "the rule of the poet's expression seems to be that it is not the revealing of him but of themselves to others, and to him the revealing of them and himself among them" (*Housewife's Opinions*, 155). In effect, Webster argues for secrecy as part of the poet's professional identity, something it shares, as Pionke shows, with other Victorian professions. The poet may not reveal himself in his work, but he offers as compensation to the reader the revelation, in the words

---

5 Augusta Webster, *A Housewife's Opinions* (London: Macmillan, 1879), 147. Hereafter cited within the text.

6 Augusta Webster, review of *Flower Pieces and Other Poems*, by William Allingham, *Athenaeum*, May 18, 1889, 623. Quoted in Patricia Rigg, "Augusta Webster and the Lyric Muse: The *Athenaeum* and Webster's Poetics," *Victorian Poetry* 42, no. 2 (Summer 2004): 150.

of the philosopher, that nothing human is alien to him. Despite this high moral aim that she assigns to lyric poetry, Webster notes that its use of the first-person singular pronoun can lead to misunderstanding and accusations of immorality: "One even hears it adduced as a fault in the moral character of poets generally that they do not feel all they write—meaning that they do not feel it in their own persons, part of their own existence. It is heartily to be hoped of most of them that they do not" (153). Though Webster argues humorously and to effect through this essay "that, as a rule, I does not mean I" (154), she nevertheless is aware that some readers will believe that the poet is "a case for the police" (155).

Daniel Karlin has demonstrated that some of Browning's virtuoso speakers, such as Mr. Sludge, may indeed be "a nightmare of what the poet might become."[7] Though Webster insists on distance between art and life, her model of the poet as assimilative consciousness, able to filter out the idiosyncratic and deliver the essence of a character and thereby make it her own, can be said to mirror some of her own less savory speakers and their all-consuming passions. Through these morbidly criminal figures, this poet, like Browning, explores monomanias less benign than the artist's wish to impose order on the arbitrary through her art. "The Snow Waste" and "With the Dead" are paired poems (like "Fra Lippo Lippi" and "Andrea del Sarto") that offer opposed extremes—both poems involve crimes of passion and resulting curses; however, in the former the protagonist is doomed to have knowledge of his crime but lack affective response, while in the latter the speaker is all affect but has no memory of why he suffers a "horrible cold dread" (39),[8] with the exception of one day each year when he remembers his past, one of those anniversaries being the occasion of the poem. Both characters are compelling speakers who tell Gothic tales of jealousy, obsession, and violent secrets linked to masculine heterosexual desire, and the speakers of both are driven to confess these secrets. In the case of "The Snow Waste," an unnamed narrator listens to the eerie tale, while in "With the Dead" the speaker is his own audience each year on the anniversary of his crime.

Van Zuylen discusses the jealous lover in language that links his monomania to the artist's or the collector's, like Browning's Duke of Ferrara:

> The obsessive lover wants to craft a marvelously sterile world, a museum of feelings, where portraits inevitably become still lifes. Knowing everything about the other is a form of framing, of freezing. It is an attempt to defy the serpentine nature of experience, a desperate insurance policy that will guarantee that some things will never change if prudently kept under glass.[9]

---

[7] Daniel Karlin, *Browning's Hatreds* (Oxford: Clarendon, 1993), 66.

[8] Augusta Webster, "The Snow Waste," in *Portraits and Other Poems,* ed. Christine Sutphin (Peterborough, ON: Broadview, 2000), 96–106. Cited hereafter in text by line number.

[9] Van Zuylen, 14.

This characterization fits "The Snow Waste" and "With the Dead" as well, two poems that explore tensions between "motion and stasis, losing and keeping" through confessional narratives about erotic triangles that end in murder and eternal hauntings.[10] In both poems, the male protagonists are agonized by the suspicion that the women they love are keeping secrets from them and, needing to know "everything about the other," they attempt to take control through violence.

"The Snow Waste" tells the uncanny story of a cursed man whose jealousy and hatred lead him to wish for the death of his wife and her brother, who both subsequently succumb to plague, the latter catching the disease after the protagonist locks him in with his sister's corpse. His curse is to wander the frozen wilderness and "mine own self unto myself reveal / In perfect knowledge," while lacking the power to "feel" (45–6). It begins abruptly with an unnamed narrator encountering a trio of figures in an unspecified frozen wasteland, a man and two "glassy-eyed" specters (11), the man with a "gaze as void as theirs" (14). Like Coleridge's Ancient Mariner, the man is compelled to confess his awful secret, "as though his voice spoke of itself / And swayed by no part of the life in him" (15–16). Both the sublime landscape and the unnatural patterns of the murderer's language—described as an "uncadenced chant" (17), a "shudderless rhythm" (237), and a "droning murmur" (368)—figure the terrible stasis of the curse and his lack of remorse. Webster's prosodic skill shows in her management of his language: while the narrator delivers his frame for the story in blank verse, the haunted man chants in eight-line iambic stanzas with a single end rhyme for the whole, and, though those many stanzas capture formally his psychic fixation and emotional flatness, they are never monotonous for the reader. In fact, Webster may work into the poem something of a jibe at Swinburne, another poet of "morbid criminality" and obsessed lovers stuck in erotic triangles, notorious for his virtuosic but hypnotic verse, when she has her protagonist describe his inability to respond emotionally to past events through an analogy to musical, but nonsensical, language:

> And I can read them with my inward eye;
> But like a book whose fair-writ phrases lie
> All shapely moulded to word-harmony
> But void of meaning in their melody,
> Vague echoes that awaken no reply
> In my laxed mind that know not what they cry. (29–35)

Under the curse, he feels only physical pain from the deadening cold, but just "one pang" of sorrow will break the spell. The figures that accompany him are effigies of his victims, through whom respectively light and dark spirits speak occasionally, trying to jar his atrophied affective responses into regret. The origins of his crime and the cold that follows him lie in jealousy, first for his friend's success—"No feat of skill in which I all had passed / But he passed me" (112–13)—and then for the sister's admiration of her brother—"she, from whom no thought of mine

---

10 Van Zuylen, 14.

could stray, / Set all her pride on him" (128–9). When he wakes one day and knows his "glory overcast" (119), he feels "as if a sudden chill north blast / had found [him] sleeping in the sun" (117–18). After he fails to secure her love exclusively, he hides his swelling hatred "from open showing of its bitter strain" (136) and plots revenge. The poem's cursed, barren landscape has been caused by his "secret thought": that "all love might die / If else he in her love must press me nigh: / Since he must bless my foe, the sun on high / Might dwindle into darkness utterly" (206–9). Though it is pronounced that his wish is fulfilled—"All love shall die from thee; thou shalt not know it / Even in thought" (266–7)—he is also offered a period of one day to repent to avoid eternal punishment. However, he cannot recant his passionate hatred, and he thereby condemns himself to wander "evermore gnawed by quick cold" (356), followed by ghosts. The poem ends with the trio leaving the narrator "with slow and even pace" (364) to cross "the boundless snows" (362) beneath an "unchanging sky" (371), the "dream of absolute possession," to use Van Zuylen's phrase, having become a nightmare.[11] The blank landscape, unnamed characters, and unspecified time of "The Snow Waste" all contribute to that impression of "universality" or the disguising of historicity that Webster argues is a necessary element of poetry in "Poets and Personal Pronouns."

Like "The Snow Waste," "With the Dead" presents a study of secrecy, jealousy, violence, and haunting that serves as a figure for passionate obsession. The poem begins with an epigraph from the third chapter of Nathaniel Hawthorne's *The Marble Faun*, where the legend of Memmius is recounted: a macabre narrative of a pagan from the early Christian era doomed to wander the catacombs for having betrayed to the Romans the woman he loved and her fellow Christians. As he roams, he forgets the reason for his sentence, but each year on the anniversary of his crime he happens upon her tomb, relives the memories, and gets a chance to repent—one such anniversary being the occasion of Webster's monologue. Hawthorne's novel deals with the power of past secrets or hidden shames to shape the present, and the legend serves to establish the malignancy of sin in the story to come; it also offers a narrative thrill of the marvelous, as the main characters encounter what they think to be the specter of the catacomb, only for him to resolve into a real person from the heroine's past come to blackmail her. Taken perhaps with what Hawthorne's heroine describes as "the most awful idea connected with the catacombs … their interminable extent, and the possibility of going astray into this labyrinth of darkness,"[12] Webster makes the supernatural story her own as another dramatic study in the monomania of heterosexual masculine desire. Unlike Hawthorne, she grounds the curse Memmius suffers not only in his denial of Christianity, but in his betrayal of the woman he loves, Lucilla, who loves instead a fellow Christian, Glaucon. This poem offers the opposite extreme of "The Snow Waste," where, obsessive desire dooms the character to an otherwise affect-less existence; here, the speaker wanders the labyrinth eternally in "slow horror" (8)

11 Van Zuylen, 13.

12 Nathaniel Hawthorne, *The Marble Faun* (Boston: Ticknor and Fields, 1860), 39.

with no knowledge of why—a secret unto himself—save for on the anniversary day, when his "memory throbs / With such a living sentience that to think / On the once themes is to be [his] once self" (118–20).[13] This intense affective experience, "this sharp knowledge of the sad foregone" (144), makes his "hour of yearly rest / From the long madness" (1–2) into a "dreadful rest, accursed, / Made weary with despair and furious / With the old hate and the old bitter love: / Because [he] must, despite [him]self, remember" (17–20). Self awareness is here figured as the ultimate punishment for the violent male. The speaker's annual return of the repressed forces him to retell and reignite the powerful hatred that has driven and doomed him, turning "even love" (160) to "one black hate" (159). Thanks to his jealousy for his rival, he tells us, he could convincingly fake his conversion (taking on a secret identity) and thereby gain the confidence of the Christians he meant to betray: "I could blend my voice / To well-put words of doubt and half belief / And trembling hope to find in that sweet creed / A happy haven for my broken soul" (186–9). By the poem's end, the power of his hate inspires him to reject once more the opportunity he is offered each year to repent and "fall asleep in Christ" (324) because he cannot imagine sharing Lucilla with Glaucon, let alone "Glaucon's god" (328). Rather, like Swinburne's defiant pagans, throughout his monologue he remains loyal to "the guardians and the worshipped of great Rome" (59) and cherishes hope for revenge.

In both these texts, then, we see linked monomania, a secretive masculinity, heterosexual violence, and the notion of poetry as revelation, if not self-revelation. Critics have found this same constellation of issues at work in Browning's poetry, and in her essay on "Robert Browning and the Lure of the Violent Lyric Voice," Melissa Valiska Gregory provides a history of "competing Victorian responses" to representations of sexual violence in Browning and others (though she doesn't mention Webster).[14] She notes that many Victorian texts depict it as "psychologically inexplicable" but argues that the dramatic monologue, especially as practiced by Browning, was disturbing because it rhetorically mirrors domestic violence in its own "dynamic of forced intimacy," thereby "luring" both poet and readers "to the theme of sexual brutality and intimate violence, giving a voice to the inner secrets of sexual dominance."[15] Gregory cites reviewers' responses to Browning's early lyrics with this theme and sums them up as a "persistent critical complaint that Browning's intense, first-person outpourings were invasive, abnormal, and immoral."[16] As I discussed above, Webster was acutely aware that such accusations

---

13 Augusta Webster, "With the Dead," in *Portraits and Other Poems*, ed. Christine Sutphin (Peterborough, ON: Broadview, 2000), 107–16. Cited hereafter in the text by line number.

14 Melissa Valiska Gregory, "Robert Browning and the Lure of the Violent Lyric Voice: Domestic Violence and the Dramatic Monologue," *Victorian Poetry* 38 no. 4 (2000): 491–510, 491.

15 Gregory, 493, 496, 494.

16 Gregory, 500.

of perversion could be leveled against the poet, and, as Pionke demonstrates in his "Introduction," the woman poet, especially, was in a double-bind when it came to self-revelation, because she was supposed to be effusive and yet not have any secrets to reveal. As she is publishing her own representations of monomaniacal masculinity, Webster carefully argues for the rhetorical independence of the poet from her creations, and, conversely, the closeness of the poem's language to the reader's own "assimilative consciousness." Gregory claims that *The Ring and the Book* found acceptance with hitherto hostile Victorian readers in part because it consoled them about the abnormality of domestic violence by turning the subjective perspective of the dramatic monologue into legal testimony that implicitly called for judgment. In his outline of Victorian "normative qualitative judgments" of secrecy, Pionke argues that "secrecy that could be located within the private sphere and attributed to individuals met with greater approbation than secrecy deemed public and associated with non-familial collectives." There is much textual evidence to support such conclusions, since domestic violence is often the dirty little secret Victorian texts dance around; one thinks, for example, of the tortured treatment of the subject in Thackeray's *The Newcomes*. With their ambiguous "I"s that implicate the poet, the reader, and the fictional character in a conspiracy of violence, the dramatic monologues of monomaniacal masculinity by Browning and Webster treat the topic with a combination of intimacy and revelation that challenge notions of a discrete "private sphere." As both "public" advocate of women's rights and "private" poet of subjectivities, Webster was concerned explicitly with the rhetoric that enabled and even normalized sexual domination, educating readers on the relation between public codes of gender and private violence. That concern, it seems to me, offers another reason for her interest in the personal pronoun of dramatic poetry, its ability to force us to inhabit the mind of another, to make us feel "what no circumstances could possibly call out in us." It also inspires, I will argue, her effort to offer an alternative to violent heterosexuality in a portrait of dissident masculinity.

Beginning with the line, "There is nothing more difficult than to protect without enslaving" (*Housewife's Opinions*, 172), Webster explores in her essay "Protection for the Working Woman" the rhetorical implications of legislation purportedly designed to "protect" working women by controlling the hours and kinds of jobs they can work. She examines how protection and domination are linked: "domination of the protector over the protected is," she observes, "in most instances, an essential condition of the protection being possible at all" (172). However, she also notes the rhetorical and behavioral slippage that can occur, turning a benevolent paternalism into a threat to women's livelihoods: "domination, starting out perhaps with the most unassuming intentions, easily out-does its part and becomes despotic" (172). As she develops her argument, Webster exposes the relationship between the kind of employer abuse that the legislation is intended to combat and the domineering behavior of husbands and fathers who are supposed to be the "'natural protectors'" of women in their charge and whose domination goes unchecked by law. Making it illegal for starving women to work the hours they choose makes no sense, she argues; making it illegal for abusive spouses or fathers to "coerce them to overwork" does (177). She ends the essay by adding her voice to Frances Power Cobbe's call to allow "magistrates, in cases of dangerous violence from a husband to a wife, to grant the victim a legal separation with alimony" (178), and she reinforces once more the rhetorical connection between the so-called "protection" that would control women's right to work and other possible kinds of "restraint on adult women's labour [that] may be justly carried on the same arguments."

An analogous rhetorical link between the language of heterosexual masculine desire and the practice of gender domination makes the personal pronoun in monologues by Browning and Webster so provocative. In the several times that she mentions "Porphyria's Lover," Gregory emphasizes how it unites "rhetorical violence and sexual cruelty,"[17] but what I have find so disturbing about that particular lyric is how the speaker's romantic secret and "non-violent" rhetoric of romantic love allow him to rationalize his murder of Porphyria, hiding his violence beneath the veneer of protection. So too, Webster's awareness of such rhetorical and behavioral continuums as those between "public" / "private" and "protection" / "despotism," inspires her wish to represent an aggressive heterosexual masculinity "in a way which shall affect us as the manifest expression of what our very selves must have felt and thought and done." Moreover, that same awareness leads her to present an alternative, dissident masculinity in another dramatic study, a portrait in which the conflict between secret desire and the dominant culture leads to a perverse combination of aggression and abjection.

"Recreant Longings": Monasticism, Masochism, and a Dissident Masculinity

As counterpoint to these depictions of a heterosexual male dominance, Webster offers monologues in the voices of men who dissent from the prescribed codes of masculine aggression, yet the dissident masculinities in these portraits become tales of the closet. "In an Almshouse," for example, presents a poor, aged scholar of modern times, who reflects on what can seem to be his failure to live an active, entrepreneurial life in "the master-Present, the strong century / That gave our lives and will have use of them" (182–3),[18] but which might also seem to the reader a valuable kind of experience, lived in repose and reflection. Though we learn at the outset of this interior monologue that he is nearly blind, we also soon discern that he has learned that "seeing can be done without the eyes" (11). One of Webster's most effective counter-narratives of masculinity, "The Manuscript of Saint Alexius," comes in another story of a life full of secrets and obsession, derived from another early Christian legend, which nevertheless speaks to these

17 Gregory, 496.

18 Augusta Webster, "In an Almshouse," in *Portraits and Other Poems*, ed. Christine Sutphin (Peterborough, OT: Broadview, 2000), 244–57. Cited in text by line number.

Victorian anxieties over social progress and the roles of both men and women. By dramatizing a perversely "feminine" religious virtuoso and examining the conflict between supposed duties to the world and the subject's private desire for spiritual "perfection" through celibacy, the poem explores at length the power of the solitary religious life—as well as the crippling power of a secret—to disrupt domestic ideology and its accompanying gender roles, including a possessive heterosexual masculinity. In a 1988 essay on the feminization of Anglo-Catholicism in post-Oxford Movement England, John Shelton Reed asserts that monastic communities of religious virtuosi were perceived by many as "symbolic affronts—and in a few cases actual threats—to central values of Victorian middle-class culture," and especially as "a challenge to Victorian family ideology and to received ideas about women's place and role."[19] Although it is based on an ancient legend, Webster's poem speaks to the Victorian controversies over the supposedly secret motives and "manliness" of virtuosi such as John Henry Newman.[20] Using the dramatic form to present the subjective perspective of the solitary as well as the voices of those around him, Webster in effect creates an *apologia pro vita contemplativa.*

The narrative Webster appropriates as the basis of her poem dates from the fifth century, though it appeared first in written form in Syria and Greece during the ninth century. In the legend, Alexius, son of Roman patrician Euphemianus, runs away from home to avoid marriage and travels to Edessa in Syria, where he lives as an ascetic for seventeen years. After becoming known for his holiness, he runs away again, this time returning home to live another seventeen years on the estate disguised as a beggar. After his death, he is discovered to be the lost son, he is immediately honored as a saint, and his father's house is converted to a church.[21] From this narrative skeleton, Webster elaborates a drama over the conflict between a patriarchal ideology that is based on normative heterosexuality and an abnormal, perverse, but religiously sanctioned, life on its very periphery. Along the way, she depicts a subject whose masochistic sainthood is constituted by a powerful desire that is structured through contradictory social discourses and which can only be expressed through a closeted identity.[22]

---

19 John Shelton Reed, "'A Female Movement': The Feminization of Nineteenth-Century Anglo-Catholicism," *Anglican and Episcopal History* 57 (June 1988): 200, 201.

20 In her review of Lewis Morris's *A Vision of Saints* (*The Athenaeum*, March 14, 1891, 339–40), Webster likened the early Christian legends to "time-honoured but time-worn fairy tales" in their ability to bear re-telling and thereby new associations and significance. For Webster, the Alexius legend combines "the spiritual problem" with "peculiar emotional interest." I'm grateful to Patricia Rigg for sending me to this review.

21 See J. P. Kirsch, "St. Alexius," in *The Catholic Encyclopedia*, vol. 1 (Robert Appleton, 1907), transcribed by Laura Ouellette for *The Catholic Encyclopedia*, <http://www.newadvent.org/cathen/01307b.htm>, copyright 2000, Kevin Knight. Accessed April 5, 2001.

22 The indispensable reference for this argument and many others on the role of the closet in nineteenth-century culture is Eve Kosofsky Sedgwick, *Epistemology of the Closet* (Los Angeles and Berkeley: U of California P, 1990).

In *Sexual Dissidence,* Jonathan Dollimore established the history of "perversion" and its significance in Western culture (and, for my purposes, especially in Victorian England) as a "destabilizing dynamic" that subverts from within discourses and institutions viewed in the mainstream as "natural."[23] Oliver S. Buckton has applied Dollimore's concept to the public feud between Newman and Charles Kingsley that resulted in the publication of the former's *Apologia Pro Vita Sua* in 1864, a few years before the appearance of Webster's portraits of aggressive and reclusive masculinities. In Buckton's view, "Kingsley's accusation of dishonesty was the culmination of a long period of widespread distrust of Newman, and…this distrust stemmed not merely from concern about his 'honesty' but also from hostility toward his perceived 'perversion'—a term that included both his religious transgression and his sexual ambiguity. Kingsley's assault on Newman…was one remarkably extreme manifestation of Victorian orthodoxies of gender and religion"[24]—orthodoxies that linked heterosexual marriage to progressive civilization and active engagement in the national and domestic economies to normal and healthy gender identities. In "The Manuscript of Saint Alexius," Webster also confronts the associations in Victorian culture and in Kingsley's attack on Newman regarding effeminacy, celibacy, and a secretive, transgressive form of homosociality.

In the manuscript he leaves behind, Webster's Alexius describes his upbringing as the only son of wealthy Romans, "learning all meet for my estate on earth, / but learning more, what they taught more, of God, / and loving most that learning" (138).[25] His wish to be given to God, a "longing" embodied in "a voice that spoke no words/ yet called me," is countermanded by the wishes of his parents that he marry and produce children, "And their words seemed God's / more than my heart's, theirs who had rule on me" (138–9). If his "natural place" were not within the patriarchal family and heterosexual society, they argue, "there would be signs which none could doubt" (140). Euphemianus insists on his son's "'living in the world'" (97), echoing a construction of normative English masculine identity as entrepreneurial and aggressive in nature, voiced in periodical articles disapproving of monasticism published from the 1840s to the 1890s. Unwilling to pick his own bride and uninterested when his father then determines the choice, Alexius submits to his parents' will when he's told that she will be his "fair playmate Claudia," for he assures himself that his indifference to her "beauty" (134) and "grace" like that of "useless goddesses perfect in stone" (135–6) will mean that his "soul shall still be … consecrate, / virgin to God until the better days / when I may live the life alone with Him" (141–3). In trying to manage his own desires and those of

---

23 Jonathan Dollimore, *Sexual Dissidence: Augustine to Wilde, Freud to Foucault* (Oxford: Clarendon, 1991), 124.

24 Oliver S. Buckton, "'An Unnatural State': Gender, 'Perversion,' and Newman's *Apologia Pro Vita Sua,*" *Victorian Studies* 35, no. 4 (Summer 1992): 360.

25 Augusta Webster, "The Manuscript of St. Alexius," in *Portraits* (London and Cambridge: Macmillan, 1870), 134–61. Hereafter cited in text by line number.

his parents, however, Alexius depends on the woman's passivity and neglects to consider the potential of Claudia's desire; after the ceremony, when she looks at him, he grows "white" and sinks "back sickly. For I suddenly / knew that I might know that which men call love" (152–4).

Rather than directly oppose his parents' "rule" (107), Alexius runs away and winds up in a "small lonely chapel, little used" (165) where he finds "patterned out in polished stones / Peter denying Christ" (167–8). Alexius thus finds himself between men (Christ and father) and the discourses with which they are identified: a homosociality imaged as a bond betrayed and a compulsory heterosexuality represented as filial duty. In the chapel, Alexius undergoes a dream vision of himself ensconced within a family circle, only to have "a carved and marble Christ / hung on a Cross" (177–8) beckon and call to him. At first, it seems, duty appears satisfied because both father, holding by the hand a grandson, "a sturdy urchin, copy of himself" (186), and mother, surrounded by other grandchildren, give him permission to "go forth" (188). However, Claudia remains to grasp his hand when the voice calls, "'Alexius, come,' loud and in wrath" (208), though indeed he otherwise "were content" (204) to follow. Conveniently imprisoned within the chapel when he comes out of this sleep or trance, Alexius hides there for two days, hearing people go by and worrying about whether, if he dies by keeping silent, he will be "self-murdered or God's martyr" (234). When Claudia comes to the chapel to pray for his return, Alexius hides, despite his sympathy for her tears, and actively plots his escape. Rather than confront Claudia and "charge her let none know" (260), he slips out when she leaves the door open, leaving his family to wander for ten years "always alone with God" (406).

In Webster's version, Alexius gains no fame during his wanderings but returns to his parents' house when he finds that the "peace" he has attained in his ten years away from home and family has become a "blankness" (411). Pondering why he "loved God more / and felt His love more near" (424–5) when he suffered, Alexius recognizes his "need of quickening pain / to stir the sluggish soul awake in" him (427–8). Realizing that his choice to follow Christ cost him "nought to give" (430), he returns to the scene of transgression to enact a secret, perverse version of family life, enclosing himself in "the beggar's shed with God" (459)—both part of and apart from his family—and watching his parents suffer from his absence for another six years. This life puts him in position to play both masochist and sadist; a victim and parodist of the cultural imperatives, as he both cloisters himself away and turns the father into a version of himself, for now Euphemianus "was changed, they said, cared not to see / friends' faces greeting him, nor join in talk, / but would be solitary" (475–8). Since his mother Aglaia likes this beggar's uncannily familiar voice, he is summoned to sing for her:

> they fetched me, I stood by her: ah my mother!
> and she so changed! nothing of her old self;
> the goodliness, the sweetness, the delight,
> gone, waned out from her, as the light of day
> was waning from her eyes long dulled by tears.

Ah, could I but have clung about her feet,
crying out "Mother, take thy son again!"
But yet for her it would have been too late. (498–505)

Much like the abject heroine of *East Lynne*, the disguised Alexius attends his own funeral, as it were, and submits to the "exquisite pain" (460) of proximity to those mourning him (both his parents and Claudia, who has remained in the household) and to the denial of his "recreant longings" (29) to be reunited. In embracing the "blessed" pain "that brought so exquisite joy!" (460)—for his "heart awoke for anguish, and felt God" (463)—he adopts the feminine self-abnegation through which—according to Sarah Ellis, John Ruskin, and others—Victorian women were to find their glory, as well as the arbitrarily "feminine attitude" Freud would assign male masochists he diagnosed as trying to "evade" their homosexuality.[26] In effect, Alexius's unusual version of family life is an arrested development that undermines the bourgeois, masculine *bildungsroman* narrative, as his refusal to deny Christ disallows his assumption of his father's place. Caught between a disembodied "voice" of homosocial desire and the opposing cultural narratives that would discipline it, Alexius lives the open secret, inventing a perverted existence—ascetic and enclosed, neither reproducing the father's life nor finally following Christ's—which parodies the choices of compulsory heterosexuality and celibate homosexuality he has been given. However, unlike Mrs. Henry Wood's Isabel Vane, Alexius completes the dynamic of abjection and arrogance that would be Freud's paradigm of male masochism by leaving behind his manuscript and thus elevating his status from marginal to central—transforming himself from the invisible "beggar Lazarus" to the bizarre spectacle of a prodigal son—and at the same time turning himself, thus outed, into a problem for the Pope and the poem to solve.

At the end of his narrative, Alexius imagines himself in death as both abject sufferer of his family's indifference (thanks to his disguise) and their persecutor, who prolongs their suffering as they "wait for lost Alexius to come home, / and mourn for him, half hating him for their grief" (535–6). Playing both submissive and dominant roles through his secret identity, he claims of Christ the "earned fruit" (537) of his sufferings and theirs: "give fruit for them I smote" (539). This half-triumphant, half-guilty admission of his aggression against the family leads Alexius for a moment to consider whether he has "written wildly" (540), but he decides that God has sanctioned his story and, by implication, the willful life of submission he has led, "for all is good, / all happy, if it be to do His will, / the suffering ye may guess, but not the bliss / till ye have tasted it" (558–61).

As a final gesture of power that ironizes his masochism, Alexius designates the Pope his messenger: "he first, / and I the last, so thereto he is called;

[26] Sigmund Freud, "'A Child is Being Beaten.' A Contribution to the Study of the Origin of Sexual Perversions," in *Collected Papers,* vol. 2, ed. Ernest Jones, trans. Joan Riviere (New York: Basic Books, 1959), 126.

servant of servants" (549–50).[27] The "poor words" (567) the Pope is to deliver, he prays, will have power both to comfort the family and, significantly, to "strengthen and stir souls / which hear Thee call and pause to count with Thee" (569–70). His perverse existence, he seems to imply, fits into both cultural narratives (domestic heterosexuality and celibate homosociality) and thus has value as a survival strategy.

"The Manuscript of Saint Alexius" is not, strictly speaking, a dramatic monologue, but rather a dramatic poem in which the main section of the text is the manuscript of the dead saint/son and a frame narrative accommodates the perspectives of other characters, including Alexius's parents, Claudia, and Pope Innocent, whom Alexius, on his deathbed, summons through a servant boy. Not surprisingly, this frame helps to shape the reader's response and the significance of Alexius's story. At the end of his manuscript, before invoking the prayer of John at the end of Revelation, "Lord Jesus come" (573), Alexius has asserted that his testimony is "forced as by the Spirit" and thus reconciles the conflicting discourses that have shaped his life. It remains to the frame narrative to corroborate the "utter truth" (25) of his story. Of the four potential interpreters, it is Claudia, the rejected wife, who first validates Alexius's actions. When the Pope confronts the family and unmasks the beggar as the son, father and mother stare and are "perplexed" (582), but Claudia reveals that she has a secret too: she recognized Alexius when he first returned home, several years earlier, and has repressed her knowledge, whereupon "one strong gust of passion" overwhelms her and she falls beside the corpse weeping. When, in the poem's conclusion, the dazed Euphemianus repeats the question, "'Yet did he well?'" (605), Claudia bears witness and is followed by the Pope:

> But Claudia rose up tearless, and replied
> "Alexius did all well: he knew God called:"
> and Innocent, not tearless, raised his hand
> and spoke "She answers wisely: he obeyed;
> he knew, being a very saint of God:
> let us bless God for him." And they all knelt.
> But still Aglaia could not understand. (608–14)

If the puzzlement of Euphemianus and Aglaia reflects the anxiety of someone like Kingsley—who was both influenced by Newman's "ideal of monastic purity" early in life,[28] and later disturbed by "the challenge he posed to Victorian classifications of gender, sexuality, and religion"[29]—Claudia's acceptance of Alexius's choice

---

[27] Thereby echoing the inversion of dominant and submissive in Matthew 19:30 (The King James Version), where in response to his complaint that the disciples have left all for Jesus, Peter is told, "But many that are first shall be last; and the last shall be first."

[28] Sheridan Gilley, *Newman and his Age* (London: Darton, 1990), 324. Quoted in Buckton, 373.

[29] Buckton, 374.

despite her love for him reminds one of the open-mindedness of Fanny Kingsley, the wife who had lent Newman's books "to her lover when she was trying to convert him back to Christianity."[30]

The Pope's agreement with Claudia's view evens the opinions on the manuscript as an interpretation of Alexius's life—two endorse it and two question it—but his presence does more to shape this seemingly open-ended poem and its implications for secret identities. In the opening section of the poem, as the child with the manuscript enters the Pope's "solemn hall" (1), the latter is listening to "angry disputing on Free-Will in man, / Grace, Purity, and the Pelagian creed" (3–4). Webster highlights the significant moment in church history that serves as a context for Alexius's narrative, when, by condemning Pelagius (who denied original sin and preached the freedom of the human will to choose and work for salvation) and implicitly favoring Augustine (who preached the total depravity of humanity and the necessary intervention of divine grace for salvation), Pope Innocent I helped to shape Catholic (and thus Western) attitudes toward dissident subjectivities. While history's Innocent I might have helped to undermine such identities as sinful, at the poem's conclusion Webster's Innocent I endorses Alexius's wish to withdraw from the dominant narrative of aggressive heterosexuality: "he obeyed; / he knew, being a very saint of God" (611–12).

Alexius's longings are, finally, "recreant"—meaning both craven and apostate—in more ways than he can know. Though by this label he means to chide himself for what he sees as his own weak wish to return to the family, the poem suggests that, in the context of Victorian compulsory heterosexuality, his yearning for celibate homosociality is, like John Henry Newman's, transgressive but can only take shape as a misunderstood, secret story of surrender.

Conclusion

In "The Snow Waste," "With the Dead," and "The Manuscript of Saint Alexius," we have a series of monologues that put into practice Webster's complicated, gendered understanding of the valence of the personal pronoun in poetry and that use Gothic and early-Christian narratives to comment on the mysteries of masculinity in her own age. In "Lay Figures," she even makes the case that such legends and myths offer the poet pre-narrated subjectivities that compel her to probe beyond the superficial levels of story and identity:

> The highest powers of creative imagination have usually found their fittest exercise in intensified pourtrayal [sic] of the men and women and events of history or of legends and tales. It seems as if the resistance, so to speak, offered to the plastic despotism of the artist by characteristics accepted, not made, called forth a subtler and a stronger skill than if he had worked with the limitlessness of free invention. The poet creates as the sculptor does; he need not make the stone as well as the statue. (*Housewife's Opinions*, 150–51)

30 Buckton, 364.

And it is in her own age that Webster sees the greatest need for such resistance, such alien forms of subjectivity. In another essay from *A Housewife's Opinions*, "Portraits," Webster complains about modern conformity as it is embodied in nineteenth-century portrait painting, and in doing so she pinpoints the paradoxical sense of identity that she thinks the true artist can capture. In their "trite and meaningless monotony," these paintings

> are like the sitters, and the sitters differ in features and complexion from each other, therefore they are not like each other; and yet they leave the impression of their having no special identity, they are portraits of anybody. Any one of them you feel could just as well be the resemblance of any other person with a similar nose and coat or dress and no matter how different a story. (169)

These portraits are bad because they have no secrets. According to Webster, the "secret of genius" in the artist is the ability "to see the unlikeness through the likeness and to render both" (170). In her monologues of masculinities, and obsessive, secret desires, she strives to achieve that uncanny balance of difference and similarity and succeeds in revealing the power of the secret in the formation of identity.

Chapter 10
Victorian Conjuring Secrets

Michael Claxton

Of all the Victorian professionals whose livelihood or public image depended upon secrets, the conjurer was perhaps the most paranoid. The nineteenth century was a critical time for magic as a form of entertainment; it slowly moved from outdoor fairs into more stable performance venues, and made dramatic transitions in terms of costume and staging, and as it witnessed the growing literature of secrets. Professor Hoffmann's 1876 book *Modern Magic* marked a watershed in the publication of magicians' methods, and, depending on the age of its reader, was either received with youthful glee as a revelation, or lamented as the death-knell of the business. The prestidigitators who made their living from the effects described in this volume had much at stake in their objections, especially during an era which would soon witness the increasing professionalization of magic and the rise of conjuring journals, organizations, and codified standards of conduct. Once a theatrical stepchild banished to the noisy fairs, streets, and taverns, magic was fighting for its acceptance as an art.

"Two of a trade must not underbid each other," says Hank Morgan in *A Connecticut Yankee at King Arthur's Court* (1889), as he waits for Camelot's legendary wizard to restore a broken fountain by magic. "Merlin has the contract; no other magician can touch it till he throws it up ..."[1] The Yankee's repeated view of magic as a viable profession almost parodies a contemporary phenomenon in the world of stage magic. In response to a century of change, performers increasingly realized the need for collective support and secrecy. The turn-of-the-century magic world saw the formation of the Society of American Magicians (1902), the Association Française des Artistes Prestidigitateurs (1903), and England's The Magic Circle (1905). One primary goal of these organizations was to prevent public exposure of magic tricks, while at the same time providing a forum for sharing such secrets within the profession. The journal *Mahatma* (1895) had appeared slightly earlier, followed by *The Sphinx* (1902), *L'Illusionniste* (1902), and *The Magic Circular* (1906), among many others. As early as 1891, French magician and film pioneer George Méliès (1861–1938) even founded a magicians' trade union, the Academy of Prestidigitation, to help stabilize the market and protect the reputations of its professionals. In 1907, Harry Houdini was rebuked by the union

[1] Mark Twain, *A Connecticut Yankee in King Arthur's Court*, ed. Bernard L. Stein, *The Works of Mark Twain*, vol. 9 (Berkeley: U of California P, 1979), 251–2.

for slandering a French magic legend during the serial publication of his book: *The Unmasking of Robert-Houdin.*[2]

As they circled the wagons professionally, those who saw themselves as true conjuring artists were often hostile to three major groups of quasi-magicians during the period, each of which became the target of a systematic debunking effort by the magic fraternity. These rivals included, first, the spirit mediums, who appropriated conjuring secrets for fraudulent ends; second, the legendary magicians of the East, who, in the age of Empire, had to be shown inferior to their Western colleagues; and finally, the card sharps and thimble-riggers, who were a visible reminder of magic's lowbrow roots. And, of course, there were rivalries within the profession itself, as magicians, then as now, played one-upmanship. The drama involved could be intense, as when, for example, the American illusionist Harry Kellar (1849–1922) brazenly walked onstage during a performance of the levitation illusion at the Egyptian Hall in London in 1901 to see how the trick worked, then hired away the assistants of his rival in order to discover the full secrets.[3] Magic historian H. J. Burlingame (1852–1915) had complained in 1891 that Kellar and his competitor Alexander Herrmann (1844–96) had stooped to exposing each other's methods to the public.[4] While magic's turf wars seem little different from the intrigues in other professions, the magician's complex proprietary attitude toward secrets seems, in part, a response to a changing world in which the desire to create wonder was increasingly in tension with the technological and literary urge to dispel it.

In his nostalgic 1842 volume *Merrie England in the Olden Times*, George Daniel mourns the passing of the English fairs, which he says had fallen prey to the sour disapproval of the Utilitarians and Evangelicals. He especially laments the disappearance of that breeding ground for a class of skilled entertainers like the magician Isaac Fawkes (c1675–1731), who had developed his skills over decades of repeated outdoor shows.[5] In so doing, Daniel describes a phenomenon in the world of conjuring that was particularly intensified during the nineteenth century. As venues for performing changed, as styles and technologies of entertainment went in and out of fashion, the conjurers had to adapt in ways that took them further from their itinerant roots. The decline of the fairs ushered two centuries of rapid successive changes in performance media. From street corners and fair booths to taverns and lecture halls, from vaudeville and full-evening shows to the new media of film and television, magicians have reinvented themselves, adapting to their ever-changing venues and audiences both in order to survive, and to elevate the status of their profession.

---

[2] Paul Hammond, *Marvelous Méliès* (London: Fraser, 1974), 63.

[3] Jim Steinmeyer, *Hiding the Elephant: How Magicians Invented the Impossible and Learned to Disappear* (New York: Carroll and Graf, 2003), 169–70.

[4] H. J. Burlingame, *Leaves from Conjurers' Scrap Books* (Chicago: Donohue, 1891), 77–8.

[5] George Daniel, *Merrie England in the Olden Times* (1842; London: Chatto and Windus, 1881), 316.

In 1876, journalist and entertainment historian Thomas Frost (1821–1908) described the perception of conjuring in the previous century:

> The social position of the professional conjuror was at this period even more dubious than that of the actor. The prejudice against his art and its professors which had been born of ignorance and superstition was dying out with the process of mental enlightenment; but he was ranked, in common with the juggler, the posturer, and the tumbler, as a vagrant, and in his provincial ramblings was sometimes in danger of being treated in that character with the stocks. He might be patronized by the upper classes, and even by the royal family; but he was not admitted into good society, or even regarded as a respectable character.[6]

In his memoir, *The Life of a Showman*, the Scottish traveling magician David Prince Miller (1808–73) confesses how much trouble he had getting "respectable people" to stop at his booth at a fair in Norwood, despite a bombastic (and false) speech about having performed before the queen.[7] At the beginning of the nineteenth century, William Wordsworth articulated the discomfort of many who felt that the fairs had declined into a noisy, chaotic freak show where "singers, rope dancers, giants and dwarfs, / Clowns, conjurers, posture-makers, harlequins" competed for attention "amid the uproar of the rabblement."[8] Increasingly drawn to more stable venues such as taverns, lecture halls, drawing rooms, and eventually theatres, magicians were fast abandoning the fairs and street corners as places to exhibit their talents. Simon During suggests several reasons for the decline in conjurers at the fairs: legal prohibitions after 1826 against the lotteries from which many magicians had benefited, the negative results of magicians giving away too many secrets, and the opportunities for expanding one's performance repertoire afforded by the fixed sites.[9] In their history of street magic, Edward Claflin and Jeff Sheridan further point out that magicians' increasing use of bulky mechanical apparatus required larger performance venues.[10] Leaving the fairs, then, was both a social and a practical move for many conjurors.

Except for *The Life of a Showman*, the voices of few itinerant magicians have been recorded; fortunately, Henry Mayhew (1812–87) interviewed two anonymous street conjurers for his *London Labour and the London Poor*. One plucky performer tells Mayhew how the chance absence of a conjurer provided his first break. The young lad calmed a noisy tavern crowd with his conjuring and was

6 Thomas Frost, *The Lives of the Conjurors* (1876; London: Chatto and Windus, 1881), 125–6.

7 David Prince Miller, *The Life of a Showman* (London: Avery, 1851), 165.

8 William Wordsworth, *The Prelude*, ed. Jonathan Wordsworth, M. H. Abrams, and Stephen Gill (1805; New York: Norton, 1979), VII: 294–7.

9 Simon During, *Modern Enchantments: The Cultural Power of Secular Magic* (Cambridge: Harvard UP, 2002), 98.

10 Edward Claflin and Jeff Sheridan, *Street Magic* (Washington, DC: Kaufman, 1977), 85.

rewarded when the hat was passed: "When the plate went round I got one shilling and sixpence. 'Hulloa! I said to myself, is this the situation?' Then I sold some penny books, explaining how the tricks was done, and I got sixpence more."[11] It was a story that was to become a staple of conjuring memoirs and magic-related fiction: the young, resourceful teenager saves the day by filling in for an inept or absent adult magician and thus begins his career.

Yet the magician here is not simply an entertainer, dazzling audiences with his mysterious skills. He is also a savvy entrepreneur, fully conscious of working for money and willing to expose his own secrets for a quick handful of coins. While the penny books he sold no doubt explained elementary tricks that were beneath his repertoire, later in the interview with Mayhew this street conjurer explains the methods behind several of his own card tricks, showing how to crimp corners, make secret passes, and force cards. It seems an impolitic confession, one potentially damaging to his livelihood. Yet as magic secrets increasingly became a marketable commodity during the century, performers such as Mayhew's conjurer sought to profit from the spirit of an increasingly secular and scientific age, which was more and more uncomfortable with mystery and anxious to probe behind the curtain of the world's seeming wonders.

We cannot be reminded too often that the Victorians and Edwardians were living in an age when industry and technology were fast becoming a new form of magic. Nineteenth-century inventions such as the electric light bulb, the telephone, the phonograph, the automobile, and the cinema gave Westerners something novel to wonder at and boosted their image of themselves as industrial magicians. In a century constantly "praised to its face" for its "unparalleled ingenuity,"[12] parlor tricks could indeed seem quaint or trivial. In fact, when extolling the accomplishments of the American whaling industry in building up the opulent town of New Bedford in *Moby-Dick* (1851), Herman Melville triumphantly asked, "Can Herr Alexander do that?"[13] *Punch* magazine made a similar observation in 1860, arguing in "Dobler Outdone," that with the increasing number of practical and amazing inventions, "the apparatus of a conjuror seems sold at every counter, and feats of legerdemain are now in everybody's hands."[14] Compared to the wonders of "Blank's Patent Coffee Pot," *Punch* believed, the magic of Austrian conjurer Ludwig Dobler (1801–64) was passé. While clearly tongue-in-cheek, the article makes the serious point that commercial innovation had the power to package the miraculous and put it into every household.

---

[11] Henry Mayhew, *London Labour and the London Poor, vol. 3* (London: Griffin, Bohn, 1861), 108.

[12] Walter Houghton, *The Victorian Frame of Mind* (New Haven: Yale UP, 1957), 39.

[13] Herman Melville, *Moby–Dick, or The Whale*, ed. Harrison Hayford et al (Evanston and Chicago: Northwestern UP and Newberry Library, 1988), 32. Herr Alexander was the stage name of German magician Johann Friedrich Heimburger (1818–1909), whose brief performing career included a tour of the United States in the mid 1840s.

[14] "Dobler Outdone," *Punch* 39 (November 17, 1860), 194.

Such confidence in technological advancement and human cleverness also accompanies a certain characteristically Victorian optimism about solving puzzles. Since the conjurer is in some ways a combative figure, brazenly challenging audiences to figure out how the illusions are accomplished, one natural response of spectators is to accept the challenge and announce that they have seen the secret. The teenage Morris, a smug would-be-magician in G. K. Chesteron's play *Magic* (1913) does exactly that. After a litany of explanations about sleeves and false bottoms, he admits to the professional conjurer that "Most mysteries are tolerably plain if you know the apparatus."[15] Such confident problem-solving is reflected, among other things, in the increasing popularity of detective fiction during the century. Sherlock Holmes certainly recognized the wonder-worker's dilemma, when, after revealing the straightforward mental process by which he had deduced information about Mr. Wilson in "The Red-Headed League" (1892), he regretted exposing his own tricks:

> Mr. Jabez Wilson laughed heavily. "Well, I never!" said he. "I thought at First that you had done something clever, but I see that there was nothing in it after all."
>
> "I begin to think, Watson," said Holmes, "that I make a mistake in explaining. '*Omne ignotum pro magnifico*,' you know, and my poor little reputation, such as it is, will suffer shipwreck if I am so candid."[16]

While many Victorians actually welcomed the opportunity to be mystified as they flocked to magic shows, that willing suspension of disbelief was balanced on the other hand by a skeptical spirit that prided itself on not being easily tricked.

Magic historians often divide conjuring history by the year 1876, when an English barrister named Angelo Lewis (1839–1919) published his magnum opus, *Modern Magic*, which had been serialized in *Every Boy's Magazine*. Using the pseudonym Professor Hoffmann, Lewis exhaustively described card tricks, coin sleights, and almost every piece of mechanical apparatus then in use in the parlor magician's repertoire. In his introduction, Hoffmann justifies his breach of secrecy:

> The more important secrets of the art have been known but to a few, and those few have jealously guarded them, knowing that the more closely they concealed the clue to their mysteries, the more would those mysteries be valued. Indeed, the more noted conjurors of fifty years ago strove to keep the secret of their best tricks not only from the outside world, but from their *confreres*. At the present day the secrets of the art are not so well kept; and there is hardly a trick performed upon the stage which the amateur may not, at a sufficient expenditure

[15] G. K. Chesterton, *Magic* (London: Martin Secker, 1913), 39.

[16] Arthur Conan Doyle, *The Complete Sherlock Holmes* (Garden City, NY: Garden City Books, 1930), 197. *Omne ignotum pro magnifico*: Everything unknown seems greater than reality.

> of shillings or guineas, procure at the conjuring depots. There being, therefore, no longer the same strict secrecy, the literature of magic has improved a little, though it still leaves much to be desired.[17]

Writing in the 1920s, magic historian Sidney Clarke (1864–1940) says the 560-page book "fell like a bombshell" among conjurers of the time and had "an almost incalculable effect in revolutionizing and revivifying the art of conjuring and improving the status of the conjurer."[18] Books explaining tricks had appeared before, but none of these earlier volumes "compared to *Modern Magic* in style, quality, and literary merit."[19] Throughout the text, Hoffmann gives advice to the amateur conjurer, always stressing the level of mastery needed to become a professional. For example, in his discussion of gimmicked cards, Hoffmann points out that "Professionals of the highest class discard them altogether, and rely wholly on the more subtle magic of their own fingers."[20] Hoffmann goes on to explain that "subtle magic" in meticulous detail, emphasizing the dramatics of presentation and poise in addition to the mechanical secrets.

Reactions were mixed. The American magician Frederick Eugene Powell (1856–1938) expressed the bitter scorn of many, who felt their pearls had been cast before swine: "I wish he had died in his mother's womb," he said years later, blaming Hoffmann for the "avalanche of books" that made secrets available to those who had not yet proven themselves.[21] Clarke cites one professional who lamented in 1876 that "the golden days of magic are over."[22] But to young readers, Hoffmann had opened a new world. In 1929, the historian Henry Ridgely Evans (1861–1949) effused that "its arrival on Christmas day, 1878 was fortuitous for it marked that particular white day as a red-letter day in the history of my life ... Prior to reading *Modern Magic*, I had picked up some little manuals on conjuring by Prof. W. H. Cremer, but found them inconclusive ... I longed to draw the veil that hid the Holy of Holies and penetrate to the very core of the magic art ... *Modern Magic* allowed me to do this."[23] William W. Durbin (1866–1937), who would become a leader in the International Brotherhood of Magicians in the 1920s, got

---

17 Professor Hoffmann, *Modern Magic* (1876; Philadelphia: McKay, c 1890), 1–2.

18 Sidney Clarke, *The Annals of Conjuring*, ed. Todd Karr and Edwin Dawes (Seattle: Miracle Factory, 2001), 350. Clarke's ground-breaking history of magic was first serialized in a British conjuring periodical, *The Magic Wand*, from 1924–28.

19 J. B. Findlay and Thomas Sawyer, *Professor Hoffmann: A Study* (Tustin, CA: Thomas Sawyer, 1977), 5.

20 Hoffmann, 62.

21 Tom Ewing, *Frederick Eugene Powell: The Man and His Magic* (NP: Tom Ewing, 1986), 29.

22 Clarke, 351.

23 Henry Ridgely Evans, *The Linking Ring* 8, no. 11 (January 1929), 869. *The Linking Ring* (1922–present) is the journal of the International Brotherhood of Magicians. William Henry Cremer (d. 1892?) authored or had ghosted for him *The Secret Out* (New York: Dick and Fitzgerald, 1859) and other conjuring manuals.

his copy in 1879 at age 13 and confessed, "I think I studied that book more than I studied my books in school … It was the first authentic work that really told you how magic was performed."[24] Shops selling conjuring apparatus had been around since the 1840s, but at least for their first few decades they had catered to a close-lipped community of professionals, who resisted both the sharing of old secrets, and, sometimes, the innovation of new ones.

To understand the progressive changes mid-to-late Victorian conjurers made in their approach to the craft, we must look at the typical image of the stage magician earlier in the century. While some magicians were abandoning the gaudy costumes favored by fairground performers like Gyngell (d. 1833), many continued the vogue epitomized by the Frenchman Phillippe (1802–78), who dressed as a wizard, complete with decorated robe and conical hat. Professor Hoffmann snidely remarked in *Modern Magic* that "the very last specimen of such a garment … is, or was, worn by the magician attached to the Crystal Palace," and he quipped that any conjurer ought to be liberally paid for such self-debasement.[25]

Since the 1840s, magicians also displayed a taste for overdone stage settings: tables loaded with cumbersome and suspicious-looking apparatus. Boxes, tubes, and cones filled the stage, even though many were not used in the performance. Clarke links the fashion for showy apparatus to a wider Orientalism and commercialism:

> The chief aim of the popular conjurer was not so much to deceive the eye of his patrons by the nimbleness of his fingers as to dazzle them by the brilliancy of his apparatus. Shining boxes, glittering cups, polished cases, all apparently constructed out of some terribly precious metal, converted the stage on which they were arranged into a scene of hybrid magnificence that artfully combined the Oriental palace with the store for the sale of shop fittings.[26]

John Henry Anderson (1814–74), the flamboyant Scotsman billed as "The Wizard of the North," was the standard-bearer for gaudy showmanship, cluttered stages, and bombastic advertising. The following description of his apparatus from an 1857 broadside is typical: "The magnificent paraphernalia of the most elaborate description, gorgeous in its golden glow and resplendent in its jeweled richness, has recently been manufactured at a cost exceeding 7000 pounds … It comprises all that is Oriental in Splendor with all that is chaste in Parisian elegance."[27]

Unfortunately, such stage settings led audiences to suspect hidden confederates under the draped tables, or false bottoms among the boxes on display. Hence the reforms of other mid-century magicians like Wiljalba Frikell (1818–1903), who became a spokesperson for eliminating cumbersome apparatus. He wrote about

---

[24] W. W. Durbin, *The Linking Ring* 15 no. 7 (September 1935), 607.

[25] Hoffmann, 8.

[26] Clarke, 203.

[27] From a broadside reproduced in Edwin Dawes, *The Great Illusionists* (Secaucus: Chartwell, 1979), 109.

the subject in 1857, with all the earnestness of a missionary appeal and with the finality of a royal decree:

> The use of complicated and cumbrous apparatus to which modern conjurors have become addicted ... greatly diminishes the amount they are enabled to produce—a defect that is not compensated by the external splendour and imposing effect of such paraphernalia ... It has been my object in my performances to restore the art to its original province ... I banish all such mechanical and scientific preparatives from my own practice, confining myself for the most part to the objects and materials of everyday life."[28]

His ideas were popularized by the Frenchman who has become known to history as the father of modern magic: Jean Eugene Robert-Houdin (1805–71). The clock-maker-turned conjurer had only a ten year career on the stage, but his innovations are still felt by magicians today. Writing in his 1868 volume *The Secrets of Conjuring and Magic*, Robert-Houdin labeled the dependence upon self-working apparatus as "the false bottom school of conjuring," and compared it to "the musician who produces a tune by turning the hands of a barrel organ."[29] He discarded the robes, melodramatic gesturing, and cluttered stage settings of an earlier generation, performing in evening dress on a stage that more closely resembled a parlor room than a Dickensian rag and bottle shop. His undraped Louis XV tables held only the props actually used during a performance, and the entire stage was well lit. This streamlined *mise en scene* had the double advantage of not only dispelling obvious suspicions about the apparatus, but also of giving a greater appearance of elegant respectability, as if the magician were inviting his spectators to tea in the parlour.

Robert-Houdin famously characterized his art by aligning it with the more venerable stage tradition. He wrote in 1868 that "A conjuror is not a juggler; he is an actor playing the part of a magician, an artist whose fingers have more need to move with deftness than with speed."[30] Distancing himself and his colleagues from the jugglers of an earlier era, whose conjuring was tied to the shifty outdoor world of the fairs, Robert-Houdin links himself to a profession that had similarly risen from disrepute into an established art. While much could be said about the implication of a magician as an actor, Robert-Houdin's emphasis seems to have been on class distinctions. As Simon During puts it, "entertainment magic has intersected with the larger processes of modernity ... increasing capitalization, urbanization, specialization, and the intensified pressure on individuals to become 'respectable.'"[31] According to Sidney Clarke, the English performer who popularized conjuring as a society entertainment was Charles Bertram (1853–1907), whose success elevated Victorian magic into a new social class:

---

[28] *Wiljalba Frikell's Lessons in Magic, or, Two Hours of Illusion without the Aid of Apparatus* (London: np, c1857), quoted in Frost, 296–7.

[29] Jean Eugene Robert–Houdin, *The Secrets of Conjuring and Magic*, 1868; reprinted in *Essential Robert–Houdin*, ed. Todd Karr (Seattle: Miracle Factory, 2006), 29.

[30] Robert-Houdin, 39.

[31] During, 74.

> Votaries of magic, especially drawing-room performers, owe much to Bertram, for it was largely due to him that fashionable society learned that conjuring would interest, even fascinate, private audiences other than those of a children's Christmas party and that a conjurer was not necessarily an uneducated, ill-dressed, and unreliable person who preferred to come in at the back door and take supper with the servants but might be a gentleman who could hold his own in any company, who would not disgrace his host or hostess, and who could be relied on to amuse and interest their guests.[32]

The distinction is clearly made in a 1912 cartoon titled "East London/West London," published by magic dealer Will Goldston (1878–1948) in his journal *The Magician*, in which a dignified parlor magician in white tie and tails is contrasted with his simian-like colleague in the slums.[33] The street conjurer, though given a voice through the interviews of Henry Mayhew, was clearly looked down upon by his elite peers.

Keenly aware of the street-performance origins of their art, Victorian and early twentieth-century magicians deliberately distanced themselves from their outdoor counterparts, just as they would reject brotherhood with the Spiritualists whom they viewed as imposters and the Eastern magicians whom they saw as overrated hacks. All three rivalries are articulated in the writings of John Nevil Maskelyne (1839–1917), the founder of a famous dynasty of magicians, and the director of Egyptian Hall, England's Home of Mystery. When the notorious American Spiritualists, the Davenport Brothers, came to England in 1865, a young Maskelyne discovered the method behind their cabinet demonstration, in which the brothers produced seeming miracles while allegedly bound in a wardrobe. Angered that mediums would use conjuring tricks to imply the existence of spirits, or, even worse, to defraud grieving séance patrons, Maskelyne dedicated many resources to exposing them. He duplicated ghostly stunts in his magic shows, much as Harry Houdini would do in the next century. He wrote *Modern Spiritualism* in 1876 and co-authored *The Supernatural?* with Lionel Weatherly in 1891. In both volumes Maskelyne excoriates the "pernicious doctrine … which has done so much to fill our lunatic asylums."[34] While much has been written about the gender politics of Spiritualism—Houdini's crusade against the Boston medium Margery, for example, is rife with implications—for Victorian magicians, exposing Spiritualist fraud was also an issue of morality and professional rivalry.[35]

---

[32] Clarke, 315.

[33] Dawes, *Stanley Collins: Conjurer, Collector, and Iconoclast* (Washington, DC: Kaufman, 2002), 33.

[34] John Nevil Maskelyne and Lionel Weatherly, *The Supernatural?* (London: Arrowsmith, 1891), 182–3.

[35] See Alex Owen, *The Darkened Room: Women, Power, and Spiritualism in Late Victorian England* (London: Virago, 1989) and Ruth Brandon, *The Life and Many Deaths of Harry Houdini* (New York: Random House, 1993).

The Mr. Sludges and the J. N. Maskelynes of the Victorian world were arch-enemies, each convinced that theirs was the only form of "true" magic, each convinced that the others' claims about being able to produce or expose spirit phenomena were grossly exaggerated, each constantly preaching to a choir of already-converted believers or skeptics. Spirit mediums insisted that they were conduits through which the dead communicated with the living, and they claimed that proof was available at every séance in the countless table raps, floating spirit hands, moving furniture, self-playing instruments, full-form ghost materializations, globs of ectoplasm, spirit photographs, slate messages, and correct answers to questions which only the departed could possibly provide. Magicians countered by arguing that the raps were caused by snapping joints, the floating hands belonged to the medium herself, the furniture and instruments were manipulated by someone in the room, the ghosts were really luminously-painted sheets on a stick, the ectoplasm was fake, the spirit photos were doctored, the slates were gimmicked, and the so-called revelations from the spirit world came from a combination of cold-reading, exchanges of private information from medium to medium, and sheer luck. In *Modern Magic,* Professor Hoffmann dismissed spiritualists as "nothing more nor less than clever but unprincipled conjurors."[36] Despite their notorious over-protectiveness of secrets, magicians were willing to tip their hands whenever exposure would help to stem the tide of belief in Spiritualism.

The willingness to expose secrets also extended to the relationship between Western magicians and their Eastern colleagues. In *The Supernatural?* Maskelyne includes a chapter on Oriental jugglery, in which he articulates one of the great clichés of Western magicians, who swore by the absolute predictability, stagnancy, and inferiority of Eastern conjuring. Over and over in print, magicians would expose mysteries like the famous Indian basket trick (in which a boy in a basket survives being pierced with swords) or the mango tree illusion (in which a seed covered with a cloth turns into a small, fruit-bearing tree). All of this was in order to squash the reputation of Asia as the alleged birthplace of magic. As Alexander Herrmann put it, the magic of India had been effectively colonized:

> Time was when the student of prestidigitation aspiring to fame in his art did not consider his education complete without a visit to India. But this is no longer necessary. The very secretiveness of the East Indian juggler, and his lack of communication with others of his art elsewhere, have lost him the prestige he once commanded. Whatever was wrested from him by close observation has been wonderfully improved upon.[37]

---

[36] Hoffmann, 557.

[37] Alexander Herrmann, "The Art of Magic," *North American Review* 153, no. 416 (July 1891), 93. Further examples of such dismissive exposures include Maskelyne, "Oriental Jugglery," *Leisure Hour* (1878), 198–301; Herrmann, "Light on the Black Art," *Cosmopolitan* 14 (December 1892), 207–14; Harry Kellar, "High Caste Indian Magic," *The North American Review* 156, no. 3 (1893), 75–86; Professor Hoffmann, "Indian Conjuring Explained," *Chambers's Journal* 78 (October 26, 1901), 757–61; and Lionel Branson, *Indian Conjuring* (London: Routledge, 1910). Victorian and early twentieth-century autobiographies by magicians also repeat this theme.

Of course, depending on the occasion, Victorian magicians could either equate secrecy with isolation and lack of development, or zealously guard it as the key to maintaining a sense of wonder in their performances. That is, as long as spectators were watching *Western* magicians. Irritated by the effusive praise given to the tricks of Asian conjurers by impressionable laymen travelers, Maskelyne snorts that "Truly, a little common sense and a five-shilling Hoffmann would save some people a world of disquietude."[38] In 1912, Maskelyne even wrote a slender volume titled *The Fraud of Theosophy Exposed and the Miraculous Rope-Trick of the Indian Jugglers Explained*, in which he equated the religion of Madame Blavatsky with the legend that Indian magicians could climb a rope into the skies and disappear in midair. The reputations of both Blavatsky and the Rope Trick were the result, Maskelyne claimed, of the exaggerated accounts of easily deluded persons, and Maskelyne's purpose in writing was to "cause the light of common sense to dispel some of the artificial glamour surrounding Indian mysticism."[39]

Numerous surviving photographs of Western magicians traveling overseas provide a telling record of the collision of two cultures. Invariably dressed in white suits and/or pith helmets, hobnobbing with street jugglers, and showing off their wealth and sleight-of-hand skills at any opportunity, these magicians adopted the pose of the cosmopolitan traveler, eager to be recognized both as Westerners and as superior wizards. With a complicated mix of rivalry and curiosity, Western magicians felt compelled to seek out their Eastern counterparts to see for themselves whether their magic was in fact as good as some laymen had claimed. "I went to India to learn," Charles Bertram confessed to *The Strand* in his article "Are Indian Jugglers Humbugs?" What he discovered, though, was that his Eastern colleagues "are very keen on getting European tricks."[40] Bertram announces his conclusion more dramatically in his posthumously published travel narrative *A Magician in Many Lands*: "I here place it unmistakably on record that I consider the Hindoo Juggler a greatly over-rated personage, around whom a fictitious glory has been cast."[41] Removing that glory, Bertram felt, was his professional duty.

A similar missionary concern over the fate of the easily-fooled prompted both Bertram and Maskelyne to expose a third group of rivals, the racetrack con artists who used sleight-of-hand to separate gullible folk from their money. Bertram dedicated a chapter titled "Dodges" in his 1899 memoir *Isn't It Wonderful?* to explaining the methods of card cheats, and even felt the need to apologize for using slang gambling terms, "which to the cultivated ear savour of vulgarity."[42] This warning comes from a seasoned society performer steeped in the delicacies

38 Maskelyne, 172.

39 Maskelyne, *The Fraud of Modern Theosophy Exposed and the Miraculous Rope-Trick of the Indian Jugglers Explained* (London: Routledge, 1912), 11.

40 Charles Bertram, "Are Indian Jugglers Humbugs?" *The Strand Magazine* 18, no. 108 (December 1899), 657.

41 Bertram, *A Magician in Many Lands* (London: Routledge, 1911), 99.

42 Bertram, *Isn't It Wonderful?* (London: Swan Sonnenschien, 1899), 142.

of fashionable London, a man who, for instance, always used a magic wand in his act to point to various persons in his audience, so that he would never commit the *gauche* blunder of pointing to a lady with his finger.[43] Maskelyne also muddied himself to pen *Sharps and Flats*, his 1894 volume that reveals the methods of card cheats, especially drawing attention to secretive mechanical devices used by the professional gambler. He believed that such exposure was a sacred duty, making the sweeping claim that there was "no subject more worthy of serious consideration, when regarded in the relation it holds to the moral well-being of mankind in general." He felt that the widespread, unchecked use of fraudulent gambling devices was a "satire upon civilization" and concluded that, "There is not the slightest necessity for anyone, however foolish, to fall victim to the wiles of the sharper in any game either of skill or chance."[44] Gambling exposes had been published before, first by ex-riverboat cheats like Jonathan Harrington Green in 1858, and later by Robert-Houdin himself in *Card-Sharping Exposed* (1861). In this book, translated into English by Professor Hoffmann, the fastidious conjurer preserved his own middle-class reputation by claiming that he had hired someone else to conduct his research in the seedy, lowbrow gambling dens of Paris.[45]

What is at work here is not only professional and class rivalry, but a struggle to define how the secrets of magic could be legitimately used. Victorian magic was fighting to establish itself as something decent people could enjoy. That is why in their autobiographies and publicity materials, magicians repeatedly told stories of their luxurious travels, boasting of their elaborate, costly stage shows, and showing off royal gifts. Queen Victoria herself saw Anderson, Frikell, and Robert-Houdin, among others. In fact, as James Cook puts it, Victorian magicians "invented parlor magic as one of the Gilded Age's most popular bourgeois hobbies."[46] Yet at the same time, one of the great ironies of the period was the desire to appropriate the magic of these three rival groups. Exhibitions of card flourishes, demonstrations of séance effects, and recreations of Eastern miracles became standard fare on the vaudeville stage. For example, all three could be seen in the stage repertoire of the highly successful American magician Howard Thurston (1869–1936), who manipulated cards, printed posters asking, "Do Spirits Come Back?," and staged a version of the Indian rope trick. In his study of magic in India, Lee Siegel puts it this way, "In India the great magic was Western; in the West the great magic

---

43 Dawes, *Charles Bertram: The Court Conjurer* (Washington, DC: Kaufman, 1997), 172. Even the street conjurers felt superior to the thimble-riggers, and the second conjurer interviewed by Mayhew comments that he is often called upon to expose the thimble-rig (Mayhew, 107–10).

44 Maskelyne, *Sharps and Flats* (London: Longmans, Green & Co, 1894), quoted in David Britland, *Phantoms of the Card Table* (London: High Stakes Publishing, 2003), 16, 32–4.

45 Robert–Houdin, *Card-Sharping Exposed* (1861); reprinted in *Essential Robert–Houdin*, 224.

46 James Cook, *The Arts of Deception: Playing with Fraud in the Age of Barnum* (Cambridge: Harvard UP, 2001), 167.

was Indian—and Westerners had a monopoly on both."[47] The dynamic between protecting and exposing secrets was complex indeed.

Ultimately, Victorian conjurers were both the proponents and the victims of exposure. Repeatedly depicted in *Punch* and other humor periodicals as a hackneyed, bombastic figure, the magician became a frequent caricature of the politician, as in an 1876 cartoon of Disraeli as an illusionist trying to make an embarrassing issue of the day disappear under a cone.[48] Literary writers were equally dismissive. When conjurers appeared in fiction at all, they were often exposed, silenced, or expelled. In *Jane Eyre* (1847), a mysterious gypsy fortune-teller turns out only to be Mr. Rochester in disguise. In *Cranford* (1853), the exotic conjurer Signor Brunoni who creates such a sensation among the community of women is eventually unmasked as a broken-down Englishman named Samuel Brown. Some fictional magicians expose their own secrets, as does *Mr. Sludge, the Medium* (1864), while the three Indian jugglers who lurk in the shadows throughout *The Moonstone* (1868), trying to recover the legendary jewel, are soon revealed to be Brahmins who have betrayed their caste by disguising themselves as street conjurers. The legendary Merlin comes off as a rank amateur in *A Connecticut Yankee* (1889), and Dorothy soon learns that the great and "terrible" Oz is no wizard at all (1900).

Such uncovering reflects a conflict in nineteenth-century culture between a desire for wonder and a quest for answers. Burlingame's complaint that exposures of magic secrets are offensive to audiences who "enjoy [magic effects] much more when in ignorance of how the tricks are performed," contrasts sharply with Strindberg's claim in the preface to *Miss Julie* (1888) that "we want to see the strings, look at the machinery, examine the double-bottom drawer, put on the magic ring to find the seam, look in the deck for the marked cards."[49] Granted, Strindberg is talking about the psychology of drama and Burlingame about the psychology of magic, but both have their finger on a central issue. As audiences, do we cheer for the magician as he or she amazes us, or is magic a more confrontational performance relationship, where spectators are dared to figure out the secrets? Ultimately, I believe, the magic show is both, and the conflicted desire both to know and to be amazed is a tension that runs throughout nineteenth-century culture. The crisis of a faith struggling to believe in a mysterious God in an increasingly demystified world, the desire to understand people of other races scientifically while still seeing them as distant and exotic, the literary debate between those who try to depict reality with exactness and those who seek a more romanticized, escapist fictional word, the human longing to be amused amidst a culture in which some are

---

[47] Lee Siegel, *Net of Magic: Wonders and Deceptions in India* (Chicago: U of Chicago P, 1991), 397.

[48] John Tenniel, "The Extinguisher Trick," *Punch* 70 (February 19, 1876), 59.

[49] Burlingame, 223. August Strindberg, Preface to *Miss Julie, The Harcourt Brace Anthology of Drama,* ed W. B. Worthen, 2nd ed (Fort Worth: Harcourt, 1996), 616.

suspicious that amusement equals idle folly—all of these tensions come to bear on how Victorian magicians present themselves and how they are in turn presented and viewed by others. Thus the conflicts over keeping—and revealing—secrets are more than just professional courtesy. They are at the heart of defining the role of an ancient entertainment art in a modern world.

Chapter 11
A Secret Censorship: The British Home Office v. *Town Talk*

Allison L. E. Wee

Literary censorship, especially of matters pertaining to homosexuality, is hardly a surprising topic to appear in a volume of essays devoted to "Victorian Secrets." Despite early assertions of Victorian candor and sincerity popularized by Emerson and others,[1] and recent widespread scholarly acceptance of Michel Foucault's theory that discourses of sexuality were not repressed during the nineteenth century but rather proliferated,[2] in popular imagination the Victorians remain famously prudish. In fact, the urge to keep homosexuality a "Victorian secret" has caused concrete historical data on the subject to be sparse; the legal record tends to reveal much of what can be discovered as to Britain's attitudes and assumptions about it. In 1857, Parliament passed an Obscene Publications Act that remarkably remained on the books for more than one hundred years. Originally intended to combat the public distribution of pornography, the Act frequently was used to prohibit representations of homosexuality in literature.[3] Though the bill was clearly a product of mid-Victorian sensibilities, the records that survive in Britain's Home Office archives regarding "indecent publications" between the years 1857 and 1900 are sparse; furthermore, as the remaining files do not involve novels, most scholars of literature only know the Obscene Publications Act for its impact on the work and careers of twentieth-century novelists James Joyce, D. H. Lawrence, and Radclyffe Hall.[4]

---

1 See Ralph Waldo Emerson, "English Traits," *The Complete Works of Ralph Waldo Emerson*, Centenary Edition, 12 vols. (Boston: Houghton Mifflin, 1903).

2 See Foucault's *History of Sexuality*: vol. 1, *An Introduction*; vol. 2, *The Uses of Pleasure*; and vol. 3, *The Care of the Self*; trans. Robert Hurley (New York: Pantheon, 1978–86).

3 For a powerful account of how pornography and homosexuality have been linked closely in the Western cultural imagination as a strategy to maintain a perceived social integrity and health, see Carolyn J. Dean, *The Frail Social Body: Pornography, Homosexuality, and Other Fantasies in Interwar France* (Berkeley: U of California P, 2000).

4 James Joyce ran into trouble in Britain in 1912 for his short story collection entitled *Dubliners*, and chose to publish *Ulysses* in Paris in 1922. The 1915 obscenity trial of D. H. Lawrence's *The Rainbow* (London: Methuen, 1915) received little public attention beyond a few mentions in the *Times*, but because of this experience Lawrence did not attempt

Though sparse, the nineteenth-century records ought not be overlooked, for they reveal all the internal and behind-the-scenes—one might call them "secret," or illicit—deliberations of Home Office officials that preceded the institution's formal, or licit, actions (or, as in the case in question here, inaction). Careful analysis of these records suggests that much of the power of the Victorian obscenity law resulted not from its formal application at all, but rather from informal strategies undertaken specifically to *avoid* the formal application of the law, as officials knew that trials would publicize that which they hoped instead to veil. This article addresses a curious incident from 1885 involving an editorial rant against homosexuality in a small London weekly newspaper called *Town Talk*. The assumption that a message preaching against homosexuality would still disseminate knowledge of it was a Foucauldian Catch-22 that led Home Office officials to circumvent the formal machinery of their own institution out of fear that prosecution would promote the very subject of homosexuality they wished to keep quiet. The success of their strategy in this modest incident seems to have led the officials to engage over time in increasingly calculated and unapologetic illicit behavior in order to preserve the "secret" of homosexuality.

The Home Office is the branch of the government responsible for initiating prosecutions against alleged obscenity on behalf of the public. It is important to note that employees of this institution vigorously disputed accusations of censorship, usually made against them by the literary elite whose works were challenged under the law. In the archival record, clerks and officials give lip service to candor, remarking time and again that there was no censorship in England, proudly affirming England's longstanding traditions of freedom of the press. They stood firm in the belief that anyone could feel free to publish anything, and saw no contradiction between this and the existence of the Obscene Publications Act designed to prosecute texts that, once published, might threaten the moral fiber of the public. Since its thirteenth-century origins, the charge of the Home Office had been to keep the "King's Peace" (or the Queen's, as was obviously the case for the Victorians), so if members of the public complained about the nature of a given publication, it was assumed to be the natural duty of this office to determine whether it seemed to meet the legal definition of obscenity, and, if so, to set in motion the machinery of the law at that time.

The evolution of Britain's obscenity law is too long and complex to explain here, but a few words about its origins and application are necessary to understand the *Town Talk* case. Though the 1857 Obscene Publications Act, also known as Lord Campbell's Act after its author, is best known for its role in banning several

---

to publish *Lady Chatterley's Lover* in England in 1928, opting instead to fund a private printing in Florence, Italy. His disgust with Home Office employees and the obscenity law is legendary, and his 1929 essays "Pornography and Obscenity" and "A Propos of *Lady Chatterley's Lover*" remain fixtures in studies of the subject. The 1928 obscenity trial of Radclyffe Hall's *The Well of Loneliness* (London: John Lane, 1928) and Hall's failed legal appeal nearly a year later was followed sensationally by the international media.

important twentieth-century novels, it was not originally intended to target serious literature; it was created in a singular effort to curb the distribution of pornographic flyers and advertisements in London's streets. The proliferation of print culture by the mid-century was due to several factors, including the gradual demise of once-heavy paper taxes, the invention of cheaper printing technologies, rising literacy rates among members of the commercial and working classes, and the railroad boom.[5] In *The English Common Reader*, Richard Altick notes that, by mid-century, "No longer was it possible for people to avoid reading matter; everywhere they went it was displayed."[6] Reading practices no longer were limited to the private drawing rooms of the well-to-do, but extended to public spaces of the city where people of different classes, genders, and ages mixed, resulting in a new marketplace in which sexually suggestive publications circulated with few restrictions. As the nature of print culture changed in this manner, middle-class concerns over its content grew, eventually prompting Sir John Campbell, a Member of Parliament and Britain's Attorney General in the 1830s, to frame new legislation against publications that explicitly intended to harm public morals.[7]

Though Campbell wished to limit the scope of his bill so as not to apply to serious literature, his intention did not survive to go on legal record. In 1868 a case designated *Regina v. Hicklin*, commonly known as the Hicklin ruling, made Lord Campbell's Act into law. The text in question, ironically, was a religious critique published by the Protestant Electoral Union, a deeply anti-Catholic religious organization, entitled "The Confessional Unmasked: Shewing the Depravity of the Roman Priesthood, the Iniquity of the Confessional and the Questions Put to Females in Confession." In short, the pamphlet pointed out the potentially sordid results of an authority figure digging for details regarding one's sins.[8] Chief Justice Alexander Cockburn acknowledged that its publisher may have had decent intentions, but those who bought the tract may have been interested solely

---

[5] For a wonderfully detailed and efficient account of these factors and more, see Simon Eliot, "The Business of Victorian Publishing," in Dierdre David, ed., *The Cambridge Companion to the Victorian Novel* (Cambidge: Cambridge UP, 2001), 37–60.

[6] Richard D. Altick, *The English Common Reader: A Social History of the Mass Reading Public, 1800–1900* (Chicago: U of Chicago P, 1957), 301.

[7] At the time, many members of Parliament expressed grave concerns that the proposed Act would be able to be used against not only pornography but also serious literature. In response to this concern, Campbell held up a copy of Alexandre Dumas' *La Dame Aux Camélias* (1855) on the floor of Parliament and explained that although the book might not be to his taste, it was not against such literature that the new law was aimed. Many accounts of censorship history retell this story in varying detail; see, for example, Norman St–John Stevas, *Obscenity and the Law* (London: Secker and Warburg, 1956), 66–9; Alan Travis, *Bound and Gagged: A Secret History of Obscenity in Britain* (London: Profile Books, 2000) 4–6; Donald Thomas, *A Long Time Burning: The History of Literary Censorship in England* (New York: Frederick A. Praeger, 1969), 239.

[8] Originals of this publication no longer exist. The British Library contains an expurgated second edition from 1869.

in its salacious details. In his landmark decision, he famously defined obscenity as "that with the tendency to deprave and corrupt those whose minds are open to such influences, and into whose hands such a work might fall."[9] For the all-male government officials of the nineteenth century, the vulnerable group with such open minds included women, youth, and the working classes. The most important aspect of the ruling is that it erased completely the question of authorial intent, placing the test of obscenity fully on the reader.

From the beginning the terminology of this decision was problematic. In *Long Time Burning: the History of Literary Censorship in England*, Donald Thomas points out the obvious:

> Of course, terms like 'deprave' and 'corrupt' have an inherent imprecision and emotive effect which makes their use in discussion hardly possible. For most purposes, certainly for the purposes of the law, they are taken to mean that a reader is encouraged by a book to imitate the behavior described, stimulated to orthodox or unorthodox acts.[10]

The unspoken assumption of the law that an obscene text is one that encourages sexual acts is central to understanding the government's concerns about *Town Talk*, one of the few records from the years 1857–1900 that remain in the Home Office archive.[11]

On November 14, 1885, a clerk filed a report stating that Adolphus Rosenberg, editor for seven years of the small weekly newspaper *Town Talk,* had submitted an advance copy of his upcoming number to the Home Office along with a written inquiry whether his editorial column was likely to run afoul of the obscenity law.[12] At a glance, the column in question does not seem to be a likely candidate for "encouraging imitation" of the behavior in question, as Thomas' assertion of a typical application of the obscenity law would imply; the column is, from start to finish, a vociferous condemnation of male homosexuality. Rosenberg complains about the presence of gays in the military, as well as in the police force and in the upper classes generally. He accuses men in positions of power of having a secret

---

[9] (1868), *Law Report* Vol. 3, Queen's Bench 360. This legal standard remained on the books until 1959.

[10] Donald Thomas, *A Long Time Burning: The History of Literary Censorship in England* (New York: Frederick A. Praeger, 1969), 312.

[11] Many files have been destroyed over the years, and it is impossible to know how many or what their contents may have been. Some files were destroyed during the second World War when paper pulp was at a premium; some were destroyed in the move from Whitehall to the new Public Record Office (PRO) in Kew; many were destroyed when the laws changed, causing earlier cases to become obsolete. Current employees of the PRO assert that the files that were kept were usually chosen due to their status as borderline cases that best revealed the complex issues at stake.

[12] The official file number is HO 144/160/A41450. The Home Office archives are housed in the Public Record Office at Kew.

conspiracy to allow the "abomination" to persist, and he expresses his intent to reveal the secret, forcing the ranks of authority to be purified.

Actually, by the end of 1885, it was difficult to call homosexuality a real secret—or at least to consider it a very well-kept one. Rosenberg may have had the sense that the time was ripe to address the subject openly due to several homosexual scandals that had rocked the country in recent years. One case in particular had kept the suggestion of homosexuality front and center in the London news for several weeks. In the spring of 1870, two young men, 22-year-old Ernest Boulton and 23-year-old Frederick William Park, were arrested at London's Strand Theater for dressing as women and, further, interacting with men "like women of the town."[13] The original charge brought against them was for "outraging public decency," a misdemeanor for public cross-dressing, but while in police custody the men were also examined for evidence of anal intercourse; in spite of inconclusive medical findings, the charges were increased to the "detestable and abominable crime of buggery not to be named among Christians," carrying the much heavier punishment of ten years to life imprisonment.[14] However, when prosecutors realized they would not be able to produce concrete evidence of a sex act between men, the charges were reduced once again to "conspiracy to commit a felony," the felony being sodomy. For their first appearance in Bow Street Magistrate's court, Boulton and Park appeared in floor-length gowns and gloves.[15] The reporter covering the case for the London *Times* noted that the following week the courtroom was full of curious spectators who must have been disappointed at their appearance in regular men's clothing.[16] In the end, the men were acquitted on the basis of a defense that claimed their actions were nothing but "a lark," and a lack of concrete evidence that a crime had been committed. Nevertheless, the media attention given to the case made the idea of homosexuality—if not the word itself—public knowledge.

In 1884, just a year before Rosenberg's editorial tirade, another homosexual scandal involving officials at Dublin Castle prompted a large demonstration in London's Hyde Park, at which the outspoken feminist Josephine Butler and

---

13 *The Times*, May 7, 1870.

14 This language originated in the Parliamentary Act from 1533 officially designated as 25 Henry VIII. The phrase has long remained a favorite euphemism to "name" the act of sodomy without explicitly naming it. The fact that the legal charges were temporarily increased has caused many to assume that the medical examiner found what he was looking for, whatever that may have been; however, in *Coming Out: Homosexual Politics in Britain, from the Nineteenth Century to the Present* (London: Quartet Books Ltd, 1977), historian Jeffrey Weeks asserts that the medical examination was inconclusive (14).

15 "When placed in the dock Boulton wore a cherry-coloured evening silk dress trimmed with white lace; his arms were bare, and he had on bracelets. He wore a wig and plaited chignon. Park's costume consisted of a dark green satin dress, low necked and trimmed with black lace, of which material he also had a shawl round his shoulders. His hair was flaxen and in curls. He had on a pair of white kid gloves." *The Times*, April 30, 1870.

16 *The Times*, May 7, 1870.

members of various social purity leagues gave speeches against male lust and its twin vices, prostitution and "sexual decadence," another contemporary euphemism for homosexual activity.[17] These scandals, the people's strong and public reactions to them, and the courts' inability to take decisive action against them were far from secrets. In fact it was their very visibility that helped prompt new legislation. In August of 1885, Parliament passed the Criminal Law Amendment Act, a law promoted by Butler designed to protect teenaged girls from prostitution; at the eleventh hour, a rider was attached to this Act called the Labouchère Amendment that for the first time explicitly criminalized all male homosexual behavior, whether in public or private.

Adolphus Rosenberg may well have felt empowered by the recent passage of the new law to speak out against male homosexuality in his newspaper. One might think that government officials, who generally shared his views, would have had no problem with Rosenberg's editorial, but indeed they did. The Home Office found the *Town Talk* issue inappropriate for circulation not for its particular position on homosexuality, but for discussing the subject at all. Government officials were determined to keep the subject as secret as was possible; since it was commonly assumed that knowledge of homosexuality would encourage the practice of it, the government's key strategy for deterrence was simply to prevent all mention of it, whether positive or negative.

The case of *Town Talk* is unusual in that Rosenberg himself sent a copy of his editorial column to the Home Office asking for their advance assessment, testing the waters rather than risking legal action after publication. The strident tone of his column, reinforced by formatting, helps explain why he was so concerned. The headline of issue #308 spells out, in bold capitals: "HORRIBLE CRIMES. THE LAWS OF GOD AND MAN DEFIED," and parenthetically, "[THIS ARTICLE HAS BEEN SUBMITTED, PREVIOUS TO PUBLICATION, TO THE PERUSAL OF THE HOME SECRETARY, SIR E.Y. HENDERSON, AND COLONEL FRASER].[18] The rhetorical invocation of the laws of both God and man would have signaled to most readers that the subject in question was homosexuality; in case some might remain unsure, Rosenberg also references the 1870 case against "Messrs Boulton and Park," and claims that, although the men were cleared of all charges, "the crime with which their names will forever be associated remains to this day a terrible factor in the vices of society." Rosenberg employs several common euphemisms of the day for homosexuality, referring, for example, to "unnatural vice" and "the most horrible crime in the list of vices of the flesh." He claims it is "generally committed by wealthy and cultured men—men whose

---

[17] Weeks, 18.

[18] Though not named in the documents themselves (probably because everyone involved with the paperwork would have known), the Home Secretary at the time was Sir Richard Assheton Cross, according to Jill Pellew's institutional history *The Home Office 1848–1914: From Clerks to Bureaucrats* (Rutherford, Madison, Teaneck: Farleigh Dickinson UP, 1982), 206.

outward lives are pure and intelligent," and he asserts that his goal is "to set before the readers of this paper an accurate account of what really takes place."

Importantly, Rosenberg claims not only that the vice assumed of Boulton and Park is practiced among men in a variety of social classes, but also that knowledge of such practices is similarly widespread. He writes, "There is not a policeman who could not, if he pleased, indicate the place where the most bestial—pardon the word, oh beasts of the field!—of men meet, but for some mysterious reason the police are silent and inert." Capitalized subheadings for subsequent sections of the article follow: EVERY NIGHT … IN THE ARMY … IN THE ROYAL NAVY … IN CHURCHES … IN ALL RANKS the vice exists, and next week I shall proceed to give detailed accounts of what I have been able to learn, and I may at the same time be able to suggest some means of putting the law into operation. The irony is that the only operation to result from Rosenberg's article is the eventual closure of his own newspaper. But how this closure came about is not quite what one might think, because the Home Office remained unwilling to put the law into operation.

For one thing, it turns out that Rosenberg already had a criminal record for publishing "indecency," a fact known by both Home Office officials and the police. Just a few years earlier he had been prosecuted for obscene libel for reporting that the actress Lillie Langtry would be divorcing her husband due to an affair with Prince Albert, Queen Victoria's son and the future king of England. Though the affair was common knowledge, the divorce rumor was officially denied, and Rosenberg was sentenced to eighteen months in prison.[19]

The injustice and hypocrisy of these events obviously rankled, for Rosenberg chose to include within his lengthy polemic against homosexuality some choice remarks against the obscenity law, and in particular those who govern its application:

> God forbid that I should attempt to write down here the slightest outline of the history and description of the crime for which the Cities of the Plain suffered, and for the inhabitants of which the Patriarch Abraham pleaded in vain with an outraged Creator. I am led to believe that this journal is read by young persons, and if I have no respect for a narrow, one-sided law, my feelings as a man and father prompt me to curb my language. But if there were a case in which this law should for a time be abrogated it is the present. For the law is peculiar. The man who discusses the great social question is placed in the same category with the individual who for the purpose of making a few shillings publicly vends a filthy picture … In these days an Isaiah or Jeremiah who addressed the people on their vices would be esteemed no better than the man who sold the semi-nude professional beauties on a coster's barrow.

---

[19] A clerical note in the file following the record of this conversation reads: "The trial of Rosenberg before Mr. Justice Hawkins on the October 25, 1879 will be found reported at page 889 of vol. 90 of the Sessions Papers (part 540—12th Session—October 1879)."

In this passage, Rosenberg acknowledges his awareness that the law of obscenity is not applied so as to promote a certain moral stance on issues regarding sexuality, but simply to maintain a strict silence—a silence that he believes only contributes to moral decay because it prevents righteous criticism. Thus, his editorial attacks not only the practice of homosexuality itself, but also the "narrow and one-sided law" that does not allow in print a serious discussion on the subject, but treats him, a godly prophet, the same as it would the proprietor of risqué penny postcards.

Rosenberg's awareness of how the law functions ultimately places him in a curious double bind. First, though he criticizes the law for making homosexuality unmentionable, he follows suit and resists mentioning it too, in the name of protecting vulnerable "young persons" into whose hands his newspaper might fall. Second, although he expresses contempt for the law, he still recognizes that he must submit to it, and thus has chosen to seek its approval. His own conscientiousness in this matter ultimately creates, rather than prevents, trouble for him. It may also be the case that Rosenberg's allusion to a "mysterious reason" behind the inactivity of the police, combined with the accusation that the "vice" is present in many of the primary social institutions whose task is to protect and uphold conventional morality, helped set members of the government—precisely one such social institution—against him.[20]

Whatever their reasons, government officials were not at all eager, for their part, to enter into communication with Rosenberg. In the absence of concrete evidence for his claims (recall that he planned to share the details "next week"), they did not want to respond in any way that would suggest the accusations were true. Furthermore, officials had no interest in opening the door in the future to petitions of this sort, requesting prior authorization to publish; this clearly flew in the face of their seriously held convictions against censorship. The first item placed in the file after the newspaper itself is a clerk's handwritten note addressed to Mr. Lushington, the Home Office's Permanent Under-Secretary, asking him to seek additional opinions.

An unsigned reply came back dated November 14, 1885.[21] It reads, in part:

> Mr. Poland is of opinion that it would not be expedient for the public prosecutor to write as suggested in the telegram—to write would involve the assumption that the Editor is acting with bona fides and can give detailed information

[20] It is also possible that anti-Semitism played a role in the tone of these interactions. Rosenberg's name certainly suggests Jewish heritage, and many British, despite Benjamin Disraeli's recent tenure as Prime Minister, still felt quite comfortable harboring anti-Semitic feelings in the late nineteenth century. However, having read several hundred pages of documents in the Home Office files marked "indecent publications," I would say that the tone taken toward Rosenberg seems no different than the tone displayed in other records concerning publications discussing homosexuality. "Indecency" seems to generate an equal-opportunity disgust from those who dislike it.

[21] The content of the message makes it fairly clear that the writer is the Director of Public Prosecutions himself, at the time a man named Augustus Stephenson.

with respect to the crimes he refers to in his article—besides it would be an invitation to the Editor to communicate on other issues with the Director of P. Prosecutions …

Mr Poland is of the opinion (and I agree with him)—that knowing the character of Mr. Rosenberg the editor of Town Talk, who has been convicted and suffered 18 months imprisonment for scandalous libels—that the only communication which should be made by me as Director of P P to Mr Rosenberg is to the effect "that the printed slip headed "Horrible Crimes" has been forwarded to me as Director of P.P by the Home Office—and that its contents are indecent and obscene, and that if he publishes it—I as Director of P.P. will prosecute him.[22]

This document offers some important clues as to the reasons behind Home Office tactics in cases of alleged indecency. One is that their lack of communication with the members of the public in question is a deliberate strategy chosen for reasons of self-protection. Writing, they feel, "would involve the assumption that the Editor is acting with bona fides," an assumption which they do not hold; and they also simply do not wish to encourage further discussion with Rosenberg, in this case or at any time in the future. The record also demonstrates that the officials know the reputation of the editor, which obviously slants their opinion of him. They seem ready to assume that one who is once guilty of publishing scandal is always guilty.

The final assertion of the Director of Public Prosecutions, that the article's "contents are indecent and obscene," is especially important, for it suggests that he finds the publisher's guilt to be an obvious and foregone conclusion. While it is no doubt the job of prosecuting attorneys to feel confident about cases they pursue, the remark is still noteworthy, given that a courtroom trial is usually considered the primary site for negotiating guilt or innocence. In these historical literary obscenity cases, however, keeping the contents of the texts in question away from the public was such a high priority that government officials viewed the courtroom not as the proper space for deliberation, but only the space in which to rubber-stamp a verdict already determined.

In the next file document, however, two men write to remind the Director of Public Prosecutions that telling Rosenberg he cannot print his article constitutes the very censorship the institution vehemently denies.[23] In the end, given the potential difficulties foreseen with any type of communication with Rosenberg, officials opted not to respond at all. Rosenberg, for his part, decided that silence meant consent, and proceeded to publish his newspaper on November 21. Three days

---

[22] I have reproduced the Home Office texts and their markings at length and as closely to the handwritten originals as I can in typescript because, although the grammar and punctuation is inconsistent, it seems more important to retain the authors' voice and style than to have summarized or edited for correctness.

[23] This document is signed by R. Webster and Harry Bodkin Poland.

after the issue was distributed, and approximately ten since Rosenberg's original inquiry, the course of events took some unexpected and interesting turns.

The next item in the file is an account by police inspector James Butcher of an encounter with Rosenberg, written on letterhead from Scotland Yard. Its contents, though somewhat lengthy, tell an important story and bear including here in full:

> At 5:30 pm Mr Adolphus Rosenberg called here and stated that it was common talk in Public Houses in Fleet Street mostly frequented by Newspaper men that a warrant had been issued for his arrest, and wished to know if it was so: he produced a copy of the St. James' Gazette of this day's issue, which contained the following paragraph: –
>
> "We are authorized to state that the recent publication in Town Talk has been placed in the hands of the Director of Public Prosecutions and the Attorney General"
>
> I said, referring to the newspaper, "There is nothing said here about a Warrant—if a Warrant has been issued no doubt it will be executed." He said, "This is very ambiguous, it makes me think proceedings have been commenced against me, I have no wish to evade the law, I come here to surrender myself." I said "are you Mr. Edwin Rosenthal? (purposely) he said "No my name is Adolphus Rosenberg, you will remember the Langtry libel case in Town Talk, and my being prosecuted for it."
>
> He then said alluding to the St. James's Gazette "this is stated to be by authority: reading "the recent publication mind—in the singular." I said "We cannot be responsible for anything that appears in the newspapers." He said "I shall go to the office of the St. James's Gazette and demand an explanation." I said "I think perhaps that will be your best course."
>
> "And understand me" he continued (I should like to have your name officially—I said Inspector Butcher) "if any breach of the Peace occurs I am not responsible, for I shall punch the first fellow on the nose who admits that they published this account, which I consider equally as bad as if I was branded a thief.—He then said Good evening and left. …
>
> Rosenberg called again at 7 o'clock he stated that he had been to the Office of the St. James's Gazette, where he was informed that the information had been supplied by Scotland Yard—I told him I had already said all that I could say in the matter, that I had no knowledge of a Warrant having been issued, and that I thought, if he considered it necessary to make any further enquiry his best bet course would be to address the Commissioner of Police in writing.

It is possible, based on the details conveyed here; that there never was a warrant issued for Rosenberg's arrest, but it is certain that the police found it convenient to let him believe there was. In fact, the statement made by the *St. James Gazette* may well have been referring to Rosenberg's own headline stating that he had sent an advance copy to the Home Secretary. But Rosenberg's belief that a warrant and arrest were once again in store for him was enough to prompt dramatic action: not punching a fellow journalist in the nose, as he had threatened, but ducking away from the impending blow he feared was coming his way from the Home Office.

> The final document in the file regarding this case, dated December 3, provides some interesting new information and also leaves some tantalizing gaps. Augustus Stephenson, the Director of Public Prosecutions, again writes to the Permanent Undersecretary, Mr. Lushington:
>
> I have to acknowledge receipt this morning of your letter of yesterday's date marked "Pressing"—acquainting me by the direction of the Secretary of State "that a letter addressed to the Publisher of "Town Talk" 11. Gough Square, has been returned through the Dead Letter Office marked "gone away"—and to state for the information of the Secretary of State that in pursuance of my instructions Detective Inspector Pope visited the premises … on Tuesday morning the 1st December and found these premises closed—with a notice on the window that the publication of Town Talk would be discontinued.
>
> The paper did not appear on that day its usual day of publication and I have not heard since that it has again appeared …
>
> It would seem that for the present the proprietors have "gone away" from Gough Square altogether.

The document addressed to Rosenberg and returned as a "dead letter" may or may not have been a warrant, but as it turns out, its contents were moot, for Rosenberg's quick disappearance and the closure of his newspaper business seem to have been all the Home Office officials needed to hear in order to consider the case closed.

Remarkably, a new publication entitled *Tittle Tattle* appeared in London a few weeks later (a name conspicuously similar to *Town Talk*) that not only made explicit reference to Rosenberg's editorial on homosexuality, but also stated that "if and when *Town Talk* reappeared, [the two newspapers] would not be enemies but publish simultaneously" against such vice. Just as the final issue of *Town Talk* had done, the first issue of *Tittle Tattle* stated that it was not afraid to take up—in its next issue, of course—the fact of this "crime hidden among the police force." Though the police never followed up on the case, it seems likely that *Tittle Tattle* was simply Rosenberg's new publishing venture, and that, rather than give up his profession, he simply changed locations and venues to evade Scotland Yard, a tactic that apparently worked like a charm.

Threatening Rosenberg with prosecution served the government's purpose well; that he closed his newspaper before providing his readers with the promised details about homosexual "vice" means that the secret was effectively preserved. But the presence of the final document in the file leaves a question unanswered. Given that officials were aware of *Tittle Tattle's* echoes of *Town Talk*—a clerk, after all, had carefully clipped the new publication's editorial referencing *Town Talk* and its mission against homosexual vice and pasted it into the *Town Talk* file—why did they choose not to pursue the matter further? The answer may lie in an important distinction between institutional actions and individual actions. Institutional actions, by their very nature, veil the actions and ideas of the individual people who work within them. Home Office employees did not always think alike or share identical values, but in order for the institution to take an action, the individuals responsible for signing off on it needed to arrive at a consensus regarding that action. One could describe as "secret" the deliberations that took place behind closed doors, to the extent that they were not public knowledge.[24] But the officials did not perceive themselves as acting "in secret"—they were merely taking the steps required in order to fulfill their obligations to the law and to their profession. One might more accurately describe the actions of the officials as "covert" in the sense of the word's original French meaning. Institutional actions, on the other hand, are public. For the Home Office to initiate contact with *Tittle Tattle* in an effort to achieve closure and punish Rosenberg would only have prolonged the issue and risked making visible to the public eye their entire interactions.

The case of *Town Talk* demonstrates that Home Office officials shared Foucault's understanding of the dynamics of power; they were keenly aware of the counterintuitive dynamic regarding discourses of sexuality that he would later articulate. In order to circumvent the problem of advertising the very thing they wished to suppress, they used the threat of the law, rather than the law itself, to cause Rosenberg to censor himself—first by submitting the text of his editorial prior to publication in hopes of gaining the government's stamp of approval, and later by shutting down (or perhaps simply moving) his entire operation. In other words, the mere existence of the Obscene Publications Act, and not its application, gave Home Office officials the means to manage the "secret" of homosexuality, supporting Foucault's argument that power is enabled at least in part by "its ability to hide its own mechanisms."[25] At its heart, the motive of the Home Office in the case against *Town Talk* is to protect national security by avoiding the spread of sexual knowledge to categories of people, such as women, the young, and the laboring classes, that could not be counted on to respond safely or appropriately to such knowledge.

At first glance, the process undertaken by employees of the Victorian Home Office concerning "indecent publications" seems to align with what we think we already know about government operations in the nineteenth century: a group of civil servants discuss, informally and behind closed doors, whether the obscenity law applies to a given publication, and when a consensus is reached, the institution either chooses not to pursue the case or takes legal action, "full formed and majestic," to echo Carlyle's phrase from *Sartor Resartus* quoted at the beginning

---

24 Interestingly, many of the files pertaining to obscene literature were sealed to the public for 75 or 100 years, a delineation for which no written legal justification can be found.

25 Michel Foucault, *History of Sexuality* vol. 1, trans. Robert Hurley (New York: Pantheon, 1978), 86.

of the introduction to this volume. While one could call this a "secret" process, in that the deliberations are veiled from the general public, it nevertheless remains licit collective behavior, to the extent that employees are simply working to fulfill their responsibilities to protect the "King's Peace."

However, the 1885 case of *Town Talk* diverged from this script, leaving us with a more complex picture with more interesting implications. Faced with the prospect of either allowing one newspaper editorial decrying male homosexual behavior to be distributed in the streets of London, or bringing the publisher to court only to have the case followed and the subject matter deliberated in *every* newspaper in town, government officials chose neither of these courses of action. Instead, they elected to draw upon the powerful threat of institutional action in order to pressure the publisher to censor himself, not only by withdrawing that number, but by closing his business and disappearing. The reluctance of government officials to set in motion the formal mechanisms of the law they represent, and to opt instead for informal—indeed, illicit—pressure, tells us that they well understood Foucault's assertion that sexual knowledge proliferates through the very gestures of suppression. Their grasp of this dynamic led them to circumvent their own "official business."

The success of this venture in 1885 led the government to engage in increasingly calculated secret actions against publications including representations of homosexuality, and especially of lesbianism. In 1909, for example, a novel called *The Hazard of the Die*, which depicted a healthy young British lad who accidentally marries a lesbian,[26] was also suppressed by the Home Office, again not through applying the mechanism of the law, but through top officials strong-arming the publisher, off the record, into recalling all unsold copies.[27] In the wake of such incidents, many prominent authors in the early decades of the twentieth century, including James Joyce and D. H. Lawrence, followed Adolphus Rosenberg's lead and in effect "went away"—choosing to publish their works containing sexually unconventional material on the continent. In 1928, Radclyffe Hall, a prominent, wealthy, and stubborn woman, decided not to "go away," and instead chose to publish her groundbreaking lesbian novel *The Well of Loneliness* in Britain, finally forcing a public obscenity trial of sensational proportions.[28] Despite the fact that the trial made the subject of lesbianism fodder for public conversation for more than a year, the archival record shows that officials talked amongst themselves to arrange ahead of time for the prosecutors and Judges at Bow Street Magistrate's Court to shut down the defense and procure the guilty verdict they desperately desired.

---

[26] Predictably, many awkward hijinks ensue until the lesbian wisely takes her own life.

[27] The record of this case can be found in the Home Office file designated HO 45/10360.

[28] For two good accounts of this obscenity trial, see Diana Souhami, *The Trials of Radclyffe Hall* (London: Weidenfeld and Nicolson, 1998); Edward de Grazia, *Girls Lean Back Everywhere: The Law of Obscenity and the Assault on Genius* (New York: Random House, 1992), 165–208.

Officially, the *Town Talk* case did not result in any legal action. No charges were brought forward; no trial occurred; the pressure exerted on Adolphus Rosenberg to close his business was ultimately pressure he put upon himself while the authorities stood by, saying as little as possible, allowing him come to conclusions on his own. In short, the whole incident was nothing but an informal conversation behind closed doors. But this is what is so interesting about the relationship between obscenity and secrecy as it played out in the late nineteenth century: the Obscene Publications Act was indeed powerful, but the application of the law itself was not precisely wherein the government's power lay. Akin to the power of the speaker in Christina Rossetti's poem "Winter: My Secret," briefly explored in the introduction to this volume, the power of the Home Office lies not in prosecuting obscenity—an act that would simultaneously reveal it—but practicing secrecy and surveillance—acts outside the formal mechanism of the law that enable officials informally to produce self-censorship. The forgotten file recording the modest case of *Town Talk*, and others like it, are of critical importance to those scholars who wish to understand fully the inner workings of historical literary censorship cases, for it is only within their handwritten pages that the government's real negotiations, concerns, and motives, long kept "secret" from the public eye, are clearly visible at last.

Chapter 12
Secrets, Silence, and the Fractured Self: Hardy's *Tess of the d'Urbervilles*

Brooke McLaughlin Mitchell

Hardy's 1891 novel, *Tess of the d'Urbervilles*, presents a female protagonist as the title character who has a secret. While many readers assert forcefully that we can narrate the experience of Tess's life, in fact portions of it are withheld from us. Of primary significance, however, is the secret of her experience in The Chase with Alec d'Urberville. This event, which takes place between—not within—a few brief paragraphs, becomes the defining secret of Tess's life. The magnitude of the experience is realized fully only in later accounts of this same event. However, these "tellings" become non-events in the novel, also taking place in "between" spaces in the text; like the initial event, the narrator tells readers only that they happened while leaving them un-narrated. Critics have offered multiple interpretations of these seeming blanks in the text, but previous analyses have overlooked the insight offered to the novel through contemporary trauma theory. Both the characterization of Tess and the structure of the narrative mimic the fractured self of a traumatized individual; trauma theory allows us to move beyond recognizing the presence of secrets and silence in the text to understanding more completely the nature of Tess's experience. This theoretical apparatus illuminates that the secret kept from the audience is also a secret kept from Tess—from herself, by herself.

Trauma, Trauma Theory and *Tess*

While psychological trauma is as old as humanity (one has only to think of Job and Medea), in its original meaning, trauma, refers to a physical wound. Only in the late-nineteenth century did the meaning change to include injury to the mind and emotions.[1] Now, post-traumatic stress disorder (PTSD) can include any of the following: an actual or perceived threat of physical injury to one's self, witnessing such an event to another person, or the death of a loved one. The element that moves these experiences from extremely distressing to traumatic is the response of the victim. One who suffers from the traumatic experience will continue to relive the event, through intrusive thoughts or dreams, and will try to avoid anything that reminds him or her of it. Generally, PTSD, which can last from a few weeks to a

---

[1] J. A. Simpson and E. S. C. Weiner, "Trauma," in *The Oxford English Dictionary*. (Oxford: Clarendon, 1989).

lifetime, disrupts everyday life.[2] Clearly, many elements of this definition apply to the story of *Tess of the d'Urbervilles*. Her experience in The Chase contains a real threat to her, not only physically and emotionally, but socially as well; while we do not know exactly what happens, we do know that she is helpless to do anything about it. Certainly, she continues to think about the event and tries to avoid anything associated with it, from talking about it, to contact with Alec d'Urberville. Perhaps most sadly, she perceives herself as separate from those around her, set apart by guilt and experience.

The move from a psychological discussion of trauma to the literary use of it rests predominantly on a shared emphasis on narrative and audience. While trauma theorists draw heavily on the clinical idea of post-traumatic stress disorder, they move beyond the clinical definition that allows us to recognize occurrences of trauma to examine the long-term effects of the experience on the individual and by extension the character or the text. Of particular importance is the shaping of identity in the face of an experience that is actually unknowable yet ever-present, resulting in repetitive yet un-illuminating narratives of an event, fragmentation, and silence in the place of speech. Cathy Caruth says that trauma "can be experienced in at least two ways: as a memory that one cannot integrate into one's own experience, and as a catastrophic knowledge that one cannot communicate to others."[3] Unfortunately, the novel and the character suffer both of these symptoms. In the most basic sense, the narrative absences (or silences) are choices made by the author and not the voice of the victim herself. However, the narrative functions almost as a "victim by proxy;"[4] the structure manifests the same fragmentation and silence as the victim—and Tess exhibits these symptoms a great deal. Over the course of the novel, Tess reveals multiple signs that she is traumatized by her experience. Of most significance is the fragmentation of her personality. However, her own narration also underlines how closely she fits Caruth's account. Although her words occur in a void, the surrounding text establishes that she is detached from her experience; while she can articulate the events of that night, her experience is, in fact, also a secret from herself, one which she can never fully come to know.[5]

---

[2] American Psychological Association, "Post Traumatic Stress Disorder," in *Diagnostic Statistical Manual*, 4th edition (Washington, D.C: American Psychological Association, 1994), 424.

[3] Cathy Caruth and Thomas Keenan, "The AIDS Crisis is not Over': A Conversation with Greg Bordorwitz, Douglas Crimp, and Laura Plinksy," in *Trauma: Explorations in Memory*, ed. Cathy Caruth (Baltimore: Johns Hopkins UP, 1995), 256.

[4] This phrase is a modification of Robert Jay Lifton's "survivor by proxy" when he discusses the relationship of the audience to the traumatized teller. In Cathy Caruth, "An Interview With Robert Jay Lifton," in *Trauma: Explorations in Memory*, ed. Cathy Caruth (Baltimore: Johns Hopkins UP, 1995), 145.

[5] While this analysis focuses particularly on silences associated with the events of The Chase and their aftermath, these are not the only silences that Hardy and his narrator maintain. Sorrow, the child born out of the night in the Chase, suddenly appears with no account of his birth. At one point, Tess verbalizes her religion, whose mix of naturalistic

This theoretical approach has much to recommend it even as it carries with it intense ethical concerns. The elements of this theory are predicated on the study of sensitive and devastating experiences of real people as a way to understand fictional texts. Significant possibilities of appropriation are inherent to any application of this nature. However, the potential gain outweighs the possible danger associated with the move between real and imaginary words. Caruth explains that trauma theory allows an audience to recognize and to take "into account the force of what is not known," to allow for and negotiate "the powerful effects of the ill-understood and the not yet known in human experience."[6] Ultimately, she privileges analysis and discourse that will lead us to an ability "to recognize and to respond to the realities of a history, a politics, and an ethics not based on straightforward understanding," a possibility that is present in the use of a very human theoretical stance.[7] Geoffrey H. Hartman also defends the use of the theory by pointing to the shared experience between art and human experience: "[I]n literature, as in life, the simplest event can resonate mysteriously, be invested with aura, and tend toward the symbolic." Ultimately, this theory allows us to develop an understanding of narrative repetition and silence (or "negative narratibility") in texts that can be used to understand the narratives of ourselves and others.[8] The appeal of trauma theory is that it allows us to escape the aporia that Deconstructionism leaves to us. Rather than simply watching a text implode, trauma theory offers a way to make meaning not only of the fragments but also of the experiences which produce them, whose meaning could easily appear to be lost in the void of senseless violence.

Fragmented Selves

The most stunning evidence that Tess is a traumatized figure comes through the multiple identities that she develops over the course of the novel. At least five different Tesses appear; the narrator, Tess herself, and Angel Clare all acknowledge the existence of Tess's multiple selves. For Tess, the only way to survive is to become a new—not altered—person, distinct from the one she was before the night in The Chase. Robert Jay Lifton explains how these selves come into being:

---

worship and Christianity is difficult to decipher, but we are not allowed to hear (252). The descriptions of the dead bodies of Prince and Alec replace the acts of killing that produced them (23, 302). Finally, the hanging of Tess is not narrated, but merely signified through the raising of a flag (314). In each case, the effect is the same—silence replaces concrete information.

6 Cathy Caruth, "Introduction: The Insistence of Reference," in *Critical Encounters: Reference and Responsibility in Deconstructive Writing*, ed. Cathy Caruth and Deborah Esch (New Brunswick: Rutgers UP, 1995), 6.

7 Caruth, "Introduction," 1.

8 Hartman, Geoffrey R., "Reading, Trauma and Pedagogy," in *The Geoffrey Hartman Reader*, eds. Geoffrey Hartman and Daniel T. O'Hara (New York: Fordham UP, 2004), 291.

> But in extreme involvements, as in extreme trauma, one's sense of self is radically altered. And there is a traumatized self that is created. Of course, it's not a totally new self, it's what one brought into the trauma as affected significantly and painfully, confusedly, but in a very primal way, by that trauma. And recovery from post-traumatic effects, or from survivor conflicts, cannot really occur until that traumatized self is reintegrated. It's a form of doubling in the traumatized person.[9]

This doubling comes in the form of self conception rather than the schizophrenia or disassociation that popular culture often associates with psychological stress. However, it shares the same motivation of distancing one part of the self from another as a means of survival.

The first and primary self is the maiden Tess. This young woman is "heart-whole," a beloved member of the village maidens who each "had a private little sun for her soul."[10] Rooted in her place, both socially and geographically, she is the daughter of an "extinct" family, pointing to the length of her heritage, and "[e]very contour of the surrounding hills was as personal to her as that of her relatives' faces" (25). Ironically, it is in going to claim kin of the faux d'Urbervilles that she experiences the very trauma that will remove her from any real, sustained connection with other people or the land in her future. However, even in this whole self, hints of future fragmentation lie. For example, in this and other phases of the novel, the narrator repeatedly emphasizes the contradiction between her virginal youth and her appearance, an issue that clearly has a significant role in the tragic events of her life. Tess has also already begun to cultivate separate social selves. This particular development is not due to trauma but to a desire to improve her station in life, and it is manifested through her language: she "spoke two languages; the dialect at home, more or less; ordinary English abroad and to persons of quality" (12). A young woman who aspires to be the village teacher must have superior speech. It is this maiden Tess, refined yet intricately bound to her home, whom Angel first sees, although unknowingly.

This original Tess experiences the death of Prince. This event, which serves as the specific catalyst to send her to the d'Urbervilles, is written almost as a figurative rape. The phallic image of the cart shaft sticking into the vaginal image of the wound is a violent foreshadowing of the sexual act that will traumatize Tess for the rest of her life. Also, after this episode, she regards "herself in the light of a murderess" (24). This self-labeling foreshadows the ultimate attempt that she will make to undo the wrong that was done to her, and by extension to Angel, when she stabs Alec near the end of the novel and bears this title in a literal sense.

Under duress and guilt, Tess follows her parents' wishes and goes to the d'Urbervilles. Alec d'Urberville takes a fancy to her, but for some time, Tess escapes his attempts to seduce her. However, the course of her life shifts during

---

9 Caruth, "An Interview," 137.

10 Thomas Hardy, *Tess of the d'Urbervilles*, ed. Scott Elledge (New York: Norton, 1991), 10, 7.

a ride home from the fair with Alec. The narrator fully describes this ride as well as Alec's revelation that he has sent a horse to her father and toys to her siblings. Clearly, he plays upon her most significant concerns: her guilt over the death of the family horse and her anxiety for the general well-being of her siblings. Alec casts himself as her protector in every sense; even when she declares that she cannot ride with him any more, he gives his coat to her as defense against the cold as he seeks a place to leave her. When he returns in the almost impenetrable dark, she is "sleeping soundly," passive and seemingly at peace (57).

The sleeping maiden gives way to Tess's second self, the girl in The Chase, the victim of Alec d'Urberville; this self becomes the initial bearer of her secret. The particularity of the narration up to Alec's return leads readers to expect that the next events will be recounted in the same detail;[11] however, there is only a series of questions leading to one awful statement: "where was Tess's guardian angel? Where was the providence of her simple faith? Perhaps, like any other god of whom the ironical Tishbite spoke, he was talking, or he was pursuing, or he was in a journey, or he was sleeping and not to be awakened" (57). The narrative absence in the text is then reinforced by the almost immediate shift from this scene to the next phase of the novel. Through the labeling of Phase the Second, it is clear to the reader that Tess is "a maiden no more." Certainly, there are many clues from which critics have drawn the standard interpretation that Tess has in fact been raped, though concrete substantiation is denied.

Because of the silence offered by the narrator, we have almost no way to describe this young woman, other than to recognize that she exists. This version of Tess lasts only between the lines of a few brief paragraphs, and her existence is specifically mentioned only late in the novel by Tess herself. After Angel has left her, she writes a letter to him, pleading her case and declaring the difference between herself and that girl: "I am the same woman, Angel, as you fell in love with; yes, the very same! Not the one you disliked, but never saw. What was the past as soon as I met you? It was a dead thing altogether. I am become another woman, filled full of new life from you. How could I be the early one?" (265).

Her third self appears as a result of the night in The Chase. Hardy's narrator carefully establishes that Tess has developed a distance between herself and that

---

[11] In "Gender and Silence in Thomas Hardy's Texts," William W. Morgan explains that "The fictional conventions within which Hardy worked for virtually his entire career included the expectation that a novelist would provide an *adequate* narrator—that is, a narrative voice whose management of action would also provide a management of wisdom and value—who could and would guide readers toward some kind of assessment of the issues raised by character and event. The voice that speaks in a work of nineteenth-century third-person realistic fiction is, by convention, expected to be wise enough—or at least knowing enough—to appraise the fictional situation and make it morally and philosophically coherent to the readers, even if the characters and events of the novel mount a forthright challenge to the values and habits of those same readers." In *Gender and Discourse in Victorian Literature and Art*, eds. Antony H. Harrison and Beverly Taylor (Dekalb: Northern Illinois UP, 1992), 168.

girl; she will continue to distance her present self from that earlier one each time that she is forced to recognize her past. Strikingly, the first time that the narrator acknowledges that Tess is capable of creating a new self comes within the final statement of "Phase the First." The narrator tells us that "An immeasurable social chasm was to divide our heroine's personality thereafter from that previous self of hers who stepped from her mother's door to try her fortune at Trantridge poultry-farm" (58). Moving from the first phase of the novel, "The Maiden," to the second, "Maiden No More," reiterates this change. Then, when Tess returns to her home, the landscape of her native place "was terribly beautiful to Tess today, for since her eyes last fell upon it she had learnt that a serpent hisses where the sweet bird sings, and her views of life had been totally changed for her by the lesson. Verily another girl than the simple one she had been at home was she who, bowed by the thought, stood still here, and turned to look behind her" (58–9).

Understandably, Tess must tell her story for both practical and psychological reasons. On one hand, she is pregnant and will be required to give an account. On the other, from the earliest study of trauma as a psychological problem, the idea of narrative has played a vital role. The speech act is integral to the diagnosis and treatment of trauma, whether in the form of the "compelled teller," who must continue to tell the experience over and over, or the "talking cure," which emphasizes that an experience must be recounted in order to be truly addressed and overcome. The frequency with which an experience is recounted is one indicator of the relationship of the person to the experience and its lasting effects. Tess recounts her story only twice in the novel, but even so these tellings can be read as symbolic representations of the compelled teller. Hartman explains such repetitions as "cathartic," even as they "suggest an unresolved shock: a rhythmic or temporal stutter" which "leave the storyteller in purgatory, awaiting the next assault, the next instance of hyperarousal."[12]

No story is created without context, and the audience of a narrative of trauma is as important to the integration process as is the telling of the experience itself. The receptivity—or lack of it—of an audience can encourage healing or ensure that it will be delayed or even denied. For example, Culbertson asserts that if a culture requires silence, then victims generally remain silent.[13] Expanding upon this idea, Jodie Wigren explains that, "stories are created in relation to the audience, sometimes the audience of the self, often an audience of others. Stories are frequently created in conversation with others. The availability of others is thus important to the creation of the story."[14] The two times that Tess tells her story support the importance of the audience to the victim; one audience demands silence much more stringently than the other.

---

[12] Geoffrey H. Hartman, "On Traumatic Knowledge and Literary Studies," *New Literary History* 26 (1995): 537–63, 543.

[13] Roberta Culbertson, "Embodied Memory, Transcendence, and Telling: Recounting Trauma, Re-establishing the Self," *New Literary History* 26, no.1 (1995): 173.

[14] Jodie Wigren, "Narrative Completion in the Treatment of Trauma," *Psychotherapy* 31, no. 3 (1994): 415–23, 416–7.

Her mother is her first audience, and this telling does not hold great possibility of judgment; therefore, Tess does not risk further fracturing the already fractured self. Even so, the reader knows only that she "told" her mother (63). The narrator then jumps from acknowledging that the story is told to Joan Durbeyfield's response: "And yet th'st not got him to marry 'ee!" (63). Her mother's response bears validation to the non-threatening nature of this audience. Her concern with the possibility that Alec will actually marry Tess seems to preclude any blame for immorality that the mother could place on the daughter. Aside from her dashed financial hopes, Tess's mother seems only mildly annoyed with her daughter. Joan Durbeyfield's simple and fatalistic view of life simply deems Tess's misfortune as something to be taken in stride.

However, Tess sees her situation differently,[15] as do other members of their community. Tess is clearly traumatized as a result of that night, but the relationship of Tess's story to the society of the novel questions the very source of her trauma. Do the fractures in her life spring from her actual experiences or from the view that society takes of them? Laura S. Brown argues that "Social context, and the individual's history within that social context, can lend traumatic meaning to events that might only be sad or troubling in another time and place."[16] To some degree, this seems to be true for Tess. Clearly, Alec does not suffer from this encounter; as a male he experiences no repercussions because of it. But, for Tess, as a female, her experience is much different. The necessity that she live in a society that judges her experiences, holding her responsible for her sexual encounter with Alec without any recognition of mitigating circumstances, creates a traumatic situation for her. In the eyes of her society, the experience would have magically become "good" if Alec had married her; in that circumstance, she would have become a local heroine who had snagged a rich man, and Tess's supposed transgression would have been forgiven.

But this is not what happens, and Tess often appears to be troubled by her perception of other people's opinions and the judgments that they subsequently pass because of them:

> [S]he looked upon herself as a figure of Guilt intruding into the haunts of Innocence. But all the while she was making a distinction where there was no difference. Feeling herself in antagonism she was quite in accord. She had been made to break an accepted social law, but no law known to the environment in which she fancied herself such an anomaly. (67)

---

15 This point is made blatantly clear when Tess writes to her mother about her situation with Angel. Her mother's response prompts the narrator to observe that "Her mother did not see life as Tess saw it. That haunting episode of bygone days was to her mother but a passing accident" (150).

16 Laura S. Brown, "Not Outside the Range: One Feminist Perspective on Trauma," in *Trauma: Explorations in Memory*, ed. Cathy Caruth (Baltimore: Johns Hopkins UP, 1995), 110.

Social law dictates that Tess should be guilty, not the law of nature, thus adding another layer of lasting pain to the already traumatic experience.

Hope returns to the text in the figure of Tess's fourth incarnation, which coincides with the promising label of "Phase the Third: The Rally." This self is loved by Angel and "filled full of new life" because of him (265). Yet, Tess resists this new creation because of the guilt that she carries. She intentionally tries to live a "repressed life," having decided that she cannot develop any romantic relationships because she feels herself bound, however unwillingly, to Alec (106). However, against her will, because "she little divined the strength of her own vitality," this new self does come into being (98).

Long before Angel and Tess are legally bound as one person, Hardy encourages us to see them as one. When the two first meet at Talbothay's Dairy, they are as different as two people can be. Although he has radical views of religion and society and desires to become a farmer, he is still a minister's son, a refined member of a certain class. Tess, on the other hand, is the almost primitive child of nature who still observes traditional religious practices. However, as they spend more time together, they move closer into a union of minds and spirits. Long before they succumb to their passion for each other, the narrator tells us that "All the while they were converging, under an irresistible law, as surely as two streams in one vale" (101). Later, after she has agreed to marry Angel, the narrator explains that, "she had caught his manner and habits, his speech and phrases, his likings and his aversions" (160). In the pages directly preceding the confession of Tess to Angel, Hardy increases the emphasis that they have become more than two halves of a whole—they are the same. Angel and Tess themselves have trouble telling the difference. When they wash their hands together after reaching the d'Urberville ancestral home, Angel muses on the sight in the basin: "'Which are my fingers and which are yours?' he said, looking up. 'They are very much mixed.'" She answers him, "They are all yours" (170). Later, the gravity of his relation to Tess begins to become clear to Angel. He thinks that he finally understands how much he and Tess are joined together: "What I am in worldly estate, she is. What I become, she must become. What I cannot be, she cannot be" (171). The last moment that we are allowed to believe that Tess has achieved unity through this development of a new self, bound with another, comes after Angel confesses his own indiscretion to Tess; the narrative claims that "He seemed to be her double!" (176).

Of course, this idea of the single self fragments at its very climax. The second time Tess narrates her experience has much more serious consequences. Telling her past to Angel Clare is infinitely more threatening to her future than telling it to her mother; she has much more to lose as she "confesses" her "fall" to him, regardless of how enlightened he appears to be.

When Tess relates her past to Angel, the reader is told that "she entered on her acquaintance with Alec d'Urberville and its results" (177). Once again, the reader is denied full access to her story. When she narrates her tale, Tess herself underlines her detachment from her story; the narrator tells us that she begins her account "murmuring the words without flinching" (177). Then, instead of including the account, the narrator jumps to the statement, "her narrative ended," echoing the earlier scene with her mother (178). After the completion of her confession to Angel—and the shift from "Phase the Fourth, The Consequence," to "Phase the Fifth, The Woman Pays"—we know only that, "Tess's voice throughout had hardly risen higher than the opening tone; there had been no exculpatory phrase of any kind, and she had not wept" (178). Tess's lack of emotion clearly marks the detachment from her narrative of which Roberta Culbertson speaks:

> The one who speaks without emotion presents only what Delbo calls an 'external' memory—socially constructed, skating along the surface of words and engaging the intellect—not the body's re-experience, which because it is a recapitulation of the past, cannot be spoken about or related at the moment, just as it could not be done originally. It is not known in words, but in the body.[17]

Tess's speech illuminates the rift between her intellectual knowledge of her experience and the experience itself. Because the story she tells is connected only to the surface of her being and not really absorbed as a part of it, Tess is able to detach herself from that person in The Chase. To her, that person no longer exists.

Angel turns away from Tess's narrative, just as she is unable to integrate her past into the present; the girl in The Chase cannot be part of his pure Tess. Angel's reaction is a visible demonstration of the turmoil that Tess experiences as she attempts to deal with her story. One of the most pitiable moments of the novel comes when the sleepwalking Angel takes Tess, believing her to be dead, and places her in an empty stone coffin (193–6). He buries her just as Tess has attempted to bury that other self (193–6). However, the impact of Angel turning from her is even greater than merely the symbolic self turning away; she sees him as her better self, and it is this self which now abandons her.

Angel's response should be no surprise to the reader. Loving acceptance by Angel would be a contradiction to Hardy's generally dim view of human relations. However, the text also alerts us that Angel will not be the willing and sympathetic audience that modern theorists now recognize as necessary to a victim's narrative. Multiple references tell us that he blatantly idealizes her, inflicting an identity on her that is not her own; Tess herself recognizes this on the day of their wedding: "for she you love is not my real self, but one in my image; the one I might have been" (168). Also, he literally has silenced her at earlier times when she has tried to narrate her past to him. Her response on one of these occasions is an illuminating representation of the victim's recognition of her audience. Even as she begins to tell him, he is flippant, although he does not mean to be hurtful; by the time she reaches the point in her history that she must tell him about Alec, she substitutes her secret that she is a descendent of one of the old families that he professes to hate. At the last moment, Tess replaces the lesser secret for the greater one because her audience simply will not hear her (147–9).

---

[17] Culbertson, 170.

The self turning away from itself through the reaction of Angel Clare goes beyond the single point of his vehement response towards her. Angel exhibits evidence of trauma as does Tess, further emphasizing the unity between them even as he tries to deny it. Tess's revelation has the same effect on Angel that the original experience had on Tess: he seems to fragment into another self. After the newlyweds part, the narrator tells us that for Angel "the picture of life had changed" and that he is disinterested in his former endeavors (203). Interestingly, his eventual "recovery" from his own fragmentation, the re-integration of his ideals and his wife into one holistic vision, comes after his own narration of the events to a sympathetic stranger. This man listens without judging, and he endorses a view of Tess opposite to that of society and against the view of Angel. This change not only heals Angel but prepares him to be a sympathetic listener to the other part of his own self, his wife, when she speaks again, which she does first through her long-delayed letters. Higgonnet marks that "symbolically, he cannot receive her letters until he is psychologically ready to answer."[18] His experience has transformed him into a sympathetic audience who can now allow his wife's trauma to have a voice.

The fifth and final self is the Tess who, standing before Angel at Sandbourne, "had ceased to recognize the body before him as hers" (299). This self is ill-defined, and it is difficult to pin point the exact moment that this self emerges. Ellen Rooney marks one sign of this new self in Tess's obliteration of her beauty when she goes into field service.[19] This physical manifestation of a new self calls to mind the earlier physical change marked by Sorrow. However, in the present case, Tess controls the sign of the new self although she has had no control over other events that led to it. Another possible point of materialization for this self is her second life with Alec. Although the narrator does not choose to convey this episode during which Tess passes as Alec's fashionable wife, it is possible that as soon as she gives in to her guilt and takes this role, this self emerges. She believes she must function as Alec's wife in the eyes of society, regardless of her legal marriage to Angel. It is also possible that this self emerges once Angel returns to her and she stabs Alec, literally creating a new role for herself as murderess.

Whatever moment that sparks the emergence of this new self, Tess's removal from her experience ties this last incarnation to the symptoms of trauma that we see in each of the earlier ones. Another very physical sign of a change appears in her clothing as she runs toward Angel after killing Alec; Angel does not recognize her in her changed clothes (303). When he questions her, Tess continues to show the detachment that she shows when she narrates her experience in The Chase;

---

[18] Margaret Higonet, "Fictions of Female Voice: Antiphony and Silence in Hardy's *Tess of the d"Urbervilles*," in *Out of Bounds: Male Writers and Gender(ed) Criticism*, eds, Laura Claridge and Elizabeth Langland (Amherst: U of Massachusetts P, 1990), 209.

[19] Ellen Rooney, "'A Little More Than Persuading': Tess and the Subject of Sexual Violence," in *Rape and Representation*, eds. Lynn A. Higgins and Brenda R. Silver (New York: Columbia UP), 108–9.

she knows that she has murdered Alec, but she cannot explain how (303–4). Also, that she does not fully understand her situation is clear as Angel seeks to hide her. However, the most telling statement of this last Tess is her command to Angel: "Don't think of what's past!" (307). Like each of her earlier selves, this one seeks to reject that past in order to write the present. Ultimately, it is fitting that the last silence of the text represents her execution.

Conclusion

Ironically, the narrator refers to Tess as "not incomplete" (191). But Tess is incomplete. She is never able to gather the fragments of her life into a single self with which she can live. Each time a new Tess appears, the old one dies, at least from Tess's point of view. Margaret Higonnet also recognizes this pattern: "Each time the past is voiced—whether in Tess's descent from aristocratic philanderers or her seduction—Tess is displaced, often physically, and wrenched from her pursuit of selfhood."[20] But, in fact, trauma occurs because the Tess that exists during the night in The Chase never really dies because she never really existed. Kilby explains, "Trauma insists on a past that has never been present. Trauma is impossible to experience at the time and difficult to grasp in the here and now."[21] Caruth labels it a "symptom of a history that [she] cannot entirely possess."[22] That Tess of the night in The Chase is acknowledged by Tess yet never really owned by her; that earlier Tess keeps returning with her burden of guilt to fracture the present existence of the living Tess. Subsequently, every time Tess tries to claim all of her parts, she is able only to fracture into a new one. She is left even more incomplete than she was previous to her attempt to claim all of her parts to form one, whole Tess. Even at the end of the novel when she eliminates the cause of her trauma through her murder of Alec, she does not regain her life but succeeds only in losing it altogether. Tess has split into multiple selves that can never exist at the same time to form a singular Tess.

When Hardy wrote *Tess of the d'Urbervilles*, he intended to present a faithful representation of a woman who had suffered at the hands of fate and her society, and he was very interested in the working of the mind. However, Hardy presents a much more faithful picture of her experience than he or the psychologists of his day would have been able to name. But we can name this depth, and our ability to recognize it opens an understanding to us that moves beyond merely recognizing that Tess suffers from her experience and that important details of it are withheld from us. On many levels, Hardy imbeds the key to understanding her experience—

[20] Margaret Higonet, "Fictions of Female Voice: Antiphony and Silence in Hardy's *Tess of the d'Urbervilles*," in *Out of Bounds: Male Writers and Gender(ed) Criticism*, eds. Laura Claridge and Elizabeth Langland (Amherst: U of Massachusetts P, 1990), 202.

[21] Jane Kilby, "The Writing of Trauma: Trauma Theory and the Liberty of Reading," *New Formations* 47 (2002), 217–30.

[22] Caruth, "The Insistence of Reference," 5.

even as he withholds it from us—in the silence of the narrator and the structure of the text. While Tess articulates her experience in The Chase, every indication in the text tells us that Tess is keeping a secret from herself that is, in turn, kept from the reader. Just as Tess struggles to make sense of an experience that she does not wholly recognize, we struggle through the interpretation of a text that we cannot fully know. In the end, our understanding of her is forced beyond an intellectual level to a psychological and emotional understanding that is beyond—and perhaps deeper than—words.

Bibliography

Adams, James Eli. *Dandies and Desert Saints: Styles of Victorian Masculinity*. Ithaca: Cornell UP, 1995.

Allderidge, Patricia. *The Late Richard Dadd 1817–1886*. London: Tate Gallery, 1974.

Allen, J B L. "Mad Robin: Richard Dadd." *Art Quarterly* 30, no. 1 (1967): 19–30.

Altick, Richard D. *The English Common Reader: A Social History of the Mass Reading Public, 1800–1900*. Chicago: U of Chicago P, 1957.

American Psychological Association. *Diagnostic Statistical Manual*. 4th ed. Washington, D.C: American Psychological Association, 1994.

Andrews, Jonathan, Asa Briggs, Roy Porter, Penny Tucker and Keir Waddington. *The History of Bethlem*. London & New York: Routledge, 1997.

Armstrong, Isobel. *Victorian Poetry: Poetry, Poetics and Politics*. London: Routledge, 1993.

Armstrong, Isobel and Virginia Blain, eds. *Women's Poetry, Late Romantic to Late Victorian: Gender and Genre, 1830–1890*. London and New York: Macmillan and St. Martin's, 1999.

Arnold, Matthew. "Byron." In *Essays in Criticism: Second Series*, 116–44. London: MacMillan, 1935.

———. *Arnold: Poetical Works*. Eds. C. B. Tinker and H. F. Lowry. New York: Oxford UP, 1945.

Augustinus, Aurelius. *The Confessions of Saint Augustine*. Trans. E. B. Pusey. 1838. London: Watkins Publishing, 2006.

Austen, Jane. *Northanger Abbey* (1818), *Lady Susan* (1871), *The Watsons* (1871), *Sanditon* (1925). Oxford: Oxford UP, 2003.

Baker, Joseph Ellis. *The Novel and the Oxford Movement*. New York: Russell & Russell, 1965.

Balee, Susan. "Wilkie Collins and Surplus Woman: The Case of Marian Halcombe." *Victorian Literature and Culture* 20 (1992): 197–215.

Baron-Cohen, Simon. "Autism and Theory of Mind." In *The Applied Psychologist*, eds. James Hartley and Alan Branthwaite, 181–94. Buckingham, UK: Open UP, 2000.

———. *Mindblindness: An Essay on Autism and Theory of Mind*. Cambridge: MIT Press, 1995.

Beckwith, Marc. "Catabasis in *Bleak House*: Bucket as Sibyl." *Dickens Quarterly* 1, no. 1 (1984): 2–6.

Bell, Charles. *Essays on the Anatomy of Expression in Painting*. London: J Murray, 1824.

Bertram, Charles. "Are Indian Jugglers Humbugs?" *The Strand Magazine* 18, no. 108 (December 1899): 657.

———. *A Magician in Many Lands*. London: Routledge, 1911.

———. *Isn't It Wonderful?* London: Swan Sonnenschien, 1899.

Blain, Virginia. "Sexual Politics of the (Victorian) Closet; *or*, No Sex, Please—We're Poets." In Armstrong and Blain, eds., *Gender and Genre*, 135–63.

Block, Jr., Ed. "Venture and Response: The Dialogical Strategy of John Henry Newman's *Loss and Gain*." In *Critical Essays on John Henry Newman*, ed. Ed Block, Jr., 23–38. British Columbia: U of Victoria P, 1992.

Bodenheimer, Rosemarie. *The Real Life of Mary Ann Evans: George Eliot, Her Letters and Fiction*. Ithaca: Cornell UP, 1994.

Bok, Sissela. *Secrets: On the Ethics of Concealment and Revelation*. New York: Pantheon Books, 1982.

Booth, Bradford. "Trollope and the Royal Literary Fund," *Nineteenth-Century Fiction* 7 (1952): 208–16.

Bown, Nicola. *Fairies in Nineteenth Century Art & Literature*. Cambridge: Cambridge UP, 2001.

Braddon, Mary Elizabeth. *Aurora Floyd*. 1863. Oxford: Oxford UP, 1999.

———. *Lady Audley's Secret*. 1862. Ware: Wordsworth, 1999.

Brandon, Ruth. *The Life and Many Deaths of Harry Houdini*. New York: Random House, 1993.

Branson, Lionel. *Indian Conjuring*. London: Routledge, 1910.

Brantlinger, Patrick. *The Reading Lesson: The Threat of Mass Literacy in Nineteenth-Century British Fiction*. Bloomington: Indiana UP, 1998.

Bray, William, ed. *Memoirs of John Evelyn: Comprising His Diary, from 1641–1705–6, and a Selection of His Familiar Letters*. London: Frederick Warne and Co., 1871.

Britland, David. *Phantoms of the Card Table*. London: High Stakes Publishing, 2003.

Brooks, Chris. *Mortal Remains: the History and Present State of the Victorian and Edwardian Cemetery*. Exeter: Wheaton, 1989.

Brooks, Peter. "The Law as Narrative and Rhetoric." In *Law's Stories: Narrative and Rhetoric in the Law*, eds. Peter Brooks and Paul Gewirtz, 14–23. New Haven: Yale UP, 1996.

———. *Reading for the Plot*. New York: Vintage Books, 1984.

Brown, Laura S. "Not Outside the Range: One Feminist Perspective on Trauma." In *Trauma: Explorations in Memory*, ed. Cathy Caruth, 100–12. Baltimore: Johns Hopkins UP, 1995.

Browne, Janet. "Darwin and the Face of Madness." In *The Anatomy of Madness: Essays in the History of Psychiatry, Vol. 1, People and Ideas*, eds. W F Bynum, Roy Porter and Michael Shepherd, 151–65. London: Tavistock, 1985.

Browning, Elizabeth Barrett. "The Mask." 1850. In *The Poetical Works of Elizabeth Barrett Browning*, Oxford Complete Edition, 287–8. London: Henry Frowde, 1904.

Bruss, Elizabeth. *Autobiographical Acts: The Changing Situation of a Literary Genre*. Baltimore: Johns Hopkins UP, 1976.

Buckton, Oliver S. "'An Unnatural State': Gender, 'Perversion,' and Newman's *Apologia Pro Vita Sua*." *Victorian Studies* 35, no. 4 (1992): 359–83.
Budge, Gavin. "Realism and Typology in Charlotte M. Yonge's *The Heir of Redclyffe*." *Victorian Literature and Culture* 31 (2003): 193–223.
Burlingame, H.J. *Leaves from Conjurers' Scrap Books*. Chicago: Donohue, 1891.
Burns, Sarah. *Painting the Dark Side. Art and the Gothic Imagination in Nineteenth-Century America*. Berkeley: U of California P, 2004.
Calinescu, Matei. *Rereading*. New Haven and London: Yale UP, 1993.
Carlyle, Thomas. *Past and Present*. 1843. In *The Works of Thomas Carlyle*. Edinburgh Edition. vol. 10. New York: Charles Scribner's Sons, 1903–04.
———. *Sartor Resartus: The Life and Opinions of Herr Teufelsdröckh in Three Books*. 1833–34. Introduction and notes by Roger L. Tarr, Text established by Mark Engel and Rodger L. Tarr. Berkeley: U of California P, 2000.
Carroll, Joseph. *Literary Darwinism: Evolution, Human Nature, and Literature*. New York and London: Routledge, 2004.
Caruth Cathy. "An Interview with Robert Jay Lifton." In *Trauma: Explorations in Memory*, ed. Cathy Caruth, 128–47. Baltimore: Johns Hopkins UP, 1995.
———. "Introduction: The Insistence of Reference." In *Critical Encounters: Reference and Responsibility in Deconstructive Writing*, eds. Cathy Caruth and Deborah Esch, 1–8. New Brunswick: Rutgers UP, 1995.
Caruth, Cathy and Thomas Keenan. "'The AIDS Crisis is not Over': A Conversation with Greg Bordorwitz, Douglas Crimp, and Laura Plinksy." In *Trauma: Explorations in Memory*, ed. Cathy Caruth, 256–71. Baltimore: Johns Hopkins UP, 1995.
Chadwick, Edwin. *A Supplementary Report on the Results of a Special Inquiry into the Practice of Interment in Towns*. London: W. Clowes, 1843.
Chambers, R. W. *Man's Unconquerable Mind*. London: Jonathan Cape, 1939.
Chapman, Maria Weston. *Memorials*. Boston: J. R. Osgood, 1877.
Charlton, Bruce. "Theory of Mind Delusions and Bizarre Delusions in an Evolutionary Perspective: Psychiatry and the Social Brain." In *The Social Brain: Evolution and Pathology*, eds. Martin Brune, Hedda Ribbert, and Wulf Schiefenhovel, 315–38. Chichester, UK: John Wiley & Sons, 2003.
Chase, Karen and Michael Levenson. *The Spectacle of Intimacy: A Public Life for the Victorian Family*. Princeton: Princeton UP, 2000.
Chesterton, Gilbert Keith. *Magic*. London: Martin Secker, 1913.
Christie's Catalogue. London: Archives Department, Christie's Auctioneers, 8 King Street, St James, SW1, London, 1870.
Claflin, Edward and Jeff Sheridan. *Street Magic*. Washington, DC: Kaufman, 1977.
Clarke, Sidney. *The Annals of Conjuring*. 1924–28. Eds. Todd Karr and Edwin Dawes. Seattle: Miracle Factory, 2001.
Cognard-Black, Jennifer. *Narrative in the Professional Age: Transatlantic Readings of Harriet Beecher Stowe, George Eliot, and Elizabeth Stuart Phelps*. New York: Routledge, 2004.

Cohen, William. *Sex Scandal: The Private Parts of Victorian Fiction*. Durham: Duke UP, 1996.

Collins, Philip. *Dickens and Crime*. 3rd ed. New York: St. Martin's, 1994.

Collins, Wilkie. *The Woman in White*. 1860. Eds. Maria K. Bachman and Don Richard Cox. Peterborough, ON: Broadview, 2004.

Collison, George. *Cemetery Interment: Containing a Concise History of the Modes of Interment Practised by the Ancients; Descriptions of Père la Chaise, the Eastern Cemeteries, and those of America; the English Metropolitan and Provincial Cemeteries, and more Particularly of the Abney Park Cemetery, at Stoke Newington, with a Descriptive Catalogue of its Plants and Arboretum*. London: Longman, Orme, Brown, Green, and Longmans, 1840.

"The Commissioners in Lunacy's Report on Bethlem Hospital." *Journal of Psychological Medicine and Mental Pathology* 6 (1853): 129–45.

Conan Doyle, Arthur. *The Complete Sherlock Holmes*. Garden City, NY: Garden City Books, 1930.

Cook, James. *The Arts of Deception: Playing with Fraud in the Age of Barnum*. Cambridge: Harvard UP, 2001.

Corbain, Alain. *The Foul and the Fragrant: Odor and the French Social Imagination*. Cambridge, MA: Harvard UP, 1988.

Culbertson, Roberta. "Embodied Memory, Transcendence, and Telling: Recounting Trauma, Re-establishing the Self," *New Literary History* 26, no.1 (1995):169–95.

Culler, A. Dwight. *The Victorian Mirror of History*. New Haven: Yale UP, 1985.

Cummins, Denise. "Social Norms and Other Minds: The Evolutionary Roots of Higher Cognition." In *The Evolution of Mind*, eds. Denise D. Cummins and Colin Allen, 30–50. New York: Oxford UP, 1999.

Curl, James Stevens. *The Victorian Celebration of Death*. Stroud, UK: Sutton, 2000.

———. ed. *Kensal Green Cemetery: the Origins and Development of the General Cemetery of All Souls Kensal Green, London, 1824–2001*. Chichester, UK: Phillimore, 2001.

Dadd, Richard. *Elimination of a Picture and its Subject – Called the Feller's Master Stroke*. Beckenham, Kent: Bethlem Royal Hospital and Maudsley Hospital Archives and Museum, 1865.

Daniel, George. *Merrie England in the Olden Times*. 1842. London: Chatto and Windus, 1881.

Dawes, Edwin. *Charles Bertram: The Court Conjurer*. Washington, DC: Kaufman, 1997.

———. *Stanley Collins: Conjurer, Collector, and Iconoclast*. Washington, DC: Kaufman, 2002.

———. *The Great Illusionists*. Secaucus: Chartwell, 1979.

de Grazia, Edward. *Girls Lean Back Everywhere: The Law of Obscenity and the Assault on Genius*. New York: Random House, 1992.

Dean, Carolyn J. *The Frail Social Body: Pornography, Homosexuality, and Other Fantasies in Interwar France*. Berkeley, Los Angeles, London: U of California P, 2000.

Delany, Paul. *British Autobiography in the Seventeenth Century*. London: Routledge and Kegan Paul, 1969.

Dickens, Charles. *Barnaby Rudge*. 1841. Ed. Gordon Spence. Harmondsworth: Penguin, 1997.

———. *Bleak House*. 1852–53. Ed. Norman Page. Harmondsworth: Penguin, 1971.

———. *Dombey and Son*. 1846–48. Ed. Peter Fairclough. Harmondsworth: Penguin, 1970.

———. *The Letters of Charles Dickens*. eds. Madeline House, Graham Storey, and Kathleen Tillotson. Pilgrim Edition. 12 vols. Oxford: Clarendon, 1969–2002.

———. *Little Dorrit*. 1855–57. Ed. Harvey Peter Sucksmith. Oxford: Oxford UP, 1979.

———. *Our Mutual Friend*. 1864–65. Ed. Stephen Gill. Harmondsworth: Penguin, 1971.

———. *A Tale of Two Cities*. 1859. Ed. Norman Page. London: J. M. Dent, 1998.

Digby, Anne. *Madness, Morality and Medicine, A Study of the York Retreat, 1796–1914*. Cambridge: Cambridge UP, 1985.

"Dobler Outdone." *Punch* 39 (17 November 1860): 194.

Dollimore, Jonathan. *Sexual Dissidence: Augustine to Wilde, Freud to Foucault*. Oxford: Clarendon, 1991.

Downes, Kerry. "Vanbrugh's India and his Mausolea for England." In *Sir John Vanbrugh and Landscape Architecture in Baroque England 1690–1730*, eds. Christopher Ridgway and Robert Williams, 114–30. Stroud, UK: Sutton Publishing, 2000.

Durbin, William W. "My Life of Magic." *The Linking Ring* 15, no. 7 (1935): 607.

During, Simon. *Modern Enchantments: The Cultural Power of Secular Magic*. Cambridge: Harvard UP, 2002.

Easley, Keith. "Dickens and Bakhtin: Authoring in *Bleak House*." *Dickens Studies Annual* 34 (2004): 185–232.

Edwards, Amelia. *Hand and Glove*. 1858. London: Rubicon Press, 2000.

Eigen, Joel Peter. *Witnessing Insanity, Madness and Mad-Doctors in the English Court*. New Haven & London: Yale UP, 1995.

Elfenbein, Andrew. *Byron and the Victorians*. Cambridge: Cambridge UP, 1995.

Eliot, George. *Felix Holt, The Radical*. 1866. Ed. Linda Mugglestone. London: Penguin, 1995.

———. *Middlemarch*. 1871–72. Ed. Gordon S. Haight. Boston: Houghton Mifflin, 1956.

———. *Selections From George Eliot's Letters*. Ed. Gordon S. Haight. New Haven: Yale UP, 1985.

Eliot, Simon. "The Business of Victorian Publishing." In *The Cambridge Companion to the Victorian Novel*, ed. Deirdre David, 37–60. Cambridge: Cambridge UP, 2001.

Elkins, James. *The Poetics of Perspective*. Ithaca & London: Cornell UP, 1994.

Emerson, Ralph Waldo. *English Traits*. 1856. In *The Complete Works of Ralph Waldo Emerson*, Centenary Edition, 12 volumes, vol. 5. Boston: Houghton Mifflin, 1903.

Emmott, Catherine. "Constructing Social Space: Sociocognitive Factors in the Interpretation of Character Relations." In *Narrative Theory and the Cognitive Sciences*, ed. David Herman, 295–321. Stanford: CSLI Publications, 2003.

Esquirol, Jean-Etienne Dominique. *Des maladies mentales, considerées sous les rapports médical, hygiénique et medico-légal*. Paris: J B Baillière, 1838.

Etlin, Richard A. *The Architecture of Death: The Transformation of the Cemetery in Eighteenth-Century Paris*. Cambridge, MA: MIT Press, 1984.

Evans, Henry Ridgley. "Flying Leaves from the Journal of an Amateur Magician and Mystic." *The Linking Ring* 8, no. 11 (1929): 869.

Evelyn, John. *Silva; or, a Discourse on Forest Trees*. 5th ed. London: J. Walthoe, J. Knapton, D. Midwinter, A. Bettesworth, J. Tonson, 1729.

Ewing, Tom. *Frederick Eugene Powell: The Man and His Magic*. NP: Tom Ewing, 1986.

Findlay, J.B. and Thomas Sawyer. *Professor Hoffmann: A Study*. Tustin, CA: Thomas Sawyer, 1977.

Finer, S. E. *The Life and Times of Sir Edwin Chadwick*. London: Methuen, 1952.

Fletcher, Robert P. "'I leave a page half-writ': Narrative Discoherence in Michael Field's *Underneath the Bough*." In Armstrong and Blain, eds., *Gender and Genre*, 164–82.

Forster, John. *The Life of Charles Dickens*. 1871–73. Collected, arranged, and annotated by B. W. Matz. 2 vols. Philadelphia: B. Lippincott, 1911.

Forsyth, Neil. "Wonderful Chains: Dickens and Coincidence." *Modern Philology* 83, no. 2 (1985): 151–65.

Foucault, Michel. *The Birth of the Clinic: An Archaeology of Medical Perception*. trans. A. M. Sheridan Smith. New York: Vintage, 1975.

———. *Discipline and Punish: The Birth of the Prison*. 1975. Trans. Alan Sheridan. New York: Random House, 1977.

———. *The History of Sexuality*. Trans. Robert Hurley. New York: Pantheon, 1978–86.

———. *Madness and Civilisation: A History of Insanity in the Age of Reason*. Trans. R. Howard. New York: Vintage, 1988.

Francis, G. H. *The Late Sir Robert Peel, Bart. A Critical Biography*. London: Parker & Son, 1852.

Frank, Lawrence. *Victorian Detective Fiction and the Nature of Evidence: The Scientific Investigations of Poe, Dickens, and Doyle*. Houndsmills: Palgrave-Macmillan, 2003.

Freud, Sigmund. "'A Child is Being Beaten.' A Contribution to the Study of the Origin of Sexual Perversions." *Collected Papers*, vol. 2, ed. Ernest Jones, Trans. Joan Riviere. New York: Basic Books, 1959.

Friend to Decency. "Bad Effects of Contracted Burying Grounds." *Imperial Magazine* 1, no. 5 (May 1819): 451–3.

Frost, Thomas. *The Lives of the Conjurors*. 1876. London: Chatto and Windus, 1881.
Fuller, Peter. "Richard Dadd: A Psychological Interpretation." *Connoisseur* 186, no. 749 (1974): 170–77.
Gallagher, Catherine. "The Duplicity of Doubling in *A Tale of Two Cities*." *Dickens Studies Annual* 12 (1983): 125–45.
Gennette, Gerard. *Narrative Discourse: An Essay in Method*. Ithaca: Cornell UP, 1983.
Gilley, Sheridan. *Newman and his Age*. London: Darton, 1990.
Gordon, Jan B. "Dickens and the Transformation of Nineteenth-Century Narratives of 'Legitimacy.'" *Dickens Studies Annual* 31 (2002): 203–65.
Gosse, Edmund. *Father and Son: A Study of Two Temperaments*. ed. William Irvine. Boston: Houghton Mifflin, 1965.
Gregory, Melissa Valiska. "Robert Browning and the Lure of the Violent Lyric Voice: Domestic Violence and the Dramatic Monologue." *Victorian Poetry* 38, no. 4 (2000): 491–510
Greysmith, David. *Richard Dadd, The Rock and Castle of Seclusion*. London: Studio Vista, 1973.
Griffin, Susan M. *Anti-Catholicism and Nineteenth-Century Fiction*. Cambridge: Cambridge UP, 2004.
Grosskurth, Phyllis. *Byron: The Flawed Angel*. Boston: Houghton Mifflin, 1997.
H. "On Crowded Churchyards, and a Metropolitan Cemetery." *Mirror of Literature, Amusement, and Instruction* 16, no. 446 (1830): 140–42.
Hall, Catherine. "At Home with History: Macaulay and the *History of England*." In *At Home with the Empire: Metropolitan Culture and the Imperial World*, eds. Catherine Hall and Sonya O. Rose, 32–52. Cambridge: Cambridge UP, 2006.
Hall, Radclyffe. *The Well of Loneliness*. London: John Lane, 1928.
Hammond, Paul. *Marvelous Méliès*. London: Fraser, 1974.
Hardy, Thomas. *Tess of the d'Urbervilles*. 1891. Ed. Scott Elledge. New York: Norton, 1991.
Hartley, Lucy. *Physiognomy and the Meaning of Expression in Nineteenth-Century Culture*. Cambridge: Cambridge UP, 2001.
Hartman Geoffrey H. "On Traumatic Knowledge and Literary Studies." *New Literary History* 26, no. 3 (1995): 537–63.
Hartman, Geoffrey R. "Reading, Trauma and Pedagogy." In *The Geoffrey Hartman Reader*, eds. Geoffrey Hartman and Daniel T. O'Hara, 291–9. New York: Fordham UP, 2004.
Harvey, William. *The Life of the Right Honourable Sir Robert Peel, Bart*. London: Routledge, 1853.
Hawthorne, Nathaniel. *The Marble Faun*. Boston: Ticknor and Fields, 1860.
Heller, Tamar. *Dead Secrets: Wilkie Collins and the Female Gothic*. New Haven: Yale UP, 1992.
Henderson, Heather. *The Victorian Self: Autobiography and Biblical Narrative*. Ithaca: Cornell UP, 1989.

Herbert, Christopher. "The Occult in *Bleak House*." *Novel: A Forum on Fiction* 17, no. 2 (1984): 101–15.

Herrmann, Alexander. "The Art of Magic." *North American Review* 153, no. 416 (July 1891): 93.

———. "Light on the Black Art." *Cosmopolitan* 14 (December 1892): 207–14.

Higgonet, Margaret. "Fictions of Feminine Voice: Antiphony and Silence in Hardy's *Tess of the d'Uberville*." In *Out of Bounds: Male Writers and Gender(ed) Criticism*, eds. Laura Claridge and Elizabeth Langland, 197–218. Amherst: U of Massachusetts P, 1990.

Hinde, Wendy. *Richard Cobden. A Victorian Outsider*. New Haven: Yale UP, 1987.

Hindmarsh, Bruce. *The Evangelical Conversion Narrative: Spiritual Autobiography in Early Modern England.* New York: Oxford UP, 2005.

HO 144/160/A41450. *Town Talk.* "Obscene Publications." Public Record Office, London, 1885.

HO 45/10360. *Hazard of the Die*. "Indecent Publications." Public Record Office, London, 1909.

Hoffmann, Professor. "Indian Conjuring Explained." *Chambers's Journal* 78 (26 October 1901): 757–61.

———. *Modern Magic*. 1876. Philadelphia: McKay, c 1890.

Holmes, Basil. *The London Burial Grounds: Notes on their History from the Earliest Times to the Present Day.* London: T. F. Unwin, 1896.

Hood, W. Charles. *Statistics of Insanity, Being a Decennial Report of Bethlem Hospital from 1846–1855 Inclusive*. London: Batten, 1862.

Hooks, Bell. "The Oppositional Gaze: Black Female Spectators." In *Reading Images*, ed. Julia Thomas, 123–37. Basingstoke & New York: Palgrave, 2001.

Hopkins, Gerard Manley. *The Poems of Gerard Manley Hopkins*. 4th ed. Eds. W. H. Gardner and N. H. MacKenzie. New York: Oxford UP, 1967.

Hotz, Mary Elizabeth. "Down Among the Dead: Edwin Chadwick's Burial Reform Discourse in Mid-Nineteenth-Century England." *Victorian Literature and Culture* 29, no.1 (2001): 21–38.

———. *Literary Remains: Representations of Death and Burial in Victorian England.* Albany, NY: SUNY Press, 2009.

Houghton, Walter. *The Victorian Frame of Mind.* New Haven: Yale UP, 1957.

Howe, Anthony. *Letters of Richard Cobden*. New York and Oxford: Oxford UP, 2007.

Howlin, Patricia, Simon Baron-Cohen, and Julie Hadwin. *Teaching Children with Autism to Mind-Read: A Practical Guide*. New York: John Wiley & Sons, 1999.

Hughes, Winifred. *The Maniac in the Cellar: Sensation Novels of the 1860s.* Princeton: Princeton UP, 1980.

Hutter, A. D. "Fosco Lives!" In *Reality's Dark Light: The Sensational Wilkie Collins*, eds. Maria K. Bachman and Don Richard Cox, 195–238. Knoxville: U of Tennessee P, 2003.

———. "The High Tower of His Mind: Psychoanalysis and the Reader of *Bleak House*." *Criticism: A Quarterly for Literature and the Arts* 19, no. 4 (1977): 296–316.

Jacyna, L S. "Somatic Theories of Mind and the Interests of Medicine in Britain, 1850–1879." *Medical History* 26 (1982): 233.

Jaffe, Audrey. *Vanishing Points: Dickens, Narrative, and the Subject of Omniscience*. Berkeley & Los Angeles: U of California P, 1991.

Jenner, Mark. "Death, Decomposition and Dechristianisation? Public Health and Church Burial in Eighteenth-Century England." *English Historical Review* 120, no. 487 (2005): 615–32.

Jones, Christine Kenyon. "Fantasy and Transfiguration: Byron and His Portraits," In *Byromania*, ed. Frances Wilson, 109–36. New York: St. Martin's, 1999.

Jones, Colin & Roy Porter, eds. *Reassessing Foucault, Power, Medicine and the Body*. New Haven & London: the Paul Mellon Centre for Studies in British Art and the Yale Center for Art, Yale UP, 1995.

Jones, Peter. "A Painter Possessed." *Observer Magazine* (London: 16 June 1974): 28–9; 31; 33–5.

Jordanova, Ludmilla. "The Representation of the Human Body: Art and Medicine in the Work of Charles Bell." In *Towards a Modern Art World*, ed. Brian Allen, 70–94. New London & New York: Routledge, 1994.

———. *The Sense of the Past in Eighteenth-Century Medicine*. Reading, UK: University of Reading, 1997.

Joyce, Simon. "Inspector Bucket versus Tom-all-Alone's: *Bleak House*, Literary Theory, and the Condition-of-England in the 1850s." *Dickens Studies Annual* 32 (2002): 129–49.

Jupp, Peter. "Enon Chapel: No Way for the Dead." In *The Changing Face of Death: Historical Accounts of Death and Disposal*, eds. Peter C. Jupp and Glennys Howarth, 90–104. New York: Palgrave Macmillan, 1997.

Justyne, William. *Guide to Highgate Cemetery*. London: Moore, 1865.

Karlin, Daniel. *Browning's Hatreds*. Oxford: Clarendon, 1993.

Karr, Todd, ed. *Essential Robert-Houdin*. Seattle: Miracle Factory, 2006.

Kee, Tara White. "No Place for the Dead: The Struggle for Burial Reform in Mid-Nineteenth-Century London." Ph.D. diss., University of Delaware, 2006.

Kellar, Harry. "High Caste Indian Magic." *The North American Review* 156, no. 3 (1893): 75–86.

Kelley, Anita. *The Psychology of Secrets*. New York: Kluwer Academic/Plenum Publishers, 2002.

Kelsall, Malcolm. "The Byronic Hero and Revolution in Ireland: The Politics of *Glenarvon*." *The Byron Journal* 9 (1981): 4–19.

Ker, Ian T. *John Henry Newman: A Biography*. New York: Oxford UP, 1990.

Kilby, Jane. "The Writing of Trauma: Trauma Theory and the Liberty of Reading." *New Formations* 47 (2002): 217–30.

Kinealy, Christine. *This Great Calamity. The Irish Famine 1845–52*. Boulder: Roberts Rinehart, 1995.

[King, Henry]. "Post-Mortem Musings." *Blackwood's Edinburgh Magazine* 48 (December 1840): 829–35.

Kirsch, J. P. "St. Alexius." *The Catholic Encyclopedia*, vol. 1. Robert Appleton, 1907. Transcribed by Laura Ouellette for *The Catholic Encyclopedia*. http://www.newadvent.org/cathen/01307b.htm.

Knight, Mark, and Emma Mason. *Nineteenth-Century Religion and Literature*. Oxford: Oxford UP, 2006.

Knoepflmacher, U. C. "The Counterworld of Victorian Fiction and *The Woman in White*." In *The Worlds of Victorian Fiction, Harvard English Studies* 6, ed. Jerome H. Buckley, 351–69. Cambridge: Harvard UP, 1975.

Kselman, Thomas A. *Death and the Afterlife in Modern France*. Princeton, NJ: Princeton UP, 1993.

Kucich, John. *The Power of Lies: Transgression in Victorian Fiction*. Ithaca and London: Cornell UP, 1994.

———. Repression *in Victorian Fiction: Charlotte Brontë, George Eliot, and Charles Dickens*. Berkeley: U of California P, 1987.

Lane, Julie and Daniel Wegner. "The Cognitive Consequences of Secrecy." *Journal of Personality and Social Psychology* 69, no. 2 (1995): 237–53.

Latimer, Hugh. *Select Sermons*. Boston: Hilliard and Gray, 1832.

Law Report Vol. 3, Queen's Bench 360, 1868.

Lawrence, D. H. *À Propos of Lady Chatterley's Lover and Other Essays*. Ed. Mark Schorer. Harmondsworth, Middlesex: Penguin, 1961.

———. *Pornography and Obscenity*. London: Faber and Faber, 1929.

———. *The Rainbow*. London: Methuen, 1915.

Leighton, Angela. *Victorian Women Poets: Writing Against the Heart*. Charlottesville: U of Virginia P, 1992.

Leighton, Angela and Margaret Reynolds, eds. *Victorian Women Poets: An Anthology*. Oxford: Blackwell, 1995.

Lewis, Thomas. *Seasonable Considerations on the Indecent and Dangerous Custom of Burying in Churches and Churchyards: with Remarkable Observations, Historical and Philosophical, Proving that the Custom is not only Contrary to the Practice of the Antients, but Fatal, in case of Infection*. London: A. Bettesworth, 1721.

Li, Hao. *Memory and History in George Eliot: Transfiguring the Past*. New York: St. Martin's, 2000.

Lippincott, Louise. "Murder and the Fine Arts; or, a Reassessment of Richard Dadd." *The J Paul Getty Museum Journal* 16 (1988): 75–94.

Logan, Deborah, ed. *The Collected Letters of Harriet Martineau*. 5 vols. London: Pickering & Chatto, 2007.

———. *Harriet Martineau's Writing on British History and Military Reform*. 6 vols. London: Pickering & Chatto, 2004.

London Grave-Yards." *Monthly Review* 1, no. 2 (February 1840): 161–8.

Macaulay, Thomas Babington. "History." In *The Works of Lord Macaulay*, ed. Lady Trevelyan, 5:121–61. London: Longmans, Green and Co., 1871.

Macgregor, John M. *The Discovery of the Art of the Insane*. Princeton: Princeton UP, 1989.

Machann, Clinton. *The Genre of Autobiography in Victorian Literature*. Ann Arbor: U of Michigan P, 1994.

Marcus, Steven. *The Other Victorians: a Study in Sexuality and Pornography in Mid-Nineteenth-Century England*. New York: Basic Books, 1966.

Margaret Thatcher Foundation. http://www.margaretthatcher.org/ speeches/ default.asp.

Margolin, Uri. "Cognitive Science, The Thinking Mind, and Literary Narrative." In *Narrative Theory and the Cognitive Sciences*, ed. David Herman, 271–94. Stanford: CSLI Publications, 2003.

Martineau, Harriet. *Harriet Martineau's Autobiography*. 1877. 2 vols. Ed. Gaby Weiner. London: Virago, 1983.

———. *Illustrations of Political Economy*. London: Charles Fox, 1832–34.

———. *Illustrations of Taxation*. London: Charles Fox, 1834.

———. *Poor Laws and Paupers Illustrated*. London: Charles Fox, 1833.

Maskelyne, John Nevil. The Fraud of Modern Theosophy Exposed and the Miraculous Rope-Trick of the Indian Jugglers Explained. London: Routledge, 1912.

———. "Oriental Jugglery." *Leisure Hour* (1878): 198–301.

Maskelyne, John Nevil and Lionel Weatherly. *The Supernatural?* London: Arrowsmith, 1891.

Maunder, Andrew, ed. *Varieties of Women's Sensation Fiction: 1855–1890. Vol.1: Sensationalism and The Sensation Debate*. London: Pickering & Chatto, 2004.

Mayhew, Henry. *London Labour and the London Poor*, vol. 3. London: Griffin, Bohn, 1861.

McGilchrist, John. *Richard Cobden, the Apostle of Free Trade*. New York: Harper, 1865.

Melling, Joseph. "Accommodating Madness, New Research in the Social History of Insanity and Institutions." In *Insanity, Institutions and Society, 1800–1914: A Social History of Madness in Comparative Perspective,* eds. Joseph Melling and Bill Forsythe, 1–4. London & New York: Routledge, 1999.

Melville, Herman. *Moby-Dick, or The Whale*. 1851. Eds. Harrison Hayford, et. al. Evanston and Chicago: Northwestern UP and Newberry Library, 1988.

Metz, Nancy Aycock. "The Blighted Tree and the Book of Fate: Female Models of Storytelling in *Little Dorrit*." *Dickens Studies Annual* 18 (1989): 221–41.

Mill, John Stuart. *Autobiography*. 1873. ed. John Robson. New York: Penguin, 1989.

Miller, D.A. "Cage Aux Folles: Sensation and Gender in Wilkie Collins's *The Woman in White*." *Representations* 14 (1986): 107–36.

———. *The Novel and the Police*. Berkeley & Los Angeles: U of California P, 1988.

———. "From *roman-policier* to *roman-police*: Wilkie Collins's *The Moonstone*." *Novel* 13, no. 2 (1980): 153–70.

Miller, David Prince. *The Life of a Showman*. London: Edward Avery, 1851.

Miller, J. Hillis. Introduction to *Bleak House*, by Charles Dickens, 11–34. Harmondsworth: Penguin, 1971.

Millstein, Denise Tischler. "Lord Byron and George Eliot: Embracing National Consciousness in *Daniel Deronda*," *Forum: The University of Edinburgh Postgraduate Journal of Culture and the Arts* October (2005). http://forum.llc.ed.ac.uk/issue1/Millstein_Byron.pdf.

Milner, George. *Cemetery Burial; or, Sepulture, Ancient and Modern*. London: Longman and Co., 1846.

Mitchell, Rosemary. *Picturing the Past: English History in Text and Image, 1830–1870*. Oxford: Clarendon, 2000.

Monk, Leland. *Standard Deviations: Chance and the Modern British Novel*. Stanford: Stanford UP, 1993.

Morgan, William W. "Gender and Silence in Thomas Hardy's Texts." In *Gender and Discourse in Victorian Literature and Art*, eds. Antony Harrison and Beverly Taylor, 161–84. New York: Norton, 1992.

Morison, Alexander. *Outlines of Lectures on Mental Diseases*. London: Longman & Co, 1826.

———. *The Physiognomy of Mental Disease*. London: Longman & Co, 1840.

Morley, John. *The Life of Richard Cobden*. 2 vols. London: Chapman and Hall, 1881.

Mulvey-Roberts, Marie and Hugh Ormsby Lennon, eds. *Secret Texts: The Literature of Secret Societies*. New York: AMS Press, 1995.

Neve, Christopher. "The Lost World of Richard Dadd." *Country Life* 156 (London: 4 July 1974): 16–17.

"New Place of Public Sepulture." *Newcastle Magazine* 8, no. 3 (May 1829): 108–14.

Newman, John Henry. *Apologia pro Vita Sua*. 1864. Ed. Frank Turner. New Haven: Yale UP, 2008.

———. *An Essay on the Development of Christian Doctrine*. 1845. Ed. C. F. Harrold. New York: Longmans, Green, 1949.

———. *Loss and Gain: The Story of a Convert*. 1848. Ed. Alan G. Hill. New York: Oxford UP, 1986.

Newton, K. M. *George Eliot: Romantic Humanist*. New York: Barnes & Noble Books, 1981.

O'Malley, Patrick. *Catholicism, Sexual Deviance, and Victorian Gothic Culture*. Cambridge: Cambridge UP, 2006.

O'Neill, Philip. *Wilkie Collins: Women, Property, and Propriety*. Totowa, NJ: Barnes and Noble Books, 1988.

Ousby, Ian. *Bloodhounds of Heaven: The Detective in English Fiction from Godwin to Doyle*. Cambridge, MA: Harvard UP, 1976.

Owen, Alex. *The Darkened Room: Women, Power, and Spiritualism in Late Victorian England*. London: Virago, 1989.

Page, Norman. *Wilkie Collins: The Critical Heritage*. London: Routledge & Kegan Paul, 1974.

Palmer, Alan. *Fictional Minds*. Lincoln: U of Nebraska P, 2004.

Parent, André. "Félix Vicq d'Azyr: Anatomy, Medicine and Revolution." *The Canadian Journal of Neurological Sciences* 34, no. 1 (2007): 30–37.

Park, Maureen. "Early Examples of Art in Scottish Hospitals, 2: Crichton Royal Hospital, Dumfries." *Journal of Audiovisual Media in Medicine* 26, no. 4 (2003):142–146.

Pascal, Roy. *Design and Truth in Autobiography*. New York: Garland, 1960.

Pascalis, Felix. *An Exposition of the Dangers of Interment in Cities: Illustrated by an Account of the Funeral Rites and Customs of the Hebrews, Greeks, Romans, and Primitive Christians; by Ancient and Modern Ecclesiastical Canons, Civil Statutes, and Municipal Regulations; and by Chemical and Physical Principles. Chiefly from the Works of Vicq d'Azyr and Prof. Scipione Piattoli with additions by Felix Pascalis*. New York: W. B. Gilley, 1823.

"Pascalis on the Danger of Interment in Cities." *The New York Medical and Physical Journal* 4, no. 13 (January-March 1825): 113–121.

Peggs, James. *A Cry from the Tombs; or, Facts and Observation on the Impropriety of Burying the Dead among the Living, in Various Ages and Nations*. London: John Snow, 1840.

Pellew, Jill. *The Home Office 1848–1914: From Clerks to Bureaucrats*. Rutherford, Madison, Teaneck: Farleigh Dickinson UP, 1982.

Pennant, Thomas. *Of London.* London: Robert Faulder, 1790.

Peterson, Linda. *Victorian Autobiography: The Tradition of Self-Interpretation.* New Haven, Connecticut: Yale UP, 1986.

Phelan, James. *Living to Tell About It*. Ithaca: Cornell UP, 2004.

Picton, J. A. "On Cemeteries." *Architectural Magazine* 4, no. 43 (September 1837): 426–37.

Pionke, Albert D. *Plots of Opportunity: Representing Conspiracy in Victorian England.* Columbus: Ohio State UP, 2004.

Poovey, Mary. "Writing about Finance in Victorian England: Disclosure and Secrecy in the Culture of Investment." *Victorian Studies* 45, no.1 (2002): 17–42.

Poovey, Mary, ed. *The Financial System in Nineteenth-Century Britain.* New York: Oxford UP, 2003.

Porter, Roy. *A Social History of Madness.* New York: Weidenfeld and Nicolson, 1987.

Pykett, Lyn. *The "Improper" Feminine: The Women's Sensation Novel and the New Woman Writing*. London: Routledge, 1992.

Reed, John Shelton. "'A Female Movement': The Feminization of Nineteenth-Century Anglo-Catholicism." *Anglican and Episcopal History* 57, no. 2 (1988): 199–238.

"The Report of Bethlem Hospital." *Journal of Psychological Medicine and Mental Pathology* 6 (1853): 595–8.

Rev. of *John Marchmont's Legacy*, by Mary Elizabeth Braddon. *Athenaeum* (12 Dec 1863): 792.

Richards, John. *Essay on Cemetery Interments*. London: Pelham Richardson, Cornhill, Richard Welch: Reading, 1843.

Richardson, Ruth. *Death, Dissection and the Destitute*. Chicago: U of Chicago P, 2000.

Ricoeur, Paul. *Freud and Philosophy: An Essay on Interpretation*. Trans. Denis Savage. New Haven: Yale UP, 1970.

Rigg, Patricia. "Augusta Webster and the Lyric Muse: The *Athenaeum* and Webster's Poetics." *Victorian Poetry* 42, no. 2 (2004): 150.

Roach, Joseph. *Cities of the Dead: Circum-Atlantic Performance*. New York: Columbia UP, 1996.

Rooney, Ellen. "'A Little More Than Persuading': Tess and the Subject of Sexual Violence." in *Rape and Representation*, eds. Lynn A. Higgins and Brenda R. Silver, 87–114. New York: Columbia UP, 1991.

Rossetti, Christina. "Winter: My Secret." 1862. In *The Complete Poems of Christina Rossetti: A Variorum Edition*, ed. R. W. Crump, 1:47. Baton Rouge, LA: Louisiana State UP, 1979.

Royle, Nicholas. *The Uncanny*. Manchester: Manchester UP, 2003.

Rugg, Julie. "A New Burial Form and Its Meanings: Cemetery Establishment in the First Half of the Nineteenth Century." In *Grave Concerns: Death and Burial in England 1700 to 1850*, ed. Margaret Cox, 44–53. York: Council for British Archaeology, 1998.

Sanchez-Eppler, Karen. "Decomposing: Wordsworth's Poetry of Epitaph and English Burial Reform." *Nineteenth-Century Literature* 42, no. 4 (1998): 414–31.

Sandbach-Dahlstrom, Catherine. *Be Good Sweet Maid: Charlotte Yonge's Domestic Fiction: A Study in Dogmatic Purpose and Fictional Form*. Stockholm: Almqvist & Wiksell International, 1984.

Sanders, Valerie. "'All-sufficient to one another'? Charlotte Yonge and the family chronicle." In *Popular Victorian Women Writers*, eds. Kay Boardman and Shirley Jones, 90–110. Manchester: Manchester UP, 2004.

Santucho, Oscar Jose. *George Gordon, Lord Byron: A Comprehensive Bibliography of Secondary Material in English 1807–1974, With a Critical Review of Research By Clement Tyson Goode, Jr*. Metuchen, NJ: Scarecrow, 1977.

Schaffer, Talia. "The Mysterious *Magnum Bonum*: Fighting to Read Charlotte Yonge." *Nineteenth-Century Literature* 55, no.2 (2000): 244–75.

Schramm, Jan-Melissa. *Testimony and Advocacy in Victorian Law, Literature, and Theology*. Cambridge: Cambridge UP, 2000.

Scull, Andrew. *Museums of Madness, The Social Organization of Insanity in Nineteenth-Century England*. London: Allen Lane, 1979.

Sedgwick, Eve Kosofsky. *Epistemology of the Closet*. Los Angeles and Berkeley: U of California P, 1990.

Shumaker, Wayne. *English Autobiography: Its Emergence, Materials, and Form*. Berkeley: U of California P, 1954.

Siegel, Lee. *Net of Magic: Wonders and Deceptions in India*. Chicago: U of Chicago P, 1991.

Simmel, Georg. *The Sociology of George Simmel*. Trans. and ed. Kurt H. Wolff. New York: Free Press, 1950.

———. "The Sociology of Secrecy and of Secret Societies." *American Journal of Sociology* 11 (1906): 441–98.

Simpson, J. A. and E. S. C. Weiner. "Trauma." In *The Oxford English Dictionary*. Oxford: Clarendon, 1989.

Skultans, Vieda. *Madness and Morals, Ideas on Insanity in the Nineteenth Century*. London: Routledge & Kegan Paul, 1975.

Smailes, Helen. *Method in Madness*. exh. cat. Edinburgh: Scottish National Portrait Gallery, 1981.

Smith, David Livingstone. *Why We Lie*. New York: Macmillan, 2004

Souhami, Diana. *The Trials of Radclyffe Hall*. London: Weidenfeld and Nicolson, 1998.

[Southey, Robert]. "Cemeteries and Catacombs of Paris." *Quarterly Review* 21, no. 42 (April 1819): 359–99.

Spengemann, William C. *The Forms of Autobiography: Episodes in the History of a Literary Genre*. New Haven, Connecticut: Yale UP, 1980.

Sperber, Dan. *Explaining Culture: A Naturalistic Approach*. Oxford: Blackwell, 1997.

Staley, Allen. "Richard Dadd of Bethlem." *Art in America* 62, no. 6 (1974): 80–82.

Steig, Michael and F. A. C. Wilson. "Hortense Versus Bucket: The Ambiguity of Order in *Bleak House*." *Modern Language Quarterly* 33, no. 1 (1972): 289–98.

Steinmeyer, Jim. *Hiding the Elephant: How Magicians Invented the Impossible and Learned to Disappear*. New York: Carroll and Graf, 2003.

Stelzig, Eugene. "Is There a Canon of Autobiography?" *a/b Auto/Biography Studies* 7, no. 1 (1992): 1–12.

Stewart, Garrett. "The New Mortality of *Bleak House*." *ELH* 45, no. 3 (1978): 443–87.

Still, Arthur and Irving Velody, eds. *Rewriting the History of Madness, Studies in Foucault's 'Histoire de la Folie'*. London & New York: Routledge, 1992.

St-John Stevas, Norman. *Obscenity and the Law*. London: Secker and Warburg, 1956.

Stone, Elizabeth. *God's Acre; or, Historical Notices Relating to Churchyards*. London: John W. Parker and Son, 1858.

Stowe, Harriet Beecher. *Lady Byron Vindicated: A History of the Byron Controversy, From Its Beginning in 1816 to the Present Time*. Boston: Osgood, Fields, & Co., 1870.

Strang, John. *Necropolis Glasguensis: with Observations on Ancient and Modern Tombs and Sepulture*. Glasgow: Atkinson, 1831.

Strindberg, August. Preface to *Miss Julie*. 1888. *The Harcourt Brace Anthology of Drama*. Ed. W. B. Worthen, 2nd ed. Fort Worth: Harcourt, 1996.

Sturrock, June. "Murder, Gender, and Popular Fiction by Women in the 1860s: Braddon, Oliphant, Yonge." In *Victorian Crime, Madness and Sensation*, eds. Andrew Maunder and Grace Moore, 73–88. Aldershot: Ashgate, 2004.

Surridge, Lisa. *Bleak Houses: Marital Violence in Victorian Fiction*. Athens: Ohio UP, 2005.

Suzuki, Akihito, "Framing Psychiatric Subjectivity: Doctor, Patient and Record-keeping at Bethlem in the Nineteenth Century." In *Insanity, Institutions and Society, 1800–1914: A Social History of Madness in Comparative Perspective*, eds. Joseph Melling and Bill Forsythe, 120–24. London & New York: Routledge, 1999.

Tambling, Jeremy. "Introduction" to *Bleak House / Charles Dickens*. Ed. Jeremy Tambling. New Casebooks. New York: St. Martin's, 1998. 1–28.

Tenniel, John. "The Extinguisher Trick." *Punch* 70 (19 February 1876): 59.

Theroux, Alexander. "Artists who Kill and Other Acts of Creative Mayhem." *Art & Antiques* (Summer 1988): 95–103.

Thomas, Donald. *Swinburne: The Poet in His World*. New York: Oxford UP, 1979.

———. *A Long Time Burning: The History of Literary Censorship in England*. New York: Frederick A. Praeger, 1969.

Thomas, Ronald R. "Detection in the Victorian Novel." In *The Cambridge Companion to the Victorian Novel*, ed. Deirdre David, 169–91. Cambridge: Cambridge UP, 2001.

———. *Detective Fiction and the Rise of Forensic Science*. Cambridge: Cambridge UP, 1999.

Thompson, E. P. *The Making of the English Working Class*. New York: Vintage, 1966.

Thoms, Peter. "'The Narrow Trace of Blood': Detection and Storytelling in *Bleak House*." *Nineteenth-Century Literature* 50, no. 2 (1995): 147–67.

Thomson, James. *The City of Dreadful Night*. 1874. Introduction by Edwin Morgan. Edinburgh: Canongate Classics, 1993.

Times [London], 30 April, 1870.

Times [London], 7 May, 1870.

Travis, Alan. *Bound and Gagged: A Secret History of Obscenity in Britain*. London: Profile Books, 2000.

Treadwell, James. *Autobiographical Writing and British Literature, 1783–1834*. Oxford: Oxford UP, 2005.

Trilling, Lionel. *Sincerity and Authenticity*. Cambridge, MA: Harvard UP, 1971.

Trodd Colin., Paul Barlow, and David Amigoni, eds. *Victorian Culture and the Idea of the Grotesque*. Aldershot: Ashgate, 1999.

Trollope, Anthony. *Autobiography*. 1883. Ed. David Skilton, Introduction by John Sutherland. London: Trollope Society, 1999.

———. *Dr Wortle's School*. 1881. Ed. Mick Imlah. London: Penguin, 1999.

———. *The Eustace Diamonds*. 1873. Ed. David Skilton, Introduction by P. D. James. London: Trollope Society, 1990.

———. *The Letters of Anthony Trollope*. Ed. John Hall. Stanford: Stanford UP, 1983.

———. *Phineas Redux*. 1873–74. Ed. John C. Whale. Oxford: Oxford UP, 2000.

Tromp, Marlene. *The Private Rod: Marital Violence, Sensation, and the Law in Victorian Britain*. Charlottesville and London: U of Virginia P, 2000.

Turner, Frank. *John Henry Newman: The Challenge to Evangelical Religion*. New Haven, Connecticut: Yale UP, 2002.

Twain, Mark. *A Connecticut Yankee in King Arthur's Court*. 1889. Ed. Bernard L. Stein, vol. 3. *The Works of Mark Twain*. Berkeley: U of California P, 1979.

Van Zuylen, Maria. *Monomania: The Flight from Everyday Life in Literature and Art*. Ithaca and London: Cornell UP, 2005.

Vanbrugh, Sir John. "Mr Van-Brugg's Proposals about Building ye New Churches." 1712. In *British Architectural Theory 1540–1750: An Anthology of Texts*, ed. Caroline van Eck, with contributions by Christy Anderson, 136–8. Aldershot: Ashgate, 2003.

Vicq d'Azyr, Félix. *Essai sur les lieux et les dangers des sépultures*. Paris: Didot, 1778.

Vincent, David. *The Culture of Secrecy: Britain 1832–1998*. Oxford: Oxford UP, 1998.

Wagner, Tamara S. "Depressed Spirits and Failed Crisis Management: Charlotte Yonge's Sensationalization of the Religious Family." *Victorians Institute Journal* 36 (2008): 275–302.

Walker, George Alfred. *Gatherings from Graveyards: Particularly those of London; with a Concise History of the Modes of Interment among Different Nations from the Earliest Periods; and a Detail of the Dangerous and Fatal Results Produced by the Unwise & Revolting Custom of Inhuming the Dead in the Midst of the Living*. London: Longman, 1839.

———. *On the Past and Present State of Intramural Burying Places: with Practical Suggestions for the Establishment of National Cemeteries*. London: Longman, 1851.

Webb, R. K. *Harriet Martineau. A Radical Victorian*. New York: Columbia UP, 1960.

Webster, Augusta. *A Housewife's Opinions*. London and Cambridge: Macmillan, 1879.

———. *Portraits and Other Poems,* ed. Christine Sutphin. Peterborough, OT, Canada: Broadview, 2000.

———. "Review of *A Vision of Saints,* by Lewis Morris." *Athenaeum*, March 14, 1891, 339–40.

———. "Review of *Flower Pieces and Other Poems*, by William Allingham." *Athenaeum*, May 18, 1889, 623.

Weeks, Jeffrey. *Coming Out: Homosexual Politics in Britain, from the Nineteenth Century to the Present*. London: Quartet Books, 1977.

Wegner, Daniel and Julie Lane. "From Secrecy to Psychopathology." In *Emotion, Disclosure, and Health*, ed. J.W. Pennebaker, 25–46. Washington, DC: American Psychological Association, 1996.

Welsh, Alexander. *George Eliot and Blackmail*. Cambridge, MA: Harvard UP, 1985.

———. *Strong Representations: Narrative and Circumstantial Evidence in England*. Baltimore: John Hopkins UP, 1992.

Wheatley, Kim. "Death and Domestication in Charlotte M. Yonge's *The Clever Woman of the Family*." *Studies in English Literature* 36, no. 4 (1996): 895–915.

Wigren, Jodie. "Narrative Completion in the Treatment of Trauma," *Psychotherapy* 31, no. 3 (1994): 415–23.

Wills, W. H. "The Modern Science of Thief-Taking." In *Hunted Down: The Detective Stories of Charles Dickens*, ed. Peter Haining, 61–70. London: Peter Owen Publishers, 1996.

Wolff, Robert Lee. *Gains and Losses: Novels of Faith and Doubt in Victorian England*. New York: Garland Publishing, 1977.

Wordsworth, William. *The Prelude*. 1805. Eds. Jonathan Wordsworth, M.H. Abrams, and Stephen Gill. New York: Norton, 1979.

———. *Wordsworth: Poetical Works*. Ed. Thomas Hutchinson, revised by Edward De Selincourt. New York: Oxford University Press, 1936.

Wynne, Deborah. *The Sensation Novel and the Victorian Family Magazine*. Houndmills, Basingstoke: Palgrave, 2001.

Yonge, Charlotte M. *The Clever Woman of the Family*. 1865. Ed. Clare A. Simmons. Peterborough, ON: Broadview, 2001.

———. *The Trial; Or, More Links of the Daisy Chain*. 1864. Doylestown: Wildside, n.d.

York, R. A. *Strangers and Secrets: Communication in the Nineteenth-Century Novel*. Madison, New Jersey: Fairleigh Dickinson UP, 1994.

Zunshine, Lisa. "Richardson's Clarissa and Theory of Mind." In *The Work of Fiction: Culture, Cognition, and Complexity*, eds. Alan Richardson and Ellen Spolsky, 127–46. Aldershot: Ashgate, 2004.

———. "Theory of Mind and Fictions of Embodied Transparency." *Narrative* 16, no. 1 (2008): 65–92.

———. *Why We Read Fiction. Theory of Mind and the Novel*. Columbus: Ohio State UP, 2006.

Index

For Product Safety Concerns and Information please contact our EU
representative GPSR@taylorandfrancis.com
Taylor & Francis Verlag GmbH, Kaufingerstraße 24, 80331 München, Germany

www.ingramcontent.com/pod-product-compliance
Ingram Content Group UK Ltd.
Pitfield, Milton Keynes, MK11 3LW, UK
UKHW021721240926
475702UK00029BA/1748
9781138250543